Gender and Sexuality in the Middle Ages

Gender and Sexuality in the Middle Ages

A Medieval Source Documents Reader

Edited by
Martha A. Brożyna

McFarland & Company, Inc., Publishers
Jefferson, North Carolina, and London

LIBRARY OF CONGRESS CATALOGUING-IN-PUBLICATION DATA

Gender and sexuality in the Middle Ages : a medieval source documents reader / edited by Martha A. Brożyna.
    p.   cm.
    Includes bibliographical references and index.

    ISBN 0-7864-2042-1 (softcover : 50# alkaline paper)

    1. Sex role — History — To 1500 — Sources.   2. Sex — History — To 1500 — Sources.   3. Sex role — Biblical teaching.   4. Sex — Biblical teaching.   5. Sex role — Religious aspects.   6. Sex — Religious aspects.   7. Civilization, Medieval — Sources.
I. Brożyna, Martha A., 1973–
HQ1075.G418   2005
305.3 — dc22   2005001973

British Library cataloguing data are available

Cover image ©2005 Pictures Now

Manufactured in the United States of America

McFarland & Company, Inc., Publishers
Box 611, Jefferson, North Carolina 28640
www.mcfarlandpub.com

For my parents,
Jan Brożyna
Hanna Więckowska Brożyna
za okazaną mi miłość

Acknowledgments

There are many people who have made this book possible and to whom I am indebted. I would like to thank my doctoral advisor, Paul Knoll, for encouraging me to pursue this project and for showing great patience when other projects were delayed because of it. I am appreciative to Fred Russell, a great mind and a good friend, for his insight and advice. I am grateful to John Romano for his invaluable suggestions and library runs. I thank Jarosław Suproniuk, my Latin co-translator, old friend, and traveling buddy; as always I am impressed by his encyclopedic knowledge of medieval eastern Europe. My thanks go out also to Ted Fram for his suggestions on the chapter on Judaism.

There are others who have witnessed the day-to-day process of this work's development and have been tremendously supportive every step of the way. My husband, Aidan McNamara, has not only been a loving, supportive spouse, but he has also accepted cheerfully the roles of translator and proofreader for this project. I thank him for taking on these tasks, and I am grateful for his devotion and his confidence in me as well as my work.

Last but certainly not least, I would like to thank my parents for a lifetime of love and encouragement. They have instilled in me a passion for books and learning, and it is to them this work is dedicated.

V. Biology, Medicine, and Science

VI. Literature

VII. Witchcraft and Heresy

Introduction

Definitions of medieval gender and sexuality are not clear-cut. Scholars often invoke "gender" as an umbrella term for the biological difference between men and women and its various social implications. Some scholars have used it synonymously with "women" in the hopes that it would give their study a more neutral tone[1]; others have utilized it to indicate that men are not excluded from a study. Probably the best definition of gender comes from modern historian Joan Wallach Scott, who writes that gender is the central element of social relationships based on perceived differences between the sexes.[2] These perceptions or "knowledges" are created by cultures and societies and refer to ideas and institutions, as well as everyday customs, ceremonies and rituals.[3] Culture and society insert these knowledges into the reality of daily life by creating principles and norms (and also by providing a framework) by which men and women are taught to conduct their lives, essentially equating biology with destiny.

An important component of gender is sexuality. The study of sexuality goes hand-in-hand with gender because gender roles govern and are governed by norms of sexuality.[4] Many medievalists take the writings of Foucault[5] as their starting point and postulate that "medieval sexuality is constructed by historical formations, produced by and embedded in specifically medieval discourses, customs, institutions, regulations, and knowledges."[6] Like gender, sexuality must be studied with a view to the variety of its social and intellectual contexts. No real understanding of medieval sexuality and

---

1. Christiane Klapisch-Zuber, "Including Women," in *A History of Women: Silences of the Middle Ages* (Cambridge, MA: Harvard University Press, 1994), p. 5.
2. Joan Wallach Scott, *Gender and the Politics of History* (New York: Columbia University Press, 1988), p. 42.
3. Scott, p. 2.
4. Ruth Mazo Karras, *Common Women: Prostitution and Sexuality in Medieval England* (New York: Oxford University Press, 1996), p. 3.
5. Michel Foucault, *The History of Sexuality*, vol. 1: *An Introduction*, tr. Robert Hurley (New York: Vintage, 1990), p. 158.
6. Karma Lochrie, Peggy McCracken, and James A. Schultz, eds., *Constructing Medieval Sexuality* (Minneapolis: University of Minnesota Press, 1997), p. ix.

gender can be gleaned from a single historic event or document. Rather, sexuality and gender together reflect a number of different societal facets and forces that are best examined in tandem.

Since both gender and sexuality are cultural constructs, understanding them requires study of the ideas, laws, and institutions of society. For example, to understand medieval sexuality and gender, it is important to examine the regulations of the Christian church as well as their interpretation in both the theoretical writings of theologians and glossators and the practical workings of ecclesiastical decrees and court decisions. Medieval medical writing is also an important source of study, since the medical community based their notions of sex and gender on the ways that physicians described anatomy (e.g., women's reproductive organs were imperfect inversions of males'), illness (children born with defects reflected their parents' immoral behavior), and therapy (treating a woman's uterus could cure her of almost any illness). In historical writing, chroniclers reflected medieval belief systems of sexuality and gender in the way they recorded events of their own time (for example, often lamenting the decline of morals), and in the lens through which they perceived events of their past or those from different cultures (such as the portrayal of the enemy as a debauched barbarian). In literature, medieval writers proved to be great social critics as they reflected or mocked norms governing sexual behavior in courtly love poetry, the carmina burana, and fabliaux. Together all these different threads weave a tapestry depicting medieval society's conceptualization of sexuality and gender.

It is that tapestry, or at least some small part of it, that this book attempts to display through the reproduction of a number of relevant medieval documents. While one can learn much from historical debates and scholarly theory, it is important to have a familiarity with the original documents on which debate and theory are based. These documents are fascinating, often difficult, and sometimes contradictory. Becoming familiar with them, and learning to scrutinize them with an historian's critical eye, can only enhance one's understanding of medieval gender and sexuality.

Students of history often find it difficult to suspend their modern viewpoints; instead, they sometimes judge past cultures by their own standards. Students looking at this collection of documents, with its subjects that are both sexually charged and controversial, will see that many debates (abortion, birth control, celibate priesthood, same-sex marriage), issues (marriage, adultery, divorce) and passions (love, lust, romance) have really not changed over time. Nevertheless, many of the sources in this book do contain strong misogynistic, anti–Semitic, and racially bigoted language, and these certainly need to be studied with the historical context in mind.

The readings in this book are cross-disciplinary. While other sourcebooks on social history tend to be organized around themes, this book is organized according to disciplines. This organization frees the reader from attention to packaged ideas and themes and allows the source to speak for itself. Thus, for example, a text written by a churchman exhorting virginity not only illustrates the Church's view of the sex act itself, but may also provide a keen insight into the medieval Church's perceptions about women, marriage, and children. Moreover, such a format allows readers to examine the sources that historians use as a group and familiarize themselves with their unique characteristics (for example, the similarities of different law codes). This is the rationale underlying the division of the book into nine sections as follows: the Bible; Christian thought; chronicles; law; biology, medicine, and science; literature; witchcraft and heresy; Judaism; and Islam.

This books stresses the diverse range of ethnic, geographic, and religious identities found in the Middle Ages, such as the late Roman, Germanic, Anglo-Norman, Byzantine, Mediterranean, Slavic, Islamic, and Jewish identities. Too often in the past, medieval studies have tended to portray the Middle Ages as a monolithic era. While they usually have taken into account geography or time period, such studies have tended to ignore religious, racial and ethnic issues.[7] This book seeks to remedy this problem by bringing together a wide range of sources from throughout the medieval world, which is not only useful for the examination of these cultures in their own right, but also facilitates their comparative analysis with other medieval cultures.

Time frames in this book depend on geography. Most chapters begin with sources from the classical period because of their later influences in the Middle Ages. Cutoff dates are not uniform among the sources because there was no particular date for the end of the Middle Ages in Europe. Each area experienced, in its own time, its own renaissance, reformation, or upheaval ushering in a new era. For Southern Europe, the sources end with the rise of humanism, which emerged roughly at the beginning of the fifteenth century. For Northern Europe, the sources continue into the early sixteenth century and the start of the Reformation. The same holds true for many segments of Eastern Europe. For Russia, sources end with the reign of Peter the Great (late seventeenth century) who initiated the process of westernization in Russia. Byzantine sources end with the conquest of Constantinople by the Ottoman Turks in 1453. In Islamic areas, the end of the Middle Ages is difficult to pinpoint because of a vast geography controlled by different dynasties. The Jews lived as a minority group throughout the European and Islamic world and were influenced by the events happening in these areas.

---

7. Steven F. Kruger, "Conversion and Medieval Sexual, Religious, and Racial Categories," in Lochrie et al., p. 158.

I.

THE BIBLE

1

Old Testament

Genesis

The Bible is the work most influential in shaping notions about gender and sexuality in the western world. For the Jews, the sacred scriptures are embodied in the Old Testament (*Tanak*), while Christians acknowledge both the Old and New testaments as sacred. Even Muslims, whose holy book is the Qur'an, recognized many biblical figures such as Abraham, Moses and Jesus Christ as prophets who experienced revelations from God and were worthy of respect. The Bible was written over a period of several centuries with certain books of the Old Testament being written as far back as 1250 CE.

The first book of the Old Testament is Genesis, which means "in the beginning." Genesis begins the history of the world with creation; it discusses the first humans and illustrates how their disobedience alienated them from God. It also discusses the early patriarchs and the covenant made between God and his people, the Israelites. Genesis was compiled over an extended period of time, probably between 1000 and 300 BCE.

Source: Scripture quotations are from the New Revised Standard Version of the Bible, copyright © 1989 by the Division of Christian Education of the National Council of Churches of Christ in the USA. Used by permission. All rights reserved.

[GENESIS 2:18-24]

18. Then the Lord God said, "It is not good that the man should be alone; I will make him a helper as his partner." 19. So out of the ground the Lord God formed every animal of the field and every bird of the air, and brought them to the man to see what he would call them; and whatever the man called every living creature, that was its name. 20. The man gave names to all cattle, and to the birds of the air, and to every animal of the field; but for the man there was not found a helper as his partner. 21. So the Lord God caused a deep sleep to fall upon the man, and he slept; then he took one of his ribs and closed up its place with flesh. 22. And the rib that the Lord God had taken from the man he made into a woman and brought her to the man. 23. Then the man said,

"This at last is bone of my bones
and flesh of my flesh;
this one shall be called Woman,
for out of Man this one was taken."

24. Therefore a man leaves his father and his mother and clings to his wife, and they become one flesh. 25. And the man and his wife were both naked, and were not ashamed.

[GENESIS 3:1-7]

Now the serpent was more crafty than any other wild animal that the Lord God had made. He said to the woman, "Did God say, 'You shall not eat from any tree in the garden'?" 2. The woman said to the serpent, "We may eat of the fruit of the trees in the garden; 3. but God said, 'You shall not eat of the fruit of the tree that is in the middle of the garden, nor shall you touch it, or you shall die.'" 4. But the serpent said to the woman, "You will not die; 5. for God knows that when you eat of it your eyes will be opened, and you will be like God, knowing good and evil." 6. So when the woman saw that the tree was good for food, and that it was a delight to the eyes, and that the tree was to be desired to make one wise, she took of its fruit and ate; and she also gave some to her husband, who was with her, and he ate. 7. Then the eyes of both were opened, and they knew that they were naked; and they sewed fig leaves together and made loincloths for themselves.

[GENESIS 3: 8-17]

8. They heard the sound of the Lord God walking in the garden at the time of the evening breeze, and the man and his wife hid themselves from the presence of the Lord God among the trees of the garden. 9. But the Lord God called to the man, and said to him, "Where are you?" 10. He said, "I heard the sound of you in the garden, and I was afraid, because I was naked; and I hid myself." 11. He said, "Who told you that you were naked? Have you eaten from the tree of which I commanded you not to eat?" 12. The man said, "The woman whom you gave to be with me, she gave me fruit from the tree, and I ate." 13. Then the Lord God said to the woman, "What is this that you have done?" The woman said, "The serpent tricked me, and I ate." 14. The Lord God said to the serpent,

"Because you have done this,
cursed are you among all animals
and among all wild creatures;
upon your belly you shall go,
and dust you shall eat
all the days of your life.
15. I will put enmity between you and the woman,

and between your offspring and hers;
he will strike your head,
    and you will strike his heel."
16. To the woman he said,
"I will greatly increase your pangs in childbearing;
    in pain you shall bring forth children,
yet your desire shall be for your husband,
    and he shall rule over you."
17. And to the man he said,
"Because you have listened to the voice of your wife,
    and have eaten of the tree
about which I commanded you,
    'You shall not eat of it,'
cursed is the ground because of you;
    in toil you shall eat of it all the days of your life...."

[GENESIS 17: 9-14]

9. God said to Abraham, "As for you, you shall keep my covenant, you and your offspring after you throughout their generations. 10. This is my covenant, which you shall keep, between me and you and your offspring after you: Every male among you shall be circumcised. 11. You shall circumcise the flesh of your foreskins, and it shall be a sign of the covenant between me and you. 12. Throughout your generations every male among you shall be circumcised when he is eight days old, including the slave born in your house and the one bought with your money from any foreigner who is not of your offspring. 13. Both the slave born in your house and the one bought with your money must be circumcised. So shall my covenant be in your flesh an everlasting covenant. 14. Any uncircumcised male who is not circumcised in the flesh of his foreskin shall be cut off from his people; he has broken my covenant."

[GENESIS 19: 1-12, 24-25]

The two angels came to Sodom in the evening, and Lot was sitting in the gateway of Sodom. When Lot saw them, he rose to meet them, and bowed down with his face to the ground. 2. He said, "Please, my lords, turn aside to your servant's house and spend the night, and wash your feet; then you can rise early and go on your way." They said, "No; we will spend the night in the square." 3. But he urged them strongly; so they turned aside to him and entered his house; and he made them a feast, and baked unleavened bread, and they ate. 4. But before they lay down, the men of the city, the men of Sodom, both young and old, all the people to the last man, surrounded the house; 5. and they called to Lot, "Where are the men who came to you tonight? Bring them out to us, so that we may know them." 6. Lot went out of the door to the men, shut the door after him, 7. and said, "I beg you, my brothers, do not act so wickedly. 8. Look, I have two daughters who have not known a man; let me bring them out to you, and do to them as you please; only do nothing to these men, for they have come under the shelter of my roof." 9. But they replied, "Stand back!" And they said, "This fellow came here as an alien, and he would play the judge! Now we will deal worse with you than with them." Then they pressed hard against the man Lot, and came near the door to break it down. 10. But the men inside reached out their hands and brought Lot into the house with them, and shut the door. 11. And they struck with blindness the men who were at the door of the house, both small and great, so that they were unable to find the door.

12. Then the men said to Lot, "Have you anyone else here? Sons-in-law, sons, daughters, or anyone you have in the city — bring them out of the place. 13. For we are about to destroy this place, because the outcry against its people has become great before the Lord, and the Lord has sent us to destroy it." 14. So Lot went out and said to his sons-in-law, who were to marry his daughters, "Up, get out of this place; for the Lord is about to destroy the city." But he seemed to his sons-in-law to be jesting.

24. Then the Lord rained on Sodom and Gomorrah sulfur and fire from the Lord out of heaven; 25. and he overthrew those cities, and all the Plain, and all the inhabitants of the cities, and what grew on the ground.

[GENESIS 38:6-10]
6. Judah took a wife for Er his firstborn; her name was Tamar. 7. But Er, Judah's firstborn, was wicked in the sight of the Lord, and the Lord put him to death. 8. Then Judah said to Onan, "Go in to your brother's wife and perform the duty of a brother-in-law to her; raise up offspring for your brother." 9. But since Onan knew that the offspring would not be his, he spilled his semen on the ground whenever he went in to his brother's wife, so that he would not give offspring to his brother. 10. What he did was displeasing in the sight of the Lord, and he put him to death also.

Leviticus

Leviticus is the third book of the Old Testament and it is named after Levi, the name of the Israelite tribe from which hereditary priests came. Leviticus is made up of ritual laws that deal with sacrifice, priesthood, and purity. It was written probably between 800 and 300 BCE.

[LEVITICUS 18: 1-23]
The Lord spoke to Moses, saying:
2. Speak to the people of Israel and say to them: I am the Lord your

marriage is functional

God. 3. You shall not do as they do in the land of Egypt, where you lived, and you shall not do as they do in the land of Canaan, to which I am bringing you. You shall not follow their statutes. 4. My ordinances you shall observe and my statutes you shall keep, following them: I am the Lord your God. 5. You shall keep my statutes and my ordinances; by doing so one shall live: I am the Lord.

6. None of you shall approach anyone near of kin to uncover nakedness: I am the Lord. 7. You shall not uncover the nakedness of your father, which is the nakedness of your mother; she is your mother, you shall not uncover her nakedness. 8. You shall not uncover the nakedness of your father's wife; it is the nakedness of your father. 9. You shall not uncover the nakedness of your sister, your father's daughter or your mother's daughter, whether born at home or born abroad. 10. You shall not uncover the nakedness of your son's daughter or of your daughter's daughter, for their nakedness is your own nakedness. 11. You shall not uncover the nakedness of your father's wife's daughter, begotten by your father, since she is your sister. 12. You shall not uncover the nakedness of your father's sister; she is your father's flesh. 13. You shall not uncover the nakedness of your mother's sister, for she is your mother's flesh. 14. You shall not uncover the nakedness of your father's brother, that is, you shall not approach his wife; she is your aunt. 15. You shall not uncover the nakedness of your daughter-in-law: she is your son's wife; you shall not uncover her nakedness. 16. You shall not uncover the nakedness of your brother's wife; it is your brother's nakedness. 17. You shall not uncover the nakedness of a woman and her daughter, and you shall not take her son's daughter or her daughter's daughter to uncover her nakedness; they are your flesh; it is depravity. 18. And you shall not take a woman as a rival to her sister, uncovering her nakedness while her sister is still alive.

19. You shall not approach a woman to uncover her nakedness while she is in her menstrual uncleanness. 20. You shall not have sexual relations with your kinsman's wife, and defile yourself with her. 21. You shall not give any of your offspring to sacrifice them to Molech, and so profane the name of your God: I am the Lord. 22. You shall not lie with a male as with a woman; it is an abomination. 23. You shall not have sexual relations with any animal and defile yourself with it, nor shall any woman give herself to an animal to have sexual relations with it: it is perversion.

Deuteronomy

Deuteronomy is the fifth book of the Old Testament and means "second law" because Moses repeats God's commandments. It is made up almost entirely of Moses' discourses. It was probably written between 650 and 300 BCE.

[DEUTERONOMY 25:5-12]

5. When brothers reside together, and one of them dies and has no son, the wife of the deceased shall not be married outside the family to a stranger. Her husband's brother shall go in to her, taking her in marriage, and performing the duty of a husband's brother to her, 6. and the firstborn whom she bears shall succeed to the name of the deceased brother, so that his name may not be blotted out of Israel. 7. But if the man has no desire to marry his brother's widow, then his brother's widow shall go up to the elders at the gate and say, "My husband's brother refuses to perpetuate his brother's name in Israel; he will not perform the duty of a husband's brother to me." 8. Then the elders of his town shall summon him and speak to him. If he persists, saying, "I have no desire to marry her," 9. then his brother's wife shall go up to him in the presence of the elders, pull his sandal off his foot, spit in his face, and declare, "This is what is done to the man who does not build up his brother's house." 10. Throughout Israel his family shall be known as "the house of him whose sandal was pulled off." 11. If men get into a fight with one another, and the wife of one intervenes to rescue her husband from the grip of his opponent by reaching out and seizing his genitals, 12. you shall cut off her hand; show no pity.

The Song of Songs (*Song of Solomon*)

The Song of Songs (also known as the Song of Solomon and Canticles) contains eight erotic love poems. These poems had different allegorical meanings for Jews and Christians. For the Jews, the book symbolized God's love for Israel; for Christians it meant Christ's love for the Church. The book is dated around 538 BCE, after the Jews were exiled to Babylon.

[SONG OF SOLOMON 1-3]

1 The Song of Songs, which is
   Solomon's.

COLLOQUY OF WOMEN
        AND FRIENDS

2 Let him kiss me with the kisses of
   his mouth!
   For your love is better than wine,

3 your anointing oils are fragrant,
   your name is perfume poured
        out;
   therefore the maidens love you.

4 Draw me after you, let us make
        haste.
   The king has brought me into his
        chambers.
   We will exult and rejoice in you;

we will extol your love more than
  wine;
rightly do they love you.

5 I am black and beautiful,
  O daughters of Jerusalem,
like the tents of Kedar,
  like the curtains of Solomon.
6   Do not gaze at me because I am
  dark,
because the sun has gazed on me.
My mother's sons were angry with me;
  they made me keeper of the vineyards,
  but my own vineyard I have not kept!
7 Tell me, you whom my soul loves,
  where you pasture your flock,
  where you make it lie down at noon;
for why should I be like one who is
  veiled
beside the flocks of your companions?
8 If you do not know,
  O fairest among women,
follow the tracks of the flock,
  and pasture your kids
beside the shepherds' tents.

COLLOQUY OF LOVERS
9 I compare you, my love,
  to a mare among Pharaoh's chariots.
10 Your cheeks are comely with ornaments,
  your neck with strings of jewels.
11 We will make you ornaments of
  gold,
  studded with silver.
12 While the king was on his couch,
  my nard gave forth its fragrance.
13 My beloved is to me a bag of myrrh
  that lies between my breasts.
14 My beloved is to me a cluster of
  henna blossoms
  in the vineyards of En-gedi.
15 Ah, you are beautiful, my love;
  ah, you are beautiful; your eyes are
  doves.
16 Ah, you are beautiful, my beloved,
  truly lovely.
  Our couch is green;

17 the beams of our house are cedar,
  our rafters are pine.

2   I am a rose of Sharon,
  a lily of the valleys.
2 As a lily among brambles,
  so is my love among maidens.
3 As an apple tree among the trees
  of the wood,
  so is my beloved among young men.
With great delight I sat in his shadow,
  and his fruit was sweet to my taste.
4 He brought me to the banqueting
  house,
  and his intention toward me was
  love.
5 Sustain me with raisins,
  refresh me with apples;
  for I am faint with love.
6 O that his left hand were under
  my head,
  and that his right hand embraced
  me!
7 I adjure you, O daughters of
  Jerusalem,
  by the gazelles or the wild does:
do not stir up or awaken love
  until it is ready!

SPRINGTIME RHAPSODY
8 The voice of my beloved!
  Look, he comes,
leaping upon the mountains,
  bounding over the hills.
9 My beloved is like a gazelle
  or a young stag.
Look, there he stands
  behind our wall,
gazing in at the windows,
  looking through the lattice.
10 My beloved speaks and says to me:
"Arise, my love, my fair one,
  and come away;
11 for now the winter is past,
  the rain is over and gone.
12 The flowers appear on the earth;
  the time of singing has come,
and the voice of the turtledove
  is heard in our land.

13 The fig tree puts forth its figs,
  and the vines are in blossom;
  they give forth fragrance.
 Arise, my love, my fair one,
  and come away.
14 O my dove, in the clefts of the
    rock,
  in the covert of the cliff,
 let me see your face,
  let me hear your voice;
 for your voice is sweet,
  and your face is lovely.
15 Catch us the foxes,
  the little foxes,
 that ruin the vineyards —
  for our vineyards are in blossom."

16 My beloved is mine and I am his;
  he pastures his flock among the lilies.
17 Until the day breathes
  and the shadows flee,
 turn, my beloved, be like a gazelle
  or a young stag on the cleft moun-
    tains.

A NIGHTTIME SEARCH
3 Upon my bed at night
  I sought him whom my soul loves;
 I sought him, but found him not;
  I called him, but he gave no answer.
 2 "I will rise now and go about the
    city,
  in the streets and in the squares;
 I will seek him whom my soul
    loves."
  I sought him, but found him not.
 3 The sentinels found me,
  as they went about in the city.
 "Have you seen him whom my soul
    loves?"
 4 Scarcely had I passed them,
  when I found him whom my soul
    loves.

I held him, and would not let him go
  until I brought him into my
    mother's house,
  and into the chamber of her that
    conceived me.
5 I adjure you, O daughters of
    Jerusalem,
  by the gazelles or the wild does:
 do not stir up or awaken love
  until it is ready!

SOLOMON'S PALANQUIN
6 What is that coming up from the
    wilderness,
  like a column of smoke,
 perfumed with myrrh and frankin-
    cense,
  with all the fragrant powders of the
    merchant?
7 Look, it is the litter of Solomon!
 Around it are sixty mighty men
  of the mighty men of Israel,
8 all equipped with swords
  and expert in war,
 each with his sword at his thigh
  because of alarms by night.
9 King Solomon made himself a
    palanquin
  from the wood of Lebanon.
10 He made its posts of silver,
  its back of gold, its seat of purple;
 its interior was inlaid with love.
  Daughters of Jerusalem,
11 come out.
 Look, O daughters of Zion,
  at King Solomon,
 at the crown with which his mother
    crowned him
  on the day of his wedding,
  on the day of the gladness of his
    heart.

2

New Testament

The Gospel According to Matthew

The Gospel according to Matthew is the first book of the New Testament and is assumed to be the oldest of the four gospels, with many scholars assuming it was written around 80 CE. Its authorship is unknown. It deals with the life and teachings of Jesus.

Source: Scripture quotations are from the New Revised Standard Version of the Bible, copyright © 1989 by the Division of Christian Education of the National Council of Churches of Christ in the USA. Used by permission. All rights reserved.

[MATTHEW 19:3–12]

3. Some Pharisees came to him, and to test him they asked, "Is it lawful for a man to divorce his wife for any cause?" 4. He answered, "Have you not read that the one who made them at the beginning 'made them male and female,'" 5. and said, "For this reason a man shall leave his father and mother and be joined to his wife, and the two shall become one flesh? 6. So they are no longer two, but one flesh. Therefore what God has joined together, let no one separate." 7. They said to him, "Why then did Moses command us to give a certificate of dismissal and to divorce her?" 8. He said to them, "It was because you were so hard-hearted that Moses allowed you to divorce your wives, but at the beginning it was not so. 9. And I say to you, whoever divorces his wife, except for unchastity, and marries another commits adultery."

10. His disciples said to him, "If such is the case of a man with his wife, it is better not to marry." 11. But he said to them, "Not everyone can accept this teaching, but only those to whom it is given. 12. For there are eunuchs who have been so from birth, and there are eunuchs who have been made eunuchs by others, and there are eunuchs who have made themselves eunuchs for the sake of the kingdom of heaven. Let anyone accept this who can."

[MATTHEW 22:23–30]

23. The same day some Sadducees came to him, saying there is no resurrection; and they asked him a question, saying, 24. "Teacher, Moses said,

'If a man dies childless, his brother shall marry the widow, and raise up children for his brother.' 25. Now there were seven brothers among us; the first married, and died childless, leaving the widow to his brother. 26. The second did the same, so also the third, down to the seventh. 27. Last of all, the woman herself died. 28. In the resurrection, then, whose wife of the seven will she be? For all of them had married her."

29. Jesus answered them, "You are wrong, because you know neither the scriptures nor the power of God. 30. For in the resurrection they neither marry nor are given in marriage, but are like angels in heaven."

The Gospel According to John

The Gospel according to John is the fourth book of the New Testament. It is not part of the synoptic gospels (Matthew, Mark, and Luke) because its arrangement and emphasis are different. It focuses less on the life of Jesus and more on spiritual concepts such as identifying the Word with Christ. It was written between 85 and 100 CE.

Source: Scripture quotations are from the New Revised Standard Version of the Bible, copyright © 1989 by the Division of Christian Education of the National Council of Churches of Christ in the USA. Used by permission. All rights reserved.

[JOHN 8:1–12]
...while Jesus went to the Mount of Olives. 2. Early in the morning he came again to the temple. All the people came to him and he sat down and began to teach them. 3. The scribes and the Pharisees brought a woman who had been caught in adultery; and making her stand before all of them, 4. they said to him, "Teacher, this woman was caught in the very act of committing adultery. 5. Now in the law Moses commanded us to stone such women. Now what do you say?" 6. They said this to test him, so that they might have some charge to bring against him. Jesus bent down and wrote with his finger on the ground. 7. When they kept on questioning him, he straightened up and said to them, "Let anyone among you who is without sin be the first to throw a stone at her." 8. And once again he bent down and wrote on the ground. 9. When they heard it, they went away, one by one, beginning with the elders; and Jesus was left alone with the woman standing before him. 10. Jesus straightened up and said to her, "Woman, where are they? Has no one condemned you?" 11. She said, "No one, sir." And Jesus said, "Neither do I condemn you. Go your way, and from now on do not sin again."

The First Epistle to the Corinthians

The First Epistle to the Corinthians was written by St. Paul to the people of Corinth, Greece, between 54 and 57 CE. Paul had established the church at Corinth several years earlier, but he learned that the Corinthian church was embroiled in factionalism and abuses. Therefore, he wrote this epistle to explain to the Corinthians his teachings on such topics as morality, marriage, and worship. Many views on marriage within Christian doctrine are based on the teachings of St. Paul.

[1 CORINTHIANS 7: 1–16]

Now concerning the matters about which you wrote: "It is well for a man not to touch a woman." 2. But because of cases of sexual immorality, each man should have his own wife and each woman her own husband. 3. The husband should give to his wife her conjugal rights, and likewise the wife to her husband. 4. For the wife does not have authority over her own body, but the husband does; likewise the husband does not have authority over his own body, but the wife does. 5. Do not deprive one another except perhaps by agreement for a set time, to devote yourselves to prayer, and then come together again, so that Satan may not tempt you because of your lack of self-control. 6. This I say by way of concession, not of command. 7. I wish that all were as I myself am. But each has a particular gift from God, one having one kind and another a different kind.

8. To the unmarried and the widows I say that it is well for them to remain unmarried as I am. 9. But if they are not practicing self-control, they should marry. For it is better to marry than to be aflame with passion.

10. To the married I give this command — not I but the Lord — that the wife should not separate from her husband 11. (but if she does separate, let her remain unmarried or else be reconciled to her husband), and that the husband should not divorce his wife.

12. To the rest I say — I and not the Lord — that if any believer has a wife who is an unbeliever, and she consents to live with him, he should not divorce her. 13. And if any woman has a husband who is an unbeliever, and he consents to live with her, she should not divorce him. 14. For the unbelieving husband is made holy through his wife, and the unbelieving wife is made holy through her husband. Otherwise, your children would be unclean, but as it is, they are holy. 15. But if the unbelieving partner separates, let it be so; in such a case the brother or sister is not bound. It is to peace that God has called you. 16. Wife, for all you know, you might save your husband. Husband, for all you know, you might save your wife.

The First Epistle to the Ephesians

The Epistle to the Ephesians is believed by many to have been written by one of St. Paul's followers between 58 and 60 CE, rather than by Paul himself. Its emphasis is on the relationship between Christ and the church and the unity of all Christians.

[EPHESIANS 5:22–33]

22. Wives, be subject to your husbands as you are to the Lord. 23. For the husband is the head of the wife just as Christ is the head of the church, the body of which he is the Saviour. 24. Just as the church is subject to Christ, so also wives ought to be, in everything, to their husbands.

25. Husbands, love your wives, just as Christ loved the church and gave himself up for her, 26. in order to make her holy by cleansing her with the washing of water by the word, 27. so as to present the church to himself in splendour, without a spot or wrinkle or anything of the kind — yes, so that she may be holy and without blemish. 28. In the same way, husbands should love their wives as they do their own bodies. He who loves his wife loves himself. 29. For no one ever hates his own body, but he nourishes and tenderly cares for it, just as Christ does for the church, 30. because we are members of his body. 31. "For this reason a man will leave his father and mother and be joined to his wife, and the two will become one flesh." 32. This is a great mystery, and I am applying it to Christ and the church. 33. Each of you, however, should love his wife as himself, and a wife should respect her husband.

The First Epistle to Timothy

The First Epistle to Timothy is part of the Pastoral Epistles, which include also the Second Epistle to Timothy and the Epistle to Titus. These letters were written for the clergy and discussed church government and teachings. Timothy was Paul's younger co-worker. Scholars are uncertain if this epistle is the actual work of St. Paul himself. It is dated between 60 and 62 CE.

[1 TIMOTHY 2:8–15]

8. I desire, then, that in every place the men should pray, lifting up holy hands without anger or argument; 9. also that the women should dress

themselves modestly and decently in suitable clothing, not with their hair braided, or with gold, pearls, or expensive clothes, 10. but with good works, as is proper for women who profess reverence for God. 11. Let a woman learn in silence with full submission. 12. I permit no woman to teach or to have authority over a man; she is to keep silent. 13. For Adam was formed first, then Eve; 14. and Adam was not deceived, but the woman was deceived and became a transgressor. 15. Yet she will be saved through childbearing, provided they continue in faith and love and holiness, with modesty.

II

CHRISTIAN
THOUGHT

you = woman
we = everyone

3

Early Church Fathers

On the Apparel of Women
Tertullian (160?–225?)

Tertullian came from North Africa, which was renowned for its rigorous moralism. According to Tertullian and other Church fathers, sexuality entered the world when Adam and Eve disobeyed God in the Garden of Eden. Thereafter, humanity became mired in temptations of the flesh, which interfered with the soul's striving for spiritual closeness with God. Although himself married, Tertullian believed that sexual intercourse was illicit even within marriage. He was a member of the Monatist sect whose members practiced extreme asceticism. *woman had more power* In the following excerpt from *On the Apparel of Women*, Tertullian argues that because sin entered the world through Eve, women should don penitential garb to reflect their collective guilt. Women were the greatest temptation, and for this reason they needed to be particularly careful not to incite lust in men. The work is addressed to women and criticizes their ostentatious dress and behavior, stating that a woman who provokes lust is guilty of the same sin as the man who lusts after her.

Source: The Ante-Nicene Fathers: *Translations of the Writings of the Fathers Down to A.D. 325. Vol. IV: Tertullian, Part Four; Minucius Felix; Commodian; Origen.* Edited by the Rev. Alexander Roberts and James Donaldson (Grand Rapids, MI: WMB Eerdmans Publishing Company). Pp. 19–20, 24–25.

[BOOK II, CHAPTER II:] PERFECT MODESTY WILL ABSTAIN FROM
WHATEVER TENDS TO SIN, AS WELL AS FROM SIN ITSELF.
DIFFERENCE BETWEEN TRUST AND PRESUMPTION. IF SECURE
OURSELVES, WE MUST NOT PUT TEMPTATION IN THE WAY OF
OTHERS. WE MUST LOVE OUR NEIGHBOUR AS OURSELF.

You must know that in the eye of perfect, that is, Christian, modesty, (carnal) desire of one's self (on the part of others) is not only not to be desired, but even execrated, by you: first, because the study of making personal grace (which we know to be naturally the inviter of lust) a mean of pleasing does not spring from a sound conscience: why therefore excite toward yourself that evil (passion)? why invite (that) to which you profess yourself a stranger? secondly, because we ought not to open a way to temptations, which, by their instancy, sometimes achieve (a wickedness) which God expels from them who are His; (or,) at all events, put the spirit into a thorough tumult by (presenting) a stumbling-block (to it). We ought indeed to walk so holily, and with so entire substantiality of faith, as to be confident and secure in regard of our own conscience, *desiring* that that (gift) may abide in us to the end, yet not *presuming* (that it will). For he who presumes feels less apprehension; he who feels less apprehension takes less precaution; he who takes less precaution runs more risk. Fear is the foundation of salvation; presumption is an impediment to fear. More useful, then, is it to apprehend that we may possibly fail, than to presume that we cannot; for apprehending will lead us to fear, fearing to caution, and caution to salvation. On the other hand, if we presume, there will be neither fear nor caution to save us. He who acts securely, and not at the same time warily, possesses no safe and firm security; whereas he who is wary will be truly able to be secure. For His own servants, may the Lord by His mercy take care that to *them* it may be lawful even to *presume* on His goodness! But why are we a (source of) danger to our neighbour? why do we import concupiscence into our neighbour? which concupiscence, if God, in "amplifying the law,"[1] do not dissociate in (the way of) penalty from the actual commission of fornication,[2] I know not whether He allows impunity to him who has been the cause of perdition to some other. For that other, as soon as he has felt concupiscence after your beauty, and has mentally already committed (the deed) which his concupiscence pointed to, perishes; and you have been made the sword which destroys him: so that, albeit you be free from the (actual) crime, you are not free from the odium (attaching to it); as, when a robbery has been committed on some man's estate, the (actual) crime indeed will not be laid to the owner's charge, while yet the domain is branded with ignominy, (and) the owner himself aspersed with the infamy. Are we to paint ourselves out that our neighbours may perish? Where, then, is (the command), "Thou shalt love thy neighbour as thyself?"[3] "Care not merely about your own (things), but (about your) neighbour's?"[4] No enunciation of the Holy Spirit ought to be (confined) to the subject immediately in hand merely, and not applied and carried out with a view to every occasion to which its application is useful.[5] Since, therefore,

1. Matt. 5:17.
2. Matt. 5:28.
3. Lev. 9:18; Matt. 19: 19, 22: 39; Mark 12: 31; Luke 10: 27; Rom. 13:9; Gal. 5:14; Jas. 2:8.
4. Cf. 1 Cor. 10: 24, 13: 5; Phil. 2:4.
5. Cf. 2 Pet. 1:20

both our own interest and that of others is implicated in the studious pursuit of most perilous (outward) comeliness, it is time for you to know that not merely must the pageantry of fictitious and elaborate beauty be rejected by you; but that of even natural grace must be obliterated by concealment and negligence, as equally dangerous to the glances of (the beholder's) eyes. For, albeit comeliness is not to be *censured*, as being a bodily happiness, as being an additional outlay of the divine plastic art, as being a kind of goodly garment[6] of the soul; yet it is to be *feared*, just on account of the injuriousness and violence of suitors: which (injuriousness and violence) even the father of the faith,[7] Abraham,[8] greatly feared in regard of his own wife's grace; and Isaac,[9] by falsely representing Rebecca as his sister, purchased safety by insult!

[BOOK II, CHAPTER XII:] SUCH OUTWARD ADORNMENTS
  MERETRICIOUS, AND THEREFORE UNSUITABLE TO MODEST WOMEN

Let us only wish that we may be no cause for just blasphemy! But how much more provocative of blasphemy is it that you, who are called modesty's priestesses, should appear in public decked and painted out after the manner of the *im*modest? Else, (if you so do,) what inferiority would the poor unhappy victims of the public lusts have (beneath you)? whom, albeit some laws were (formerly) wont to restrain them from (the use of) matrimonial and matronly decorations, now, at all events, the daily increasing depravity of the age has raised so nearly to an equality with all the most honourable women, that the difficulty is to distinguish them. And yet, even the Scriptures suggest (to us the reflection), that meretricious attractivenesses of form are invariably conjoined with and appropriate to bodily prostitution. That powerful state which presides over the seven mountains and very many waters, has merited from the Lord the appellation of a prostitute.[10] But what kind of garb is the instrumental mean of her comparison with that appellation? She sits, to be sure, "in purple, and scarlet, and gold, and precious stone." How accursed are the things without (the aid of) which an accursed prostitute could not have been described! It was the fact that Thamar "had painted out and adorned herself" that led Judah to regard her as a harlot,[11] and thus, because she was hidden beneath her "veil," — the quality of her garb belying her as if she had been a harlot, — he judged (her to be one), and addressed and bargained with (her as such). Whence we gather an addi-

---

6. Cf. Gen. 27:15
7. Cf. Rom. 4: 11, 16
8. Gen. 12: 10-20, and 20.
9. Gen. 26: 6-11
10. Cf. Rev. 17
11. Cf. Gen. 38: 12-30.

tional confirmation of the lesson, that provision must be made in every way against all immodest associations and suspicions. For why is the integrity of a chaste mind defiled by its neighbour's suspicion? Why is a thing from which I am averse hoped for in me? Why does not my garb pre-announce my character, to prevent my spirit from being wounded by shamelessness through (the channel of) my ears? Grant that it be lawful to assume the appearance of a modest woman: to assume that of an *im*modest is, at all events, *not* lawful.

"Letter to Eustochium"
St. Jerome (c. 340–420)

Jerome was born in Stridon, Dalmatia, and converted to Christianity after arriving in Rome in his early twenties. He traveled around the Roman Empire for study and at one point lived as an ascetic in the desert for two years. Upon returning to Rome, he became spiritual advisor to a circle of Roman aristocratic women and secretary to Pope Damascus. Later in life he founded a monastery in Bethlehem with the help of some of his women patrons. Jerome's writings are passionate and controversial. He once wrote, "A man who loves his wife too much takes her as a whore." His writings indicate a belief that marriage and sexual intercourse are morally inferior to a life of virginity and asceticism. He discusses this view in the following passage, which comes from his famous letter written to one of his female followers, Eustochium.

Source: *A Select Library of Nicene and Post-Nicene Fathers of the Christian Church. Second Series. Vol. IV. St. Jerome: Letters and Select Works,* under the editorial supervision of Philip Schaff and Henry Wace, (Grand Rapids, MI: WM.B. Eerdmans, reprint 1961), pp. 24–25, 27–28, 30.

7. How often, when I was living in the desert, in the vast solitude which gives to hermits a savage dwelling-place, parched by a burning sun, how often did I fancy myself among the pleasures of Rome! I used to sit alone because I was filled with bitterness. Sackcloth disfigured my unshapely limbs and my skin from long neglect had become as black as an Ethiopian's. Tears and groans were every day my portion; and if drowsiness chanced to overcome my struggles against it, my bare bones, which hardly held together, clashed against the ground. Of my food and drink I say nothing: for, even in sickness, the solitaries have nothing but cold water, and to eat one's food cooked is looked upon as self-indulgence. Now, although in my fear of hell I had consigned myself to this prison, where I had no companions but scorpions and wild beasts, I often found myself amid bevies of girls. My face was pale and my frame chilled with fasting; yet my mind was burning with desire,

and the fires of lust kept bubbling up before me when my flesh was as good as dead. Helpless, I cast myself at the feet of Jesus, I watered them with my tears, I wiped them with my hair: and then I subdued my rebellious body with weeks of abstinence. I do not blush to avow my abject misery; rather I lament that I am not now what once I was. I remember how I often cried aloud all night till the break of day and ceased not from beating my breast till tranquility returned at the chiding of the Lord. I used to dread my very cell as though it knew my thoughts; and, stern and angry with myself, I used to make my way alone into the desert. Wherever I saw hollow valleys, craggy mountains, steep cliffs, there I made my oratory, there the house of correction for my unhappy flesh. There, also — the Lord Himself is my witness — when I had shed copious tears and had strained my eyes towards heaven, I sometimes felt myself among angelic hosts, and for joy and gladness sang: "because of the savour of thy good ointments we will run after thee."[12]

8. Now, if such are the temptations of men who, since their bodies are emaciated with fasting, have only evil thoughts to fear, how must it fare with a girl whose surroundings are those of luxury and ease? Surely, to use the apostle's words, "She is dead while she liveth."[13] Therefore, if experience gives me a right to advise, or clothes my words with credit, I would begin by urging you and warning you as Christ's spouse to avoid wine as you would avoid poison. For wine is the first weapon used by demons against the young. Greed does not shake, nor pride puff up, nor ambition infatuate so much as this. Other vices we easily escape, but this enemy is shut up within us, and wherever we go we carry him with us. Wine and youth between them kindle the fire of sensual pleasure. Why do we throw oil on the flame-why do we add fresh fuel to a miserable body which is already ablaze. Paul, it is true, says to Timothy "drink no longer water, but use a little wine for thy stomach's sake, and for thine often infirmities."[14] But notice the reasons for which the permission is given, to cure an aching stomach and a frequent infirmity. And lest we should indulge ourselves too much on the score of our ailments, he commands that but little shall be taken; advising rather as a physician than as an apostle (though, indeed, an apostle is a spiritual physician). He evidently feared that Timothy might succumb to weakness, and might prove unequal to the constant moving to and fro involved in preaching the Gospel. Besides, he remembered that he had spoken of "wine wherein is excess,"[15] and had said, "it is good neither to eat flesh nor to drink wine."[16] Noah drank

12. Cant. 1: 3,4.
13. 1 Tim. 5:6.
14. 1 Tim. 5:23.
15. Eph. 5: 18.
16. Rom. 14: 21.

wine and became intoxicated; but living as he did in the rude age after the flood, when the vine was first planted, perhaps he did not know its power of inebriation. And to let you see the hidden meaning of Scripture in all its fulness (for the word of God is a pearl and may be pierced on every side) after his drunkenness came the uncovering of his body; self-indulgence culminated in lust.[17] First the belly is crammed; then the other members are roused. Similarly, at a later period, "The people sat down to eat and to drink and rose up to play."[18] Lot also, God's friend, whom He saved upon the mountain, who was the only one found righteous out of so many thousands, was intoxicated by his daughters. And, although they may have acted as they did more from a desire of offspring than from love of sinful pleasure — for the human race seemed in danger of extinction — yet they were well aware that the righteous man would not abet their design unless intoxicated. In fact he did not know what he was doing, and his sin was not wilful. Still his error was a grave one, for it made him the father of Moab and Ammon,[19] Israel's enemies, of whom it is said: "Even to the fourteenth generation they shall not enter into the congregation of the Lord forever."[20]

13. I cannot bring myself to speak of the many virgins who daily fall and are lost to the bosom of the church, their mother: stars over which the proud foe sets up his throne,[21] and rocks hollowed by the serpent that he may dwell in their fissures. You may see many women widows before wedded, who try to conceal their miserable fall by a lying garb. Unless they are betrayed by swelling wombs or by the crying of their infants, they walk abroad with tripping feet and heads in the air. Some go so far as to take potions, that they may insure barrenness, and thus murder human beings almost before their conception. Some, when they find themselves with child through their sin, use drugs to procure abortion, and when (as often happens) they die with their offspring, they enter the lower world laden with the guilt not only of adultery against Christ but also of suicide and child murder. Yet it is these who say: "'Unto the pure all things are pure;'[22] my conscience is sufficient guide for me. A pure heart is what God looks for. Why should I abstain from meats which God has created to be received with thanksgiving?"[23] And when they wish to appear agreeable and entertaining they first drench themselves with wine, and then joining the grossest profanity to intoxication, they

---

17. Gen. 9:20, 21.
18. Ex. 32:6.
19. Gen. 19: 30-38.
20. Deut. 23:3.
21. Isa. 14:13.
22. Tit. 1:15.
23. 1 Tim. 4:3.

say: "Far be it from me to abstain from the blood of Christ." And when they see another pale or sad they call her "wretch" or "manichaean"; quite logically, indeed, for on their principles fasting involves heresy. When they go out they do their best to attract notice, and with nods and winks encourage troops of young fellows to follow them. Of each and all of these the prophet's words are true: "Thou hast a whore's forehead; thou refusest to be ashamed."[24] Their robes have but a narrow purple stripe, it is true; and their head-dress is somewhat loose, so as to leave the hair free. From their shoulders flutters the lilac mantle which they call "maforte"; they have their feet in cheap slippers and their arms tucked up tight-fitting sleeves. Add to these marks of their profession an easy gait, and you have all the virginity that they possess. Such may have eulogizers of their own, and may fetch a higher price in the market of perdition, merely because they are called virgins. But to such virgins as these I prefer to be displeasing.

14. I blush to speak of it, it is so shocking; yet though sad, it is true. How comes this plague of the agapetae to be in the church? Whence come these unwedded wives, these novel concubines, these harlots, so I will call them, though they cling to a single partner? One house holds them and one chamber. They often occupy the same bed, and yet they call us suspicious if we fancy anything amiss. A brother leaves his virgin sister; a virgin, slighting her unmarried brother, seeks a brother in a stranger. Both alike profess to have but one object, to find spiritual consolation from those not of their kin; but their real aim is to indulge in sexual intercourse. It is on such that Solomon in the book of proverbs heaps his scorn. "Can a man take fire in his bosom," he says, "and his clothes not be burned? Can one go upon hot coals and his feet not be burned?"[25]...

16. Do not court the company of married ladies or visit the houses of the high-born. Do not look too often on the life which you despised to become a virgin. Women of the world, you know, plume themselves because their husbands are on the bench or in other high positions. And the wife of the emperor always has an eager throng of visitors at her door. Why do you, then, wrong your husband? Why do you, God's bride, hasten to visit the wife of a mere man? Learn in this respect a holy pride; know that you are better than they. And not only must you avoid intercourse with those who are puffed up by their husbands' honors, who are hedged in with troops of eunuchs, and who wear robes inwrought with threads of gold. You must also shun those who are widows from necessity and not from choice. Not that they ought to have desired the death of their husbands; but that they have

24. Jer. 3:3.
25. Prov. 6:27, 28.

not welcomed the opportunity of continence when it has come. As it is, they only change their garb; their old self-seeking remains unchanged. To see them in their capacious litters, with red cloaks and plump bodies, a row of eunuchs walking in front of them, you would fancy them not to have lost husbands but to be seeking them. Their houses are filled with flatterers and with guests. The very clergy, who ought to inspire them with respect by their teaching and authority, kiss these ladies on the forehead, and putting forth their hands (so that, if you knew no better, you might suppose them in the act of blessing), take wages for their visits. They, meanwhile, seeing that priests cannot do without them, are lifted up into pride; and as, having had experience of both, they prefer the license of widowhood to the restraints of marriage, they call themselves chaste livers and nuns. After an immoderate supper they retire to rest to dream of the apostles....

20. I praise wedlock, I praise marriage, but it is because they give me virgins. I gather the rose from the thorns, the gold from the earth, the pearl from the shell. "Doth the plowman plow all day to sow?"[26] Shall he not also enjoy the fruit of his labor? Wedlock is the more honored, the more what is born of it is loved. Why, mother, do you grudge your daughter her virginity? She has been reared on your milk, she has come from your womb, she has grown up in your bosom. Your watchful affection has kept her a virgin. Are you angry with her because she chooses to be a king's wife and not a soldier's? She has conferred on you a high privilege; you are now the mother-in-law of God. "Concerning virgins," says the apostle, "I have no commandment of the Lord."[27] Why was this? Because his own virginity was due, not to a command, but to his free choice. For they are not to be heard who feign him to have had a wife; for, when he is discussing continence and commending perpetual chastity, he uses the words, "I would that all men were even as I myself." And farther on, "I say, therefore, to the unmarried and widows, it is good for them if they abide even as I."[28] And in another place, "have we not power to lead about wives even as the rest of the apostles?"[29] Why then has he no commandment from the Lord concerning virginity? Because what is freely offered is worth more than what is extorted by force, and to command virginity would have been to abrogate wedlock. It would have been a hard enactment to compel opposition to nature and to extort from men the angelic life; and not only so, it would have been to condemn what is a divine ordinance.

26. Isa. 28: 24.
27. 1 Cor. 7: 25.
28. 1 Cor. 7:7, 1 Cor. 7:8.
29. 1 Cor. 9:5.

The Good of Marriage *and* The City of God
St. Augustine (354–430)

Born in North Africa, converted to Christianity at the age of thirty-two, and later elected Bishop of Hippo, Augustine was one of the most influential thinkers in the history of the Church. In his view of sexuality Augustine diverged from Church fathers like Tertullian and Jerome, which suggests that no consensus existed within the early Church on sexuality. Augustine believed that sexual relations between husband and wife were part of God's plan and not an aberration that afflicted humans after Adam and Eve's expulsion from the Garden of Eden. Rather, Augustine was more concerned about lust, which he saw as the irrational and uncontrollable companion to sex. In his *Against Julian*, Augustine stated that following the fall of Adam, lust became inextricably intertwined with sex. As a result, the sin of lust is passed inexorably to a newborn child in the form of original sin.

The first excerpt below comes from *The Good of Marriage*, in which Augustine outlines the positive aspects of married life — children, companionship, and fidelity. In the second excerpt, from *The City of God*, Augustine explains what the nature of sex would have been if Adam and Eve had not been expelled from the Garden of Eden.

Source: *St. Augustine on Marriage and Sexuality*, edited by Elizabeth A. Clark (Washington, D.C.: Catholic University of America Press, 1996), pp. 19–20, 45–48, 74–78. Reprinted with permission.

The Good of Marriage

3. This is what we now say, that according to the present condition of birth and death, which we know and in which we were created, the marriage of male and female is something good. This union divine Scripture so commands that it is not permitted a woman who has been dismissed by her husband to marry again, as long as her husband lives, nor is it permitted a man who has been dismissed by his wife to marry again, unless she who left has died. Therefore, regarding the good of marriage, which even the Lord confirmed in the Gospel,[30] not only because He forbade the dismissal of a wife except for fornication, but also because He came to the marriage when invited,[31] there is merit in inquiring why it is a good.

This does not seem to me to be a good solely because of the procreation of children, but also because of the natural companionship between the two sexes. Otherwise, we could not speak of marriage in the case of old

30. Cf. Mt. 19:9.
31. Cf. Jn. 2.

people, especially if they had either lost their children or had begotten none at all. But, in a good marriage, although one of many years, even if the ardor of youth has cooled between man and woman, the order of charity still flourishes between husband and wife. They are better in proportion as they begin the earlier to refrain by mutual consent from sexual intercourse, not that it would afterwards happen of necessity that they would not be able to do what they wished, but that it would be a matter of praise that they had refused beforehand what they were able to do. Suppose, then, that the promise of respect and of services due to the other by either sex is observed. In that case, even though both members weaken in health and become almost corpse-like, chastity, that of souls rightly joined together, continues — and it becomes more pure, the more it has been proved, and more secure, the more it has been calmed.

Marriage has also this good, that carnal or youthful incontinence, even if it is bad, is turned to the honorable task of begetting children, so that marital intercourse makes something good out of the evil of lust. Finally, the concupiscence of the flesh, which parental affection tempers, is repressed and becomes inflamed more modestly. For a kind of dignity prevails when, as husband and wife they unite in the marriage act, they think of themselves as mother and father.

4. There is the added fact that, in the very debt which married persons owe each other, even if they demand its payment somewhat intemperately and incontinently, they owe fidelity equally to each other. And to this fidelity the Apostle has attributed so much right that he called it authority, when he said: "The wife has not authority over her body, but the husband; the husband likewise has not authority over his body, but the wife."[32] But the violation of this fidelity is called adultery, when, either by the instigation of one's own lust or by consent to the lust of another, there is intercourse with another contrary to the marriage compact. And so the fidelity is broken which even in material and base things is a great good of the soul; and so it is certain that it ought to be preferred even to the health of the body wherein his life is contained. For, although a small amount of straw as compared to much gold is as nothing, fidelity, when it is kept pure in a matter of straw, as in a matter of gold, is not of less importance on this account because it is kept in a matter of less value.

But, when fidelity is employed to commit sin, we wonder whether it ought to be called fidelity. However, whatever its nature may be, if even against this something is done, it has an added malice; except when this is abandoned with the view that there might be a return to the true and lawful

32. 1 Cor. 7:4.

fidelity, that is, that the sin might be amended by correcting the depravity of the will.

For example, if anyone, when he is unable to rob a man by himself, finds an accomplice for his crime and makes an agreement with him to perform the act together and share the loot, and, after the crime has been committed, he runs off with everything, the other naturally grieves and complains that fidelity had not been observed in his regard. In his very complaint he ought to consider that he should have observed his fidelity to human society by means of a good life, so that he would not rob a man unjustly, if he feels how wickedly fidelity was not kept with him in an association of sin. His partner, faithless on both counts, is certainly to be judged the more wicked. But, if he had been displeased with the wickedness which they had committed and so had refused to divide the spoils with his partner in crime on this account, that he could return them to the man from whom they were taken, not even the faithless man would call him faithless.

So, in the case of a woman who has broken her marriage fidelity but remains faithful to her adulterer, she is surely wicked, but, if she is not faithful even to her adulterer, she is worse. On the contrary, if she repents of her gross sin and returns to conjugal chastity and breaks off all adulterous unions and purposes, I cannot conceive of even the adulterer himself thinking of her as a violator of fidelity.

5. The question is also usually asked whether this case ought to be called a marriage: when a man and woman, neither of whom is married to anyone else, because of incontinence have intercourse with each other not for the purpose of procreating children but only for the sake of sex itself, with this pledge between them, that neither of them will have sex with anyone else. Yet perhaps not without reason this can be called wedlock, if this has been agreed upon between them that this arrangement should last even until the death of one of them and if, although they do not have intercourse for the purpose of having children, they at least do not avoid it, so that they do not refuse to have children nor act in any evil way so that they will not be born. But, if both or either one of these conditions is lacking, I do not see how we can call this a marriage.

For, if man lives with a woman for a time, but only until he finds another worthy either of his high station in life or his wealth, whom he can marry as his equal, in his very soul he is an adulterer, and not with the one whom he desires to find but with her with whom he now lives though not in a real marriage. The same is true for the woman, who, knowing the situation and willing it, still has sexual relations unchastely with him, with whom she has no vow as a wife. On the other hand, if she remains faithful to him and, after he has taken a wife, refuses to marry and is prepared to refrain absolutely from such an act, surely I would not lightly dare to call her an adulteress. Yet who would not say that she had sinned, when he knows that she had relations with a man though she was not his wife?

If from the union, however, she wants nothing except children and whatever she endures beyond the reason of procreation she endures unwillingly, surely this woman ranks above many matrons, who although they are not adulteresses, nevertheless force their husbands, who often desire to be continent, to have sexual intercourse, not with any hope of progeny, but though an intemperate use of their right under the passion of lust, still, in the marriage of these women there is this good, that they are married. They are married for this purpose, that lust may be brought under a lawful bond and may not waver disgracefully and loosely. Lust has in itself a weakness of the flesh that cannot be curbed, but in marriage there is an association of fidelity that cannot be dissolved. Of itself, lust leads to immoderate intercourse, but in marriage it becomes a means of reproducing chastely. For, although it is disgraceful to make use of a husband for purposes of lust, it is nevertheless honorable to refuse to have intercourse except with a husband and not to give birth except from a husband.

There also are men incontinent to such a degree that they do not spare their wives even when pregnant. Whatever immodest, shameful, and sordid acts the married commit with each other are the sins of the married persons themselves, not the fault of marriage.

6. Furthermore, in the more immoderate demand of the carnal debt, which the Apostle enjoined on them not as a command but conceded as a favor, to have sexual intercourse even without the purpose of procreation, although evil habits impel them to such intercourse, marriage protects them from adultery and fornication. For this is not permitted because of the marriage, but because of the marriage it is pardoned. Therefore, married people owe each other not only the fidelity of sexual intercourse for the purpose of procreating children — and this is the first association of the human race in this mortal life — but also the mutual service, in a certain measure, of sustaining each other's weakness, for the avoidance of illicit intercourse, so that, even if perpetual continence is pleasing to one of them, he may not follow this urge except with the consent of the other. In this case, "The wife has not authority over her body, but the husband; the husband likewise has not authority over his body, but the wife." So, let them not deny either to each other, what the man seeks from matrimony and the woman from her husband, not for the sake of having children but because of weakness and incontinence, lest in this way they fall into damnable seductions through the temptations of Satan because of the incontinence of both or one of them.

In marriage, intercourse for the purpose of generation has no fault attached to it, but for the purpose of satisfying concupiscence, provided with a spouse, because of the marriage fidelity, it is a venial sin; adultery or fornication, however, is a mortal sin. And so, continence from all intercourse is certainly better than marital intercourse itself which takes place for the sake of begetting children.

The City of God

[BOOK 14, CHAPTER 16]

There are, then, many kinds of lusts for this or that, but when the word is used by itself without specification it suggests to most people the lust for sexual excitement. Such lust does not merely invade the whole body and outward members; it takes such complete and passionate possession of the whole man, both physically and emotionally, that what results is the keenest of all pleasures on the level of sensation; and, at the crisis of excitement, it practically paralyzes all power of deliberate thought.

This is so true that it creates a problem for every lover of wisdom and holy joys who is both committed to a married life and also conscious of the apostolic ideal, that every one should "learn how to possess his vessel in holiness and honor, not in the passion of lust like the Gentiles who do not know God."[33] Any such person would prefer, if this were possible, to beget his children without suffering this passion. He could wish that, just as all his other members obey his reason in the performance of their appointed tasks, so the organs of parenthood, too, might function in obedience to the orders of will and not be excited by the ardors of lust.

Curiously enough, not even those who love this pleasure most — whether legitimately or illegitimately indulged — can control their own indulgences. Sometimes, their lust is most importunate when they least desire it; at other times, the feelings fail them when they crave them most, their bodies remaining frigid when lust is blazing in their souls. And so, strangely, lust serves neither the will to generate, nor lust for its own source; and the very passion that so often joins forces to resist the soul is sometimes so divided against itself that, after it has roused the soul to passion, it refuses to awaken the feelings of the flesh.

[CHAPTER 21]

No one, then, should dream of believing that the kind of lust which made the married couple in the Garden ashamed of their nakedness was meant to be the only means of fulfilling the command which God gave when

---

33. 1 Thes. 4:4.

He "blessed them, saying: 'Increase and multiply, and fill the earth.'"[34] The fact is that this passion had no place before they sinned; it was only after the fall, when their nature had lost its power to exact obedience from the sexual organs, that they fell and noticed the loss and, being ashamed of their lust, covered these unruly members. But God's blessings on their marriage, with the command to increase and multiply and fill the earth, was given before the fall. The blessing remained even when they had sinned, because it was a token that the begetting of children is a part of the glory of marriage and has nothing to do with the penalty for sin.

[CHAPTER 24]

In Paradise, then, generative seed would have been sown by the husband and the wife would have conceived as need required, and all would have been achieved by deliberate choice and not by uncontrollable lust. After all, it is not only our hands and fingers, feet and toes, made up of joints and bones that we move at will, but we can also control the flexing and stiffening of muscles and nerves, as when we voluntarily wrinkle our face or pout with our lips. So, too, with the lungs, which are the most delicate of human organs next to the brain, and need the protection of a wall of ribs. Whether we inhale or exhale or make or modify sounds as in puffing, panting, talking, shouting and singing, the lungs obey our will as readily as the bellows obey a blacksmith or an organist. It is worth mentioning in passing that some of the animals can move their skin in a particular spot where something is felt that ought to be removed as when they shake off a fly or, in some cases, even expel a spear from where it is lodged. Merely because men have no such power is no reason why God could not give it to any animals He wanted to. Nor is there any reason why man should not have had control even over those lowly organs which have been so rebellious ever since man's own rebellion against God. As far as God is concerned, there was no difficulty in making men in such a way that organs which are now excited only by lust could have been completely controlled by deliberate choice....

[CHAPTER 26]

Now, the point about Eden was that a man could live there as a man longs to live, but only so long as he longed to live as God willed him to live. Man in Eden lived in the enjoyment of God and he was good by a communication of the goodness of God. His life was free from want, and he was free to prolong his life as long as he chose. There were food and drink to keep away hunger and thirst and the tree of life to stave off death from senescence. There was not a sign or a seed of decay in man's body that could be

34. Gn. 1:28.

a source of any physical pain. Not a sickness assailed him from within, and he feared no harm from without. His body was perfectly healthy and his soul completely at peace. And as in Eden itself there was never a day too hot or too cold, so in Adam, who lived there, no fear or desire was ever so passionate as to worry his will. Of sorrows there was none at all and of joys none that was vain, although a perpetual joy that was genuine flowed from the presence of God, because God was loved with a "charity from a pure heart and a good conscience and faith unfeigned."[35] Family affection was ensured by purity of love; body and mind worked in perfect accord; and there was an effortless observance of the law of God. Finally, neither leisure nor labor had ever to suffer from boredom or sloth.

How in the world, then, can any one believe that, in a life so happy and with men so blessed, parenthood was impossible without the passion of lust? Surely, every member of the body was equally submissive to the mind and, surely, a man and his wife could play their active and passive roles in the drama of conception without the lecherous promptings of lust, with perfect serenity of soul and with no sense of disintegration between body and soul. Merely because we have no present experience to prove it, we have no right to reject the possibility that, at a time when there was no unruly lust to excite the organs of generation and when all that was needed was done by deliberate choice, the seminal flow could have reached the womb with as little rupture of the hymen and by the same vaginal ducts as is at present the case, in reverse, with the menstrual flux. And just as the maturity of the fetus could have brought the child to birth without the moanings of the mother in pain, so could connection and conception have occurred by a mutually deliberate union unhurried by the hunger of lust.

Perhaps these matters are somewhat too delicate for further discussions. It must suffice to have done the best that I could to suggest what was possible in the Garden of Eden, before there was any need for the reins of reticence to bridle a discussion like this. However, as things now are, the demands of delicacy are more imperative than those of discussion. The trouble with the hypothesis of a passionless procreation controlled by will, as I am here suggesting it, is that it has never been verified in experience, not even in the experience of those who could have proved that it was possible. Actually, they sinned too soon and brought on themselves exile from Eden. Hence, today it is practically impossible even to discuss the hypothesis of voluntary control without the imagination being filled with the realities of rebellious lust. It is this last fact which explains my reticence; not, certainly, any lack of proof for the conclusion my mind has reached.

35. 1 Tm. 1:5.

4

Reformers, Scholastics, and Preachers

The Book of Gomorrah
Peter Damian (1007–1072)

Damian was an Italian monk and reformer. His *Book of Gomorrah* was addressed to Pope Leo IX, and can be dated therefore between 1048 and 1154. Although it was formally addressed to the pope, *The Book of Gomorrah* was also directed at churchmen who engaged in homosexual acts. Throughout the work, Damian argues that priests who behaved in this fashion should be removed from their offices because they were unable to fulfill their spiritual duties properly. He ends his treatise by asking the pope to appoint a committee to investigate the problem. Damian did not receive the reaction he had hoped from the pope. The pope thanked him for his work, but stated that churchmen engaging in such acts perhaps should be treated "more humanely" than Damian had suggested. The following sections show how Peter Damian defined homosexual behavior and the manner in which he condemned homosexuality among churchmen.

Source: *Book of Gomorrah: An Eleventh-Century Treatise against Clerical Homosexual Practices: Peter Damian*, translated by Pierre J. Payer (Waterloo, Ont., Canada: Wilfrid Laurier University Press, 1982), pp. 29, 63–65, 72–73. Reprinted with permission.

THE DIFFERENT TYPES OF THOSE WHO SIN AGAINST NATURE

Four types of this form of criminal wickedness can be distinguished in an effort to show you the totality of the whole matter in an orderly way: some sin with themselves alone; some commit mutual masturbation; some commit femoral fornication; and finally, others commit the complete act against nature. The ascending gradation among these is such that the last mentioned are judged to be more serious than the preceding. Indeed, a greater penance is imposed on those who fall with others than on those who defile only themselves; and those who complete the act are to be judged more severely than those who are defiled through femoral fornication. The devil's artful fraud devises these degrees of falling into ruin such that the higher the level the unfortunate soul reaches in them, the deeper it sinks in the depths of hell's pit.

A DESERVING CONDEMNATION OF ABOMINABLE SHAMEFULNESS

Truly, this vice is never to be compared with any other vice because it surpasses the enormity of all vices. Indeed, this vice is the death of bodies, the destruction of souls. It pollutes the flesh; it extinguishes the light of the mind. It evicts the Holy Spirit from the temple of the human heart; it introduces the devil who incites to lust. It casts into error; it completely removes the truth from the mind that has been deceived. It prepares snares for those entering; it shuts up those who fall into the pit so they cannot get out. It opens hell; it closes the door of heaven. It makes a citizen of the heavenly Jerusalem into an heir of infernal Babylon. It makes of the star of heaven the stubble of eternal fire; it cuts off a member of the Church and casts it into the consuming fire of boiling Gehenna. This vice tries to overturn the walls of the heavenly homeland and is busy repairing the renewed bulwarks of Sodom. For it is this which violates sobriety, kills modesty, strangles chastity, and butchers irreparable virginity with the dagger of unclean contagion. It defiles everything, stains everything, pollutes everything. And as for itself, it permits nothing pure, nothing clean, nothing other than filth. "To the clean all things are clean, but to the defiled unbelievers nothing is clean."[1]

This vice casts men from the choir of the ecclesiastical community and compels them to pray with the possessed and with those who work for the devil. It separates the soul from God to join it with devils. This most pestilential queen of the sodomists makes the followers of her tyrannical laws filthy to men and hateful to God. She commands to join in evil wars against God, to carry the military burden of a most evil spirit. She separates from the companionship of angels and captures the unhappy soul under the yoke of her domination away from its nobility. She deprives her soldiers of the arms of the virtues and exposes them to the piercing spears of all the vices. She humiliates in church, condemns in law, defiles in secret, shames in public, gnaws the conscience as though with worms, sears the flesh as though with fire.

She pants to satisfy her desire for pleasure, but on the other hand she fears lest she become exposed and come out in public and become known to men. Should he not fear her, he who dreads with anxious suspicion the

---

1. Tit. 1:15

very participant in their common ruin? A person who himself participates in a sinful act ought not to be a judge of the crime in confession as long as he hesitates in any way to confess that he has sinned himself by joining in the sin of another. The fact is that the one partner could not die in sin without the other dying also; nor can one provide an opportunity for the other to rise without rising himself. The miserable flesh burns with the heat of lust; the cold mind trembles with the rancour of suspicion; and in the heart of the miserable man chaos boils like Tartarus, while as often as he is pierced with mental stings he is tormented in a certain measure with painful punishment. In fact, after this most poisonous serpent once sinks its fangs into the unhappy soul, sense is snatched away, memory is borne off, the sharpness of the mind is obscured. It becomes unmindful of God and even forgetful of itself. This plague undermines the foundation of faith, weakens the strength of hope, destroys the bond of charity; it takes away justice, subverts fortitude, banishes temperance, blunts the keenness of prudence.

And what more should I say since it expels the whole host of the virtues from the chamber of the human heart and introduces every barbarous vice as if the bolts of the doors were pulled out. To be sure, the view of Jeremiah which concerns the earthy Jerusalem is suitably adapted to this case, "The foe stretched out his hand to all her treasures; she has seen those nations enter her sanctuary whom you forbade to come into your assembly."[2]

Indeed, whomever this most atrocious beast once seizes upon with bloodthirsty jaws, it restrains with its bonds from every form of good work and immediately unleashes him down the steep descent of the most evil depravity. In fact, when one has fallen into this abyss of extreme ruin he becomes an exile from the heavenly homeland, separated from the body of Christ, confounded by the authority of the whole Church, condemned by the judgment of all the holy fathers. He is despised among men on earth and rejected from the community of heavenly citizens. Heaven becomes like iron for him and the earth like bronze.[3] Burdened with the weight of the crime, he cannot arise nor conceal his evil for long in the hiding-place of ignorance. He cannot rejoice here while he lives nor can he hope there when he dies, since he is compelled to bear the disgrace of human derision now and afterwards the torment of eternal damnation. The lamentation of the prophet clearly applies to this soul, "Look O Lord, upon my distress: my stomach is in ferment, my heart recoils within me because I am full of bitterness: the sword kills without, and at home death is similar."[4]

2. Lam. 1:10.
3. Lev. 26:19.
4. Lam. 1:20.

THE SERVICE OF AN UNWORTHY PRIEST IS THE RUIN OF THE PEOPLE

O guilty, carnal men, why do you desire the height of ecclesiastical dignity with so much burning ambition? Why is it that you try with such desire to ensnare the people of God in the bonds of your own ruin? Is it not enough for you to throw yourselves down the steep cliffs of outrageous crime without having to involve others in the peril of your own ruin?

Suppose someone comes to ask us to intercede for him with a powerful man who is angry with him, and suppose we do not know this powerful man. We would immediately respond: We are unable to come to intercede because we are not familiar with him. So, if someone is bashful about interceding with a man of whom he presumes little, in what frame of mind does a person who does not know whether he is a friend of God's grace through the merits of his life occupy the place of intercession with God for the people? Or how can anyone who does not know whether he himself is pleasing to God ask God for forgiveness for others? In this something else must be more anxiously feared, namely, that the one who is believed to be able to placate anger merit it himself because of his own guilt. We all know clearly that when anyone who is displeasing is sent to intercede, the irritated soul is provoked to worse things.

Therefore, the person who is still bound by earthly desires should beware lest, by more gravely igniting the anger of the strict Judge, he become the author of the ruin of his subordinates while he takes pleasure in his exalted position. So, if culpable vice still rules over him, a person should prudently take stock of himself before he dares to assume the position of the sacerdotal office, lest one who is perverted by his own crime should desire to become the intercessor for the faults of others. Be careful, be careful, and be afraid of igniting inextinguishably God's fury towards you; fear lest you provoke more sharply by your very prayers the one you offend openly by acting evilly. Intent on your own ruin, beware of becoming responsible for the ruin of another. The more moderately you now fall into sin, the more easily will you rise by means of the outstretched hand of penance through the mercy of God.

"Letter to Bishop Otto of Constance"
Pope Gregory VII (c. 1020/5–85)

Hildebrand, who was born in Tuscany, became Pope Gregory VII in 1073. He set about the goal of reforming abuses in the church, particularly simony and clerical sexual activity. His reign marked the beginning of an era of papal supremacy that would last for two centuries. The following letter dates from 1075 and is addressed to a bishop in Germany, one of the places that evidenced the worst abuses. It was here that the papacy was embroiled in the

Investiture Controversy with Emperor Henry IV involving a dispute over who should have the power to appoint bishops. While the letter does not mention that issue, it does discuss the question of whether the bishop should allow churchmen to keep mistresses. It is important to note that Gregory divides the world not according to social, economic, or political classes, but on the basis of sexual status.

Source: *The Epistolae Vagantes of Pope Gregory VII,* edited and translated by H.E.J. Cowdrey (Oxford: Clarendon Press, 1972), pp. 19, 21, 23. Reprinted by permission of Oxford University Press.

To Bishop Otto of Constance

Gregory, bishop, servant of the servants of God, to Bishop Otto of Constance, greeting and apostolic blessing.

Tidings have reached us about you which I have been most reluctant and sad to hear, and which if they came to our ears about even the lowliest member of the Christian people we should undoubtedly punish by a most stern judgement of stringent discipline. For, urged by our apostolic authority and the truthful judgements of the holy fathers, we were enkindled according to the duty of our office to extirpate the simoniac heresy and to enforce the chastity of the clergy. We laid it as bounden duty upon our brother the venerable archbishop of Mainz, whose suffragans are many and far flung, that both by himself and through his coadjutors he should impress this decree of the Roman church with all zeal upon his whole clergy and insist that it should be inviolably observed. We also thought fit to write a special letter, sealed with our seal, concerning this matter to you as ruler of the numerous clergy of the see of Constance and of its widely dispersed people, so that upheld by its authority you might the more safely and boldly obey our commands by driving out from the Lord's sanctuary the simoniac heresy and the foul defilement of polluting lust. For the apostolic authority of St. Paul is decisive when, including fornicators and adulterers with other vicious men, he went on to make this clear and final prohibition: "not even to eat with such a one."[5] Moreover the whole company of the catholic church are either virgins or chaste or married. Whoever stands outside these three orders is not numbered amongst the sons of the church or within the bounds of the Christian religion. Thus, if we know for a certainty that even the least of laymen is companying with a mistress, we rightly debar him from the sacraments of the altar until he repents, as a member severed from the Lord's body. This being so, how can a man be a dispenser or minister of the holy sacraments, when he can on no account be even a partaker of them? The ruling of the blessed Pope Leo is binding upon us, by which he absolutely

5. Cf. 1 Cor. 5:11.

withheld from subdeacons the liberty to marry; and subsequent popes of the holy Roman church, especially the distinguished doctor Gregory, have so established the blessed Pope Leo's decree as law that thereafter the bonds of marriage are altogether forbidden to the three ecclesiastical orders of priests, deacons, and subdeacons.

Yet when we passed on all these things for you to observe by your pastoral oversight, you, setting your heart not on things above but on the earth below,[6] relaxed the reins of lust, as we have heard, to all these orders, allowing those who had joined themselves to women to continue in their shame and those who had not taken women to have no fear of your prohibition. O the impudence! O the unparalleled insolence! that a bishop should despise the decrees of the apostolic see, should set at naught the precepts of the holy fathers, and in truth should impose upon his subjects from his lofty place and from his episcopal chair things contrary to these precepts and opposed to the Christian faith! We accordingly command you by apostolic authority to present yourself at our next council in the first week of Lent, to answer canonically respecting both this disobedience and contempt of the apostolic see, and all the charges that have been laid against you.

Policratus
John of Salisbury (1115 –1180)

John was an English philosopher who studied in Paris in his youth with philosophers and theologians such as Peter Abelard and William of Conches. John became the secretary to Theobald of Canterbury after he was introduced to him by Bernard of Clairvaux, and he later became secretary to Thomas Becket.

His book *Policratus*, a book on the art of ruling, is dedicated to Thomas Becket. In it, John argued that good government is based on the personal character of the ruler. It is not based on adherence to laws and institutions created by humans, but on obedience to divine law. In this work, he includes chapters on the vices of rulers such as gaming, hunting, entertainment, and their receptiveness to flattery. The following excerpt comes from a section on flatterers, whom John compared to prostitutes and sexual deviants.

Source: *Frivolities of Courtiers and Footprints of Philosophers Being a Translation of the First, Second, and Third Books and Selections from the Seventh and Eighth Books of the Policraticus of John of Salisbury*, by Joseph B. Pike (Minneapolis: University of Minnesota Press, 1938), copyright © 1938 University of Minnesota Press, pp. 197–202.

6. Cf. Col. 3:1-2.

[BOOK III, CHAPTER 13:] SUIT MAY BE BROUGHT TO RECOVER WHAT
   HAS BEEN EXACTED BY FLATTERY; PERVERTS AND PROCURERS;
   THEIR PUNISHMENT; CHASTITY INVIOLABLE UNLESS THE MIND
   ITSELF CONSENTS

And yet he can by no means appear to be a flatterer who desires nothing except to please his victim, by his own unaided effort if possible, if not
by employing a substitute, wife or some other woman connected by duty or
affection. Affection is the more effective bond because it approaches closer
to nature, and whatever is joined by the tie of affection is united to the very
soul. There is assuredly no more deadly form of adulation than that which
proceeds by the path of affection. Consequently husbands are often too cor-
dial, expose themselves too readily to rivals, and quite often invite to their
table the destroyers of their domestic happiness; as the proverb runs, "The
unsuspicious lover trusts his chaste bride rather than the eyes which play him
false."

Is he not effectively hoodwinked who allows his own eyes to be blinded
by the assertion of a woman who deceives quite constantly for the sole reason that she is very rarely caught? As a domestic tyrant[7] she is at her best;
in delivering a curtain lecture she can outtalk the professional orator and is
a veritable artist when it comes to giving a scene the exact coloring she
desires. The more cautious she is the more she is to be suspected.

If fraud[8] is the basis of a contract it is null and void, and every action
that has proceeded from it or on account of it is revoked. The heirs of the
deceased[9] are liable jointly and forever with regard to the property which
was acknowledged to have come into their possession. But who more fraud-
ulent than the flatterer? Possibly you object and say that I am not acquainted
with all of them. Conceded; but I feel that from many samples I have learned
to know them all.

Duillius,[10] advanced in years, decrepit in body, and with a weak heart,
returned home plunged in grief because in the course of a quarrel he had
been taunted with having a foul mouth and evil smelling breath. He complained bitterly to his wife that she had never suggested asking medical
advice. "I would have done so" she replied "had I not thought that such was
the odor of all men's breath." One may praise the chastity of that union and
laud a woman for bearing such an infliction in her husband with great
patience, so that he learned of this bodily infirmity not as a result of his wife's
disgust but by the abuse of his enemy.

7. Petronius, *Sat.* 37.
8. *Dig.* 4.3. Cf. 18.1.43.
9. *Cod. Justinian,* 4.17.
10. Jerome, *Ad Jovin.* 1.46.

I make some such reply to flatterers for I consider all of them in bad odor. They are all redolent of fraud and deception, and whithersoever they turn they waft to sensitive nostrils not a smell but a stench. Therefore all that is acquired by the art of flattery may with justice be torn from the clutches even of the heir. I do not imagine that plaintiffs would meet with any obstacle should they be bold enough to lay claim to all that they have bestowed upon sycophants. But "Who is wise and he shall understand these things?"[11] And who is capable enough to meet the situation, when not only in every home but in every social gathering the army of flatterers is so numerous that if even a discreet person should venture so much as to open his lips in condemnation,

> Their host would well defend them and their wall
> Of close locked shields.[12]

As it is, the man who has a conscience and pursues the path of virtue suffers cold, thirst, and the many insults of angry fortune; but

> On purple broidered couch the flatterer
> Is basely stretched in drunken sleep.[13]

He becomes intoxicated with good things, is flushed with wine, and by various shifts fashions a heaven to suit himself. He has the first places[14] at feasts and the seat of importance at gatherings; he is familiarly announced by his first name; he receives the first salutations; he pronounces his opinions first in courts of law; all that he says is wit unalloyed; all that he does is the essence of justice and liberty.

Come now! Just venture to display a bit of common sense. Straightway a great crowd of sycophants will come and, like the Jews, will force you to submit to their superior throng.[15] So they are safe by reason of their great numbers and their craft. The result is that they have power to conquer even kings and princes. By a miracle the unarmed element of the people prevails over the armed and makes a powerful attack upon manhood by the medium of effeminacy. I had intended to pass perverts by in silence who, being dishonorable, are and are seen to be worthy of their dishonor. Respect for morals imposes silence, and modesty by natural instinct diverts its gaze from them. Need more be said?

11 Os. 14:10, 2 Cor. 2:16.
12 Juvenal, *Sat.* 2.46.
13 Petronius, *Sat.* 83.
14 Matt. 23:6.
15 Horace, *Sat.* 1.4.141-43.

If talent fail us, then rage makes us write.[16]

Their profession is that of prostituting their own chastity and of assaulting and violating that of others. Yet not simply their own chastity, since marriage itself is defiled and the one mate abets the adultery of the other. As the bride leaves the bridal chamber do not imagine her consort to be a husband; he is a procurer. It is he who leads her forth, exposes her to libidinous eyes, and if the hope[17] of tainted money flashes before his vision, with crafty display of affection he sells her into prostitution.

A daughter at all comely, or any one else of the household that takes the fancy of a man of property, is merchandise displayed for sale to attract the customer.[18] But though natural resentment causes a twinge of pain to those who admit or allure sharers to their couch, resentment is assuaged by the money made in the transaction, or at least it mitigates their suffering. If the matter is discussed seriously and all parties are free to express their views, the sorrow[19] is not like that with which one sees his own body defiled by another's lust. For other sins[20] are without the body but he that committeth fornication sinneth against his own body. This, Adam says, is bone of my bone and flesh of my flesh,[21] so that there are no longer two, man and woman, but one flesh. This assuredly cannot be sundered without pain nor shared without ill will;

A throne, and love, cannot be shared by two.[22]

As good faith[23] exists not for those who share a throne, so it is with those who share a couch. It is in reality easier to cede to another the treasures of a kingdom than the affection of a mate. But these are no mates, they are procurers. The final surrender to the wealthy is supposed to have been made when the violation of faith inspires faith in faith.

Why do I complain that they sell their wives and daughters into prostitution when as a matter of fact, though the laws forbid, yet nature, in a sort of way, puts up with it. They rise against nature herself like a new set of giants waging a new war against heaven. They make an offering of their sons to Venus and compel them to pave the way for the virgins with their offering of dolls. In the one case they do wait for maturity but in the other

16. Juvenal, *Sat.* 1.79.
17. Persius, *Prol.* 12.
18. Sallust, *Jug.* 35.10.
19. Lam. 1:12.
20. Gen. 2:23; Matt. 19:6.
21. Lam. 1:12.
22. Juvenal, *Sat.* 1.79.
23. Lucan, *Phars.* 1.92.

it is enough if the craving of another's lust can be assuaged. It is a shame that men who have reached years of discretion do not withdraw from such foul connections; nature created them in the image of the nobler, but so far as they can they sink down into the weaker sex, effeminate as the result of vice and corruption of morals, though thanks to nature they have not the power to lose their sex completely.

When the rich lascivious wanton is preparing to satisfy his passion he has his hair elaborately frizzled and curled[24]; he puts to shame a courtesan's make-up, an actor's costume, the dress of a noble, the jewels of a maiden, and even the triumphal robes of a prince. Thus arrayed he takes the feet of the figure reclining by him in his hands, and in plain view of others caresses them and, not to be too explicit, the legs as well. The hand that had been encased in glove to protect it from the sun and keep it soft for the voluptuary's purpose extends its exploration. Growing bolder he allows his hand to pass over the entire body with lecherous caress, incites the lascivious thrill that he has aroused, and fans the flame of languishing desire.[25]

Such abomination should be spat upon rather than held up to view, and I would have been ashamed to insert an account of it in this work had not the apostle, in his epistle to the Romans, written even more explicitly on the theme. "For their women have changed the natural use into that use which is against nature. In like manner the men, also leaving the natural use of women, have burned in their lusts one toward another, men with men working that which is filthy, so that they were given to a reprobate sense and did those things which were not convenient, and being under the domination of all vices they provoked the indignation of God and the sting of punishments upon themselves."[26]

The trumpet of the apostle did indeed make this proclamation loudly in the ears of the Romans, at the time when Nero, most impious of emperors, and notorious for his savage excesses, endeavored to make the boy Sporus[27] into a woman by castrating him. From that period dates the proverb, "The use of handsome boys is abuse." And another: "The attraction of beauty is less attractive to the man of wisdom, the more attractive it is to the sordid seducer." It is indeed more difficult for a weaker force of defenders to protect what is sought by a superior force. It is easier for a cheat to secure it by stealth and deception from one off his guard, or for the violator of chastity to wrest it from the unwilling by violence.

The Fathers however long ago laid down the rule that chastity[28] cannot

---

24. Jerome, *Ep.* 54.13.
25. Juvenal, *Sat.* 11.167.
26. Rom. 1:26-28.
27. Suetonius, *Nero*, 28.
28. Augustine, *De Civ. Dei*, 1.18.

be lost unless there is first corruption of the mind. When, as the great Augustine pointed out, a body suffers violence with no preceding lust on its part, it is a case of tribulation rather than contamination. It is possible therefore that chastity be preserved where no corruption can exist unless it be voluntary, to wit in purity of mind, and there chastity can be preserved forever. Nor is it anything to boast of if the flesh remains intact where the mind is polluted with foul corruption.

As it is now, even if there be no one to seduce or violate, the training of our youth from their earliest years is so bad that they with lascivious glances, expression, bodily movements, the very dress they wear, and enticements scarcely permitted harlots, themselves solicit seduction.

The many laws directed against this evil are held in no respect nor are they feared, although the Emperor had decreed that it be severely punished. For he says "When a male becomes a bride and a female groom, what is their desire? When sex loses its place and it is not wrong to know that which is not for one's good, when the act of love is perverted and love is sought and is not found, then do we order statutes to rear their heads and teeth to be put into the law, that those who are guilty or likely to be, may be cowed by the avenging sword and stern penalties."[29]

Nor does he spare them that consent, but imposes capital punishment, since even divine law[30] inflicts like punishment upon them that do and them that consent. On the authority of the great bishop, I mean Ambrose of Milan, he defined those that consent as they who conceal an error of which they are cognizant, or condone when they have the power to correct it.

But why continue the discussion of a shameful and odious theme? To bring the matter to a fitting conclusion, without doubt God shall rain snares[31] upon them that they escape not; fire and brimstone and storms of wind shall be the portion of their cup. Along with their instigators, whom Sodom has devoured, they will be a stench and everlasting reproach[32] to the ages. How then, I pray, will the favor of the rich profit them? What enjoyment or pleasure can there be in things temporal which is not blotted out by such pain and shame?

Exempla from "Sermones vulgares"
Jacques de Vitry (1160 or 1170–1240)

Jacques was a churchman hailing from northern France. A powerful speaker, he preached against the Albigensian heresy and for the instigation of the

29. *Cod. Justinian*, 9.9.31.
30. Lev. 20:15; Rom. 1:32.
31. Ps. 10:7.
32. Jer. 23:40.

Fifth Crusade. His abilities in oratory were instrumental in helping him become elected Bishop of Acre, a city on the Syrian coast. He later returned west and became cardinal bishop of Tusculum. He wrote a history of the Fifth Crusade, but he is most famous for his sermons. Hundreds of these survive in four separate collections. The following excerpts come from his *Sermones vulgares*, which is one of his earliest collections. Here he provides colorful examples from literary sources and real life in order to exhort priests to chastity and married people to fidelity.

Source: *The Exempla or Illustrative Stories from the Sermones Vulgares of Jacques de Vitry*, edited by Thomas Frederick Crane (London: Pub. for the Folklore Society, by D. Nutt, 1890), pp. 234–235, 241, 245, 256–257.

A priest took his concubine with him to the house of an honest woman, and at night asked where a bed had been prepared for them. The hostess showed them the privy, and declared they could sleep nowhere else. They withdrew in great confusion.

Another priest was given his option by the bishop to abandon his concubine or give up his parish. He preferred to quit his parish; but when the woman saw that he had resigned a rich parish, and become poor, she forsook him.

In some places the concubines of priests are so hated that no one will give them or take from them the kiss of peace. It is the common opinion that to do so deprives one of his share in the mass. Hence, for their derision, people are wont to use a certain charm by which the mice are kept away from the grain. It is as follows:

"I conjure you, rats and mice,
To have no part in these heaps of grain,
Any more than he has part in the mass,
Who receives the kiss of peace from the priestess."

The wild cat has a handsome skin, but when it is tamed and lies by the fire, it burns its tail and fur. Like this animal are women who permit liberties to be taken with them.

There was a demoniac who publicly denounced the sins of those who came before him. A certain knight suspected a soldier of his of adultery with his wife, and asked the soldier to go with him to the demoniac. The guilty soldier first went to confession and then to the demoniac, who proclaimed the guilt of the wife, but could not discover the name of the man with whom she had sinned, saying: "A short time ago I knew, but now I do not," and inspecting his papers he found that the soldier's sin was blotted out.

A pious matron and a monk, the guardian and treasurer of his monastery, frequently met in the church and talked over religious matters. The devil, envying their virtue and fame, tempted them and changed their spiritual into carnal love, so that they eloped taking with them the treasures of the church and the property of the husband. When the monks and the husband discovered their loss they pursued the fugitives, captured them with their plunder and threw them into prison. The scandal and harm caused by this sin were far greater than the sin itself. The monk and matron in prison soon came to themselves and began to invoke the aid of the Blessed Virgin, whose devoted worshippers they had always hitherto been. At last she appeared to them in great anger saying that she might obtain pardon for their sin from her Son, but what reparation could be made for so great a scandal, which was an almost irremediable injury. The pious Virgin overcome at last by their prayers summoned the demons who had caused the harm, and ordered them to remove the infamy which they had made. The demons could not resist her power and anxiously pondered upon the means of remedying the scandal. Finally they conveyed at night the monk to the church and restored the broken treasure-chest intact to the monastery; and likewise the matron to her own home, repairing and fastening the box from which she had taken her husband's money. When the monks found their treasure and the monk praying as usual, and the husband discovered his wife and property, they were amazed, and hastening to the prison found the monk and matron in chains as they had left them, at least it seemed so to them, for one of the demons had transformed himself into the figure of the monk, and another into the shape of the matron. When the whole city flocked to see this wonder, the demons cried in the hearing of all: "Let us depart, long enough have we deceived these people, and caused ill to be thought of religious persons." With these words they vanished and every one hastened to fall at the feet of the monk and matron and beg their pardon.

Summa Theologica
St. Thomas Aquinas (1225–1274)

A Dominican monk and a professor of theology at the University of Paris, St. Thomas Aquinas was one of the great thinkers of the thirteenth century. In his *Summa Theologica*, a handbook of theology inspired by Aristotle, whose works had been gradually entering the West (Aquinas refers to him as The Philosopher in his text), Aquinas would pose a question, then list all the objections, which negated the basis on which his question was asked. He would then state his position on this issue. Finally, using authoritative texts, Aquinas would throw out each of the objections and recapitulate his own position. The *Summa Theologica* covered a wide range of topics in philosophy, theology, morality, and political theory.

Source: *The Summa Theologica of St. Thomas Aquinas, Second Part of the Second Part,
QQ. CXLI– CLXX*, translated by Fathers of the English Dominican Province (New York:
Benziger Brothers, 1921), pp. 133–138, 140–145.

WHETHER SIMPLE FORNICATION IS A MORTAL SIN?

Objection 1. It seems that simple fornication is not a mortal sin. For
things that come under the same head would seem to be on a par with one
another. Now fornication comes under the same head as things that are not
mortal sins: for it is written[33]: *That you abstain from things sacrificed to idols,
and from blood, and from things strangled, and from fornication.* But there is
not mortal sin in these observances, according to 1 Tim. 4:4, *Nothing is
rejected that is received with thanksgiving.* Therefore fornication is not a mortal sin.

Obj. 2. Further, No mortal sin is the matter of a Divine precept. But
the Lord commanded[34]: *Go take thee a wife of fornications, and have of her
children of fornications.* Therefore fornication is not a mortal sin.

Obj. 3. Further, No mortal sin is mentioned in Holy Writ without disapprobation. Yet simple fornication is mentioned without disapprobation by
Holy Writ in connection with the patriarchs. Thus we read[35] that Abraham
went in to his handmaid Agar; and further on[36] that Jacob went in to Bala
and Zelpha the handmaids of his wives; and again[37] that Juda was with
Thamar whom he thought to be a harlot. Therefore simple fornication is
not a mortal sin.

Obj. 4. Further, Every mortal sin is contrary to charity. But simple fornication is not contrary to charity, neither as regards the love of God, since
it is not a sin directly against God, nor as regards the love of our neighbour,
since thereby no one is injured. Therefore simple fornication is not a mortal sin.

Obj. 5. Further, Every mortal sin leads to eternal perdition. But simple fornication has not this result: because a gloss of Ambrose on 1 Tim. 4:8,
Godliness is profitable to all things, says: *The whole of Christian teaching is
summed up in mercy and godliness: if a man conforms to this, even though he
gives way to the inconstancy of the flesh, doubtless he will be punished, but he
will not perish.* Therefore simple fornication is not a mortal sin.

Obj. 6. Further, Augustine says[38] that *what food is to the well-being of the
body, such is sexual intercourse to the welfare of the human race.* But inordinate use of food is not always a mortal sin. Therefore neither is all inordinate

33. Acts 15:29.
34. Osee 1:2 (Hosea 1:2).
35. Gn. 16:4.
36. Gn. 30:5,9.
37. Gn. 38:18.
38. *De Bono Conjug.* 16.

sexual intercourse; and this would seem to apply especially to simple fornication, which is the least grievous of the aforesaid species.

On the contrary, It is written[39]: *Take heed to keep thyself ... from all fornication, and beside thy wife never endure to know a crime.* Now crime denotes
a mortal sin. Therefore fornication and all intercourse with other than one's
wife is a mortal sin.

Further, Nothing but mortal sin debars a man from God's kingdom.
But fornication debars him, as shown by the words of the Apostle,[40] who
after mentioning fornication and certain other vices, adds: *They who do such
things shall not obtain the kingdom of God.* Therefore simple fornication is a
mortal sin.

Further, It is written in the Decretals: *They should know that the same
penance is to be enjoined for perjury as for adultery, fornication, and wilful murder and other criminal offenses.* Therefore simple fornication is a criminal or
mortal sin.

I answer that, Without any doubt we must hold simple fornication to
be a mortal sin, notwithstanding that a gloss on Deut. 23: 17, says: *This is
a prohibition against going with whores, whose vileness is venial.* For instead
of *venial* it should be *venal,* since such is the wanton's trade. In order to make
this evident, we must take note that every sin committed directly against
human life is a mortal sin. Now simple fornication implies an inordinateness that tends to injure the life of the offspring to be born of this union.
For we find in all animals where the upbringing of the offspring needs care
of both male and female, that these come together not indeterminately, but
the male with a certain female, whether one or several; such is the case with
all birds: while, on the other hand, among those animals, where the female
alone suffices for the offspring's upbringing, the union is indeterminate, as
in the case of dogs and like animals. Now it is evident that the upbringing
of a human child requires not only the mother's care for his nourishment,
but much more the care of his father as guide and guardian, and under whom
he progresses in goods both internal and external. Hence human nature
rebels against an indeterminate union of the sexes and demands that a man
should be united to a determinate woman and should abide with her a long
time or even for a whole lifetime. Hence it is that in the human race the
male has a natural solicitude for the certainty of offspring, because on him
devolves the upbringing of the child: and this certainly would cease if the
union of sexes were indeterminate.

This union with a certain definite woman is called matrimony; which

39. Tob. 4:13.
40. Gal. 5:21.

for the above reason is said to belong to the natural law. Since, however, the union of the sexes is directed to the common good of the whole human race, and common goods depend on the law for their determination, as stated above,[41] it follows that this union of man and woman, which is called matrimony, is determined by some law. What this determination is for us will be stated in the Third Part of this work,[42] where we shall treat of the sacrament of matrimony. Wherefore, since fornication is an indeterminate union of the sexes, as something incompatible with matrimony, it is opposed to the good of the child's upbringing, and consequently it is a mortal sin. Nor does it matter if a man having knowledge of a woman by fornication, make sufficient provision for the upbringing of the child: because a matter that comes under the determination of the law is judged according to what happens in general, and not according to what may happen in a particular case.

Reply Obj. 1. Fornication is reckoned in conjunction with these things, not as being on a par with them in sinfulness, but because the matters mentioned there were equally liable to cause dispute between Jews and Gentiles, and thus prevent them from agreeing unanimously. For among the Gentiles, fornication was not deemed unlawful, on account of the corruption of natural reason: whereas the Jews, taught by the Divine law, considered it to be unlawful. The other things mentioned were loathsome to the Jews through custom introduced by the law into their daily life. Hence the Apostles forbade these things to the Gentiles, not as though they were unlawful in themselves, but because they were loathsome to the Jews, as stated above.[43]

Reply Obj. 2. Fornication is said to be a sin, because it is contrary to right reason. Now man's reason is right, in so far as it is ruled by the Divine Will, the first and supreme rule. Wherefore that which a man does by God's will and in obedience to His command, is not contrary to right reason, though it may seem contrary to the general order of reason: even so, that which is done miraculously by the Divine power is not contrary to nature, though it be contrary to the usual course of nature. Therefore just as Abraham did not sin in being willing to slay his innocent son, because he obeyed God, although considered in itself it was contrary to right human reason in general, so, too, Osee sinned not in committing fornication by God's command. Nor should such a copulation be strictly called fornication, though it be so called in reference to the general course of things. Hence Augustine says[44]: *When God commands a thing to be done against the customs or agreement of any people, though it were never done by them heretofore, it is to be done*; and afterwards

41. I-II, 90, 2.
42. Supp., Q. 29. *seqq.*
43. I-II, 103, 4, ad 3.
44. Confess. 3, 8.

he adds: *For as among the powers of human society, the greater authority is obeyed in preference to the lesser, so must God in preference to all.*

Reply Obj. 3. Abraham and Jacob went in to their handmaidens with no purpose of fornication, as we shall show further on when we treat of matrimony. As to Juda there is no need to excuse him, for he also caused Joseph to be sold.

Reply Obj. 4. Simple fornication is contrary to the love of our neighbor, because it is opposed to the good of the child to be born, shown in the *Article*, since it is an act of generation accomplished in a manner disadvantageous to the future child.

Reply Obj. 5. A person, who, while given to works of piety, yields to the inconstancy of the flesh, is freed from eternal loss, in so far as these works dispose him to receive the grace to repent, and because by such works he makes satisfaction for his past inconstancy; but not so as to be freed by pious works, if he persist in carnal inconstancy impenitent until death.

Reply Obj. 6. One copulation may result in the begetting of a man, wherefore inordinate copulation, which hinders the good of the future child, is a mortal sin as to the very genus of the act, and not only as to the inordinateness of concupiscence. On the other hand, one meal does not hinder the good of a man's whole life, wherefore the act of gluttony is not a mortal sin by reason of its genus. It would, however, be a mortal sin, if a man were knowingly to partake of a food which would alter the whole condition of his life, as was the case with Adam.

Nor is it true that fornication is the least of the sins comprised under lust, for the marriage act that is done out of sensuous pleasure is a lesser sin.

Whether There Can Be Mortal Sin in Touches and Kisses?

Objection 1. It seems that there is no mortal sin in touches and kisses. For the Apostle says[45]: *Fornication and all uncleanness, or covetousness, let it not so much as be named among you, as becometh saints,* then he adds: *Or obscenity* (which a gloss refers to kissing and fondling), *or foolish talking* (as soft speeches), *or scurrility* (which fools call geniality — i.e. jocularity), and afterwards he continues[46]: *For know ye this and understand that no fornicator, or unclean, or covetous person (which is the serving of idols), hath inheritance in the kingdom of Christ and of God,* thus making no further mention of obscenity, as neither of foolish talking or scurrility. Therefore these are not mortal sins.

Obj. 2. Further, Fornication is stated to be a mortal sin as being prejudicial to the good of the future child's begetting and upbringing. But these

45. Eph. 5:3.
46. verse 5.

are not affected by kisses and touches or blandishments. Therefore there is no mortal sin in these.

Obj. 3. Further, Things that are mortal sins in themselves can never be good actions. Yet kisses, touches, and the like can be done sometimes without sin. Therefore they are not mortal sins in themselves.

On the contrary, A lustful look is less than a touch, a caress or a kiss. But according to Mt. 5:28, *Whosoever shall look on a woman to lust after her hath already committed adultery with her in his heart.* Much more therefore are lustful kisses and other like things mortal sins.

Further, Cyprian says,[47] *By their very intercourse, their blandishments, their converse, their embraces, those who are associated in a sleep that knows neither honour nor shame, acknowledge their disgrace and crime.* Therefore by doing these things a man is guilty of a crime, that is of mortal sin.

I answer that, A thing is said to be a mortal sin in two ways. First, by reason of its species, and in this way a kiss, caress, or touch does not, of its very nature, imply a mortal sin, for it is possible to do such things without lustful pleasure, either as being the custom of one's country, or on account of some obligation or reasonable cause. Secondly, a thing is said to be a mortal sin by reason of its cause: thus he who gives an alms, in order to lead someone into heresy, sins mortally on account of his corrupt intention. Now it has been stated above,[48] that it is a mortal sin not only to consent to the act, but also to the delectation of a mortal sin. Wherefore since fornication is a mortal sin, and much more so the other kinds of lust, it follows that in such-like sins not only consent to the act but also consent to the pleasure is a mortal sin. Consequently, when these kisses and caresses are done for this delectation, it follows that they are mortal sins, and only in this way are they said to be lustful. Therefore in so far as they are lustful, they are mortal sins.

Reply Obj. 1. The Apostle makes no further mention of these three because they are not sinful except as directed to those that he had mentioned before.

Reply Obj. 2. Although kisses and touches do not by their very nature hinder the good of the human offspring, they proceed from lust, which is the source of this hindrance: and on this account they are mortally sinful.

Reply Obj. 3. This argument proves that such things are not mortal sins in their species.

WHETHER NOCTURNAL POLLUTION IS A MORTAL SIN?

Objection 1. It seems that nocturnal pollution is a sin. For the same things are the matter of merit and demerit. Now a man may merit while he

---

47. *Ad Pompon, de Virgin.*, i., Ep. II.
48. I-II, Q. 74., AA. 7,8.

sleeps, as was the case with Solomon, who while asleep obtained the gift of wisdom from the Lord.[49] Therefore a man may demerit while asleep; and thus nocturnal pollution would seem to be a sin.

Obj. 2. Further, Whoever has the use of reason can sin. Now a man has the use of reason while asleep, since in our sleep we frequently discuss matters, choose this rather than that, consenting to one thing, or dissenting to another. Therefore one may sin while asleep, so that nocturnal pollution is not prevented by sleep from being a sin, seeing that it is a sin according to its genus.

Obj. 3. Further, It is useless to reprove and instruct one who cannot act according to or against reason. Now man, while asleep, is instructed and reproved by God, according to Job 33:15,16, *By a dream in a vision by night, when deep sleep is wont to lay hold of men... Then He openeth the ears of men, and teaching instructeth them in what they are to learn.* Therefore a man, while asleep, can act according to or against his reason, and this is to do good or sinful actions, and thus it seems that nocturnal pollution is a sin.

On the contrary, Augustine says (*Gen. ad lit.* xii.): *When the same image that comes into the mind of a speaker presents itself to the mind of the sleeper, so that the latter is unable to distinguish the imaginary from the real union of bodies, the flesh is at once moved, with the result that usually follows such motions; and yet there is as little sin in this as there is in speaking and therefore thinking about such things while one is awake.*

I *answer that,* Nocturnal pollution may be considered in two ways. First, in itself; and thus it has not the character of a sin. For every sin depends on the judgment of reason, since even the first movement of the sensuality has nothing sinful in it, except in so far as it can be suppressed by reason; wherefore in the absence of reason's judgment, there is no sin in it. Now during sleep reason has not a free judgment. For there is no one who while sleeping does not regard some of the images formed by his imagination as though they were real, as stated above in I, 84, 8, ad 2. Wherefore what a man does while he sleeps and is deprived of reason's judgment, is not imputed to him as a sin, as neither are the actions of a maniac or an imbecile.

Secondly, nocturnal pollution may be considered with reference to its cause. This may be threefold. One is a bodily cause. For when there is excess of seminal humor in the body, or when the humor is disintegrated either through overheating of the body or some other disturbance, the sleeper dreams things that are connected with the discharge of this excessive or disintegrated humor: the same thing happens when nature is cumbered with

49. 3 Kgs. 3:2, Par. 1.

other superfluities, so that phantasms relating to the discharge of those superfluities are formed in the imagination. Accordingly if this excess of humor be due to a sinful cause (for instance excessive eating or drinking), nocturnal pollution has the character of sin from its cause: whereas if the excess or disintegration of these superfluities be not due to a sinful cause, nocturnal pollution is not sinful, neither in itself nor in its cause.

A second cause of nocturnal pollution is on the part of the soul and the inner man: for instance when it happens to the sleeper on account of some previous thought. For the thought which preceded while he was awake, is sometimes purely speculative, for instance when one thinks about the sins of the flesh for the purpose of discussion; while sometimes it is accompanied by a certain emotion either of concupiscence or of abhorrence. Now nocturnal pollution is more apt to arise from thinking about carnal sins with concupiscence for such pleasures, because this leaves its trace and inclination in the soul, so that the sleeper is more easily led in his imagination to consent to acts productive of pollution. In this sense the Philosopher says[50] that *in so far as certain movements in some degree pass from the waking state to the state of sleep, the phantasms of good men are better than those of any other people*: and Augustine says[51] that *even during sleep, the soul may have conspicuous merit on account of its good disposition.* Thus it is evident that nocturnal pollution may be sinful on the part of its cause. On the other hand, it may happen that nocturnal pollution ensues after thoughts about carnal acts, though they were speculative, or accompanied by abhorrence, and then it is not sinful, neither in itself nor in its cause.

The third cause is spiritual and external; for instance when by the work of a devil the sleeper's phantasms are disturbed so as to induce the aforesaid result. Sometimes this is associated with a previous sin, namely the neglect to guard against the wiles of the devil. Hence the words of the hymn at even:

> Our enemy repress, that so
> Our bodies no uncleanness know

On the other hand, this may occur without any fault on man's part, and through the wickedness of the devil alone. Thus we read in the *Collationes Patrum*[52] of a man who was ever wont to suffer from nocturnal pollution on festivals, and that the devil brought this about in order to prevent him from receiving Holy Communion. Hence it is manifest that nocturnal pollution is never a sin, but is sometimes the result of a previous sin.

---

50. *Ethic.* I, 13.
51. *Gen. ad lit.* 12, 15.
52. Coll. 22, 6.

Reply Obj. 1. Solomon did not merit to receive wisdom from God while he was asleep. He received it in token of his previous desire. It is for this reason that his petition is stated to have been pleasing to God,[53] as Augustine observes.[54]

Reply Obj. 2. The use of reason is more or less hindered in sleep, according as the inner sensitive powers are more or less overcome by sleep, on account of the violence or attenuation of the evaporations. Nevertheless it is always hindered somewhat, so as to be unable to elicit a judgment altogether free, as stated in I, 84, 8, ad 2. Therefore what it does then is not imputed to it as a sin.

Reply Obj. 3. Reason's apprehension is not hindered during sleep to the same extent as its judgment, for this is accomplished by reason turning to sensible objects, which are the first principles of human thought. Hence nothing hinders man's reason during sleep from apprehending anew something arising out of the traces left by his previous thoughts and phantasms presented to him, or again through Divine revelation, or the interference of a good or bad angel.

Archpriest of Talavera or Whip
Alfonso Martinez de Toledo (1398–1466)

He was the Archpriest of Talavera de la Reina, chaplain to King Juan II and King Enrique IV of Castile. His writings heralded the Spanish Golden Age of literature. His best known work is *Archpriest of Talavera or Whip* (*Arcipreste de Talavera o Corbacho*), a work that points to the dangers of lust. The first part focuses on how lust plays a major role in people's behavior and is the root of all evil. The second part, while feigning praise of virtuous women, in fact attacks feminine foibles. In 1427 a jealous priest reported to Pope Martin V that Alfonso was cohabiting and asked the pope to remove him from his position as Archpriest of Talavera. Alfonso was not actually punished in this way, but the incident may have inspired the topics in his work. Alfonso's work provoked the indignation of Queen Maria because of its antifeminism. The following excerpt is from part I and takes the form of sermons.

Source: *Little Sermons on Sin: The Archpriest of Talavera*, translated by Lesley Byrd Simpson, pp. 22–25, 28–32. Copyright © 1977 The Regents of the University of California. Reprinted with permission.

How Love Is the Cause of Death, Violence, and War

...none should pursue the love of women or desire it, for because of such love we see friendships broken daily, and quarrels between lovers and their

---

53. 3 Kgs. 3:10.
54. Gen. ad lit. 12, 15.

mistresses, between brothers and sisters, fathers and sons; and we see mortal enmities arise, and many deaths occur, and an infinity of other evils. Read the ancients and listen to men still living. Consider well that there is no man alive, however close a friend he may be, or how cordially he may esteem you, even a close kin — and to this rule there is no exception, be he cousin, nephew, brother, or even, I say, your father — who, when he discovers that you are in love with his mistress, or show her any affection, does not forthwith conceive for you in his heart a mortal dislike, hatred, and rancor. From that moment he will strive to do you hurt in every way he can, publicly or privately, according to his station; for a man will openly attack his equal, but dares not act against his betters except in secret. And this is the source of many dark deeds and Italian tricks, and of murders and stabbings, and of so many other things that it would be tedious to recount them.

Woe to the unlucky wretch who for a moment of carnal pleasure and his unbridled love for an inconstant woman would dishonor his friend, make of him an enemy for life, and lose him forever! From such a man, therefore, as from a brutish beast and enemy of the human race, all persons of judgment should fly, as from a venomous serpent or rabid dog that poisons everyone it bites or touches. What is more useful or profitable for a man to have than faithful friends whom he can trust? According to Cicero the Roman, neither water, fire, nor money is more necessary to a man than his friend, loyal and true, who, if such a one is discovered among a thousand, is to be cherished above all treasures. There is nothing to be compared with him, nor can anything be found. On the other hand, many, many are called friends, upon whom the name is thrust, as well as the deeds, but the name lacks truth, for their friendship vanishes in time of need; it has the appearance but lacks the substance. A true friend is proved in time of trouble and is then the more loyal and kind, for, as the ancient saying has it: "Whilst thou art rich, oh, how many friends thou hast! But, when the weather changes and the sky is overcast, alas, how alone thou shalt be!"

The worth of a true friend is well brought out by Tully, in a book of his called *De amicitia*. In his friendship, then, you will know what kind of friend you have. Verily, the name of friend should be withheld from that friend of yours, whatever or whoever he may be, and he should be held in small esteem, who, to satisfy a bit of vain appetite, loses God and ruins his friend. Such a one should never have shown his face among men, or even have been born! Other sins kill the body, but this one kills the body and damns the soul as well. The body, in lechery, suffers in all its five natural senses. First, a man loses his sight and his sense of smell, for he can no longer smell as he used. He loses his taste and even his power of eating, entirely. His hearing fades and it seems to him that he has bumble bees in his ears.

His hands and his whole body lose the strength they once had and begin to tremble. All three powers of the soul are disturbed, for he has hardly any understanding or memory left, and cannot remember tomorrow what he does today. He can no longer exercise the seven virtues: faith, hope, charity, prudence, temperance, fortitude, and justice, and thus he is turned into an irrational beast. Worse, the vile act of lechery causes the wretch to become callous in sin, not only in this one but in others by contamination, and he grows old in them. Many, therefore, are damned who die suddenly when they least expect it or think they are most secure, and they say: "Today or tomorrow I will mend my way, or get rid of such and such a vice." Thus by putting things off from day to day the poor wretch ends in the arms of Satan, which is the worst fate of all, it is needless to say. So not without reason does the Divine Authority cry out to us, saying: "There is no graver crime than fornication, for it leads man to perdition."

How Lovers, Loving, Lose the Respect of Others

I have yet another argument, very contrary and indeed inimical to love, that is, we see that love brings about a great shrinking of one's estate, and that many have fallen, and are still falling, into deep poverty because of their mad love, freely giving, neglecting their commerce and property, and are now sunken and diminished in their estates. And often we see lovers dissipate their wealth in gifts just to display their great liberality to their mistresses; but in their own houses or elsewhere God knows how closefisted they are! They give where they should not and fail to give where they should. They are, therefore, prodigal and not liberal or generous — all this from love.

It even happens that a lover will give his mistress what is not his, and to get it from God or His saints, by hook or by crook, he will do things he should not do and expose himself to such dangers that it would be a good thing for him to give up his mad love altogether. Imagine a rich man wasting his money on such a love and having his mistress learn that he is now poor, not regaling her as he used, and she insulting him, as we see every day! What do you think of that? How painful it is, how harrowing, to see this fellow, for the whole world turns dark for him, green turns white, vermilion black, and purple yellow! And I believe that in his desperation he would not hesitate to commit any crime whatever to recover if he can his misspent wealth, making no mention now of his mistress, for the loss of his estate is more painful to him than the loss of his mad beauty. God help us! There are married men who give their wives and families an evil time, and consume their substance with mistresses and, when their money is gone, have their mistresses jeer at them. And so they go back to their houses and their proper wives, moaning and cursing, with their tails between their legs! How

they suffer, having lost their love as well as their goods! How they weep and
roar about the house! Sometimes like madmen they run away to foreign
parts, leaving their wives and children in poverty. And now their wives face
ruin and become prostitutes to support themselves and their children! And
if the husband stays at home and does not abandon his wife, he must hold
his tongue and put up with it, pretending not to see, keeping out of the way,
and consenting.

This is what comes of mad and unbridled love, for there is not a lover
in the world who does not try to get money wherever he can, in order to
support his mistress and keep his mad one happy — not only her, but the
woman who covers them, and the messenger, and the procuress, and the
woman who offers her house for their madness and sin, and the servant of
the servant of her cook. Thus he must spend money in all directions, according to the place, and the rank and habits of his person. In short, he who
loves must not only give to his mistress, but must keep a hundred others
happy, even the neighbors, and work for them, also their neighbors' wives,
so that they will not see what they see, or hear what they hear. So many
tribulations are in store for the wretch who loves, not counting the infinity
of dangers to which he must expose himself day and night, that it would be
quite impossible to describe them, so many and so varied are they. And,
after all, what good does it do him, if he is held in such contempt that no
one gives a fig for him? For what will be the reputation of him who exposes
himself to the said dangers and evils for the sake of a love that is neither
enduring nor constant, and who refuses to heed the teachings of others,
wiser, older, and more worthy than he? And what good does it do the
wretched lover or his mistress, even though he achieves his love and gains
the whole world, if his unlucky soul must spend eternity in lasting torment?

5

Mysticism

Sermons on the Song of Songs
Bernard of Clairvaux (1090–1153)

A prominent figure in the twelfth century, Bernard was born near Dijon in Burgundy to a French noble family. He became founding abbot of the Clairvaux Abbey, preached for the initiation of the Second Crusade, attacked Peter Abelard for his rationalistic approach to theology, and was a prolific writer. About five hundred of his letters to various churchmen, kings, and emperors are extant, and he wrote over a dozen treatises.

Bernard of Clairvaux was also a mystic. Mystics believed that they personally experienced and connected with Jesus Christ and the Holy Spirit, which gave them a deeper understanding of Christ's teachings and love. Bernard's best known work is the *Sermons on the Song of Songs*, which were commentaries on the book of the Song of Songs (also known as the Song of Solomon and Canticles). This Song of Songs, found in the Old Testament, contains eight erotic love poems. It had different allegorical meanings for Jews and Christians. For the Jews, the book symbolized God's love for Israel; for Christians it meant Christ's love for the Church.

The following excerpt comes from Bernard's commentary on the opening sentence of chapter two of the Song of Songs. Although Bernard worked on these for the last eighteen years of his life and completed a total of eighty-six sermons, he never got further than chapter two in the Song of Songs.

Source: *Sermons on the Song of Songs*, vol. 3, Cistercian Fathers Series 31, translated by Kilian Walsh and Irene Edmonds (Kalamazoo, MI: Cistercian Publications Inc., 1979), pp. 3–4, 6–7. Reprinted with permission.

"I am the flower of the field and the lily of the valleys."[1] I feel that these words refer to the bride's commendation of the bed for its adornment with

1. Sg 2:1.

flowers. For lest she should commend herself for these flowers, with which the bed was bedecked and the room made beautiful, the Bridegroom states that he is the flower of the field, that the flowers were a product of the field, not of the room. Their splendor and perfume result from his favor and contribution. Lest anyone should reproach her and say: "What do you have that you did not receive? If you received it, then why do you boast as if it were not a gift?"[2] he, a concerned lover and kindly teacher, lovingly and courteously tells his beloved who it is to whom she should ascribe the splendor of which she boasted and the sweet perfume of the bed. "I am the flower of the field," he said: "it is of me that you boast." We are well advised from this that one ought never to boast,[3] and if one does boast he should boast of the Lord.[4] So much for the literal meaning; let us now with the help of him of whom we speak, examine the spiritual meaning that it conceals....

But listen, if you please, to another explanation of this problem, in my opinion not to be slighted. It is not without reason that the spirit is called manifold by the Wise Man,[5] if only because it usually contains different meanings under the text's one shell. Therefore, in accord with the aforesaid distinction concerning the flower's situation, the flower is virginity, it is martyrdom, it is good work: in the garden, virginity; in the field, martyrdom; in the room, good work. And how suitable the garden is for virginity that has modesty for companion, that shuns publicity, is happy in retirement, patient under discipline. The flower is enclosed in the garden, exposed in the field, strewn about in the room. You have "a garden enclosed, a fountain sealed."[6] In the virgin it seals up the doorway of chastity, the safeguard of untainted holiness, provided however that she is one who is holy both in body and spirit.[7] Suitable the field too for martyrdom, for the martyrs are exposed to the ridicule of all, made a spectacle to angels and to men.[8] Is not theirs the pitiful voice of the psalm: "We have become a taunt to our neighbors, mocked and derided by those round about us"?[9] Suitable, too, is the room for good works that foster a safe and quiet conscience. After a good work one rests more securely in contemplation, and the more a man is conscious that he has not failed in works of charity through love of his own ease, the more faithfully will he contemplate things sublime and make bold to study them.

2. 1 Cor 4:7.
3. 2 Cor 12:1.
4. 1 Cor 1:31.
5. Wis 7:22
6. Sg 4:12
7. 1 Cor. 7:34
8. 1 Cor. 4:9.
9. Ps 78:4.

And all these, in each way, mean the Lord Jesus. He is the flower of the garden, a virgin shoot sprung from a virgin. He is the flower of the field, martyr and crown of martyrs, the exemplar of martyrdom. For he was led outside the city, he suffered "outside the camp,"[10] he was raised on the cross to be stared by all, to be mocked by all.[11] He is also the flower of the room, the mirror and the model of all helpfulness, as he himself testified to the Jews: "I have done many good works among you,"[12] and Scripture says of him: "he went about doing good and healing all."[13] If the Lord then is all three of these, what was the reason that of the three he preferred to be called "flower of the field"? Surely so that he might inspire in her[14] the endurance to suffer the persecution that he knew was imminent if she wished to live a godly life in Christ.[15] Hence he eagerly proclaims himself to be that for which he especially wishes to have a following; and that is what I have said elsewhere: she always longs for quietness and he arouses her to labor, impressing on her that through many tribulations we must enter the kingdom of heaven.[16] When he had arranged to return to the Father, then, he said to the young Church on earth which he had recently betrothed to himself: "The hour comes when whoever kills you will think he is offering service to God";[17] and again: "If they persecuted me they will persecute you."[18] You too can gather many texts in the Gospels similar to this proclamation of evils to be endured.

Visions of Hadewijch
Hadewijch (early thirteenth century)

Little is known about this mystic from Brabant who wrote in Middle Dutch. She was a Beguine, a member of the movement of laywomen found primarily in the towns of Germany and the Low Countries, who lived communally and in chastity and dedicated themselves to helping the sick and poor. Along with over thirty letters and dozens of poems, Hadewijch left behind fourteen visions. These visions make plain that her seeking mystical union with God had strong erotic overtones, and they were probably influenced by the romantic literature popular at the time.

10. Heb. 13:12-13.
11. Jer 20:7, Ps 21:8.
12. Jn. 10:32.
13. Acts 10:38.
14. the Church of Sermon 46.
15. 2 Tim 3:12.
16. Acts 14:21.
17. Jn 16:2.
18. Jn 15:20.

VISION 7: ONENESS IN THE EUCHARIST

On a certain Pentecost Sunday I had a vision at dawn. Matins were being sung in the church, and I was present. My heart and my veins and all my limbs trembled and quivered with eager desire and, as often occurred with me, such madness and fear beset my mind that it seemed to me I did not content my Beloved, and that my Beloved did not fulfill my desire, so that dying I must go mad, and going mad I must die.... I desired to have full fruition of my Beloved, and to understand and taste him to the full. I desired that his Humanity should to the fullest extent be one in fruition with my humanity, and that mine then should hold its stand and be strong enough to enter into perfection until I content him, who is perfection itself, by purity and unity, and in all things to content him fully in every virtue. To that end I wished he might content me interiorly with his Godhead, in one spirit, and that for me he should be all that he is, without withholding anything from me. For above all the gifts that I ever longed for, I chose this gift: that I should give satisfaction in all great sufferings. For that is the most perfect satisfaction: to grow up in order to be God with God. For this demands suffering, pain, and misery, and living in great new grief of soul: but to let everything come and go without grief, and in this way to experience nothing else but sweet love, embraces, and kisses. In this sense I desired that God give himself to me, so that I might content him....

Then he came from the altar, showing himself as a Child; and that Child was in the same form as he was in his first three years. He turned toward me, in his right hand took from the ciborium his Body, and in his left hand took a chalice, which seemed to come from the altar, but I do not know where it came from.

With that he came in the form and clothing of a Man, as he was on the day when he gave us his Body for the first time; looking like a Human Being and a Man, wonderful, and beautiful, and with glorious face, he came to me as humbly as anyone who wholly belongs to another. Then he gave himself to me in the shape of the Sacrament, in its outward form, as the custom is; and then he gave me to drink from the chalice, in form and taste, as the custom is. After that he came himself to me, took me entirely in his arms, and pressed me to him; and all my members felt his in full felicity, in accordance with the desire of my heart and my humanity. So I was outwardly satisfied and fully transported. Also then, for a short while, I had the strength to bear this; but soon, after a short time, I lost that manly beauty outwardly in the sight of his form. I saw him completely come to nought and so fade and all at once dissolve that I could no longer recognize or perceive him outside me, and I could no longer distinguish him within me. Then it was to me as if we were one without difference. It was thus: outwardly, to see, taste, and feel, as one can outwardly taste, see, and feel in the reception of the outward Sacrament. So can the Beloved, with the loved one, each wholly receive the other in all full satisfaction of the sight, the hearing, and the passing away of the one in the other.

After that I remained in a passing away in my Beloved, so that I wholly melted away in him and nothing any longer remained to me of myself; and I was changed and taken up in the spirit, and there it was shown me concerning such hours.

The Flowing Light of the Godhead
Mechthild of Magdeburg (1210?–c.1282)

Mechthild came from Saxony and wrote in Low German. She stated that her first encounter with the Holy Spirit came at the age of twelve and these encounters then continued for the next thirty years. She joined the Beguines in her twenties and lived in that community for forty years before she retired to a Cistercian convent at Helfta. The following excerpt comes from *The Flowing Light of the Godhead*, in which Mechthild describes Jesus in terms of courtly love as if he were a handsome suitor. The "flowing" refers not only to the light, but also to all things that flow as a metaphor for God's bestowing on humanity.

Source: *Mystics, Visionaries, and Prophets: A Historical Anthology of Women's Spiritual Writings*, edited by Shawn Madigan (Minneapolis: Augsburg Fortress, 1998), pp. 138–139. Reprinted with permission.

OF THE MISSION OF THE VIRGIN MARY AND HOW THE HUMAN SOUL
    WAS MADE IN THE HONOR OF THE TRINITY

The sweet dew of the uncreated Trinity is distilled from the spring of the eternal Godhead in the flower of the chosen maid. And the fruit of this flower is the immortal God and a mortal man, Jesus. This man is a living comfort of everlasting love. Jesus is our Redeemer who is at the same time our Bridegroom!

The sight of the bride is intoxicated by the sight of the glorious countenance. In her greatest strength, my soul is overcome; in my blindness, I see most clearly. In my greatest clearness, I am still both dead and yet alive. The richer I become, the poorer I am. The more I protest in storm, the more loving God becomes to me. The higher I soar, the brighter I shine from the reflection of the Godhead and the nearer I am to him.

The more I labor, the more sweetly I am able to rest. The more I understand, the less do I speak. The louder I call to the Lord, the greater the wonder that is worked through me, with the power of the Lord. The more deeply God loves me, the more glorious is the course of love. Then, I am nearer to the resting place and I am closer to the embrace of God.

The closer I am to the embrace of God, the sweeter is the kiss of God. The more lovingly we both embrace, the more difficult it is for me to depart. The more God gives me, the more I can give and still have more. The more quickly I leave the Lord, the sooner I must return. The more the fire burns, the more my own light increases. The more that I am consumed by love, the brighter I shall shine! The greater my praise of God, the greater my desire is to love the Lord.

How does our Bridegroom share in the jubilation of the Holy Trinity? God willed to no longer remain in himself alone. This is why the Lord created the soul and gave himself in great love to her. Of what are you made, O soul, that you are blessed to soar so high above all creatures of the earth? Yet, while you remain yourself, how are you somehow mingled with the most holy Trinity?

SOUL: You have spoken of my beginning. I was created in love and therefore nothing can express or liberate my nobility except Love alone. Blessed Mary, you are the Mother of this wonder. When did this all happen to you?

THE VIRGIN MARY: The Father's joy was darkened by Adam's fall and he was angry. The everlasting wisdom of God was provoked. It was then that the Father chose me as a bride so that he might have someone to love. This was because his noble bride, the soul, was dead. So the Son chose me as mother and the Holy Spirit accepted me as friend.

Thus, I alone was the bride of the Holy Trinity. I was the mother of orphans that I presented before the sight of God, so that they might not be lost as others before them.

I became the mother of so many noble children! I was full of the milk of compassion that nurtured the wise as well as the prophets who came before the birth of the Son of God. After that, I nurtured Jesus in my youth. As the Bride of God, I nurtured the holy church at the foot of the cross. Then, I became as a dry desert, full of pain and sorrow as the human agony of my son, Jesus, spiritually pierced my soul...

But my soul was reborn through his life-giving wounds and would live again, young and childlike in a new way! If another soul were to fully recover, the mother of God would also be its mother and its nurse as well. Ah, my God, h ow just and how true! You, my God, are my true Father and my soul is your rightful bride! I resemble you in all my sorrows over the son.

Revelations of Divine Love
Julian of Norwich (c. 1342–1416)

Julian was an English anchoress (religious recluse) and mystic. At the age of
thirty, when she was ill and near death, she experienced sixteen visions as
the local priest held a crucifix before her. Recovering from her illness, she
wrote a shorter version of these visions immediately after her experience, but
then wrote a longer one over the next twenty years. In her longer version,
she describes God as both mother and father. It is God the father whom
humans fear, but it is God the mother who comforts men and women and
in whom they find sanctuary.

Source: *Revelations of Divine Love by Julian of Norwich*, translated by Elizabeth Spearing
(Harmondsworth, Middlesex, England: Penguin Classics, 1998), © Elizabeth Spearing,
1998, pp. 140–142. Reprinted with permission.

HOW WE ARE REDEEMED AND ENLARGED BY THE MERCY AND GRACE OF
OUR SWEET, KIND AND EVER-LOVING MOTHER JESUS; AND OF THE
PROPERTIES OF MOTHERHOOD; BUT JESUS IS OUR TRUE MOTHER,
FEEDING US NOT WITH MILK, BUT WITH HIMSELF, OPENING HIS SIDE
FOR US AND CLAIMING ALL OUR LOVE

But now it is necessary to say a little more about this enlargement, as I understand it in our Lord's meaning, how we are redeemed by the motherhood
of mercy and grace and brought back into our natural dwelling where we
were made by the motherhood of natural love; a natural love which never
leaves us. Our natural Mother, our gracious Mother (for he wanted to become
our mother completely in every way), undertook to begin his work very
humbly and very gently in the Virgin's womb. And he showed this in the
first revelation, where he brought that humble maiden before my mind's eye
in the girlish form she had when she conceived; that is to say, our great God,
the most sovereign wisdom of all, was raised in this humble place and dressed
himself in our poor flesh to do the service and duties of motherhood in every
way. The mother's service is the closest, the most helpful and the most sure,
for it is the most faithful. No one ever might, nor could, nor has performed
this service fully but he alone. We know that our mothers only bring us into
the world to suffer and die, but our true mother, Jesus, he who is all love,
bears us into joy and eternal life; blessed may he be! So he sustains us within
himself in love and was in labour for the full time until he suffered the
sharpest pangs and the most grievous sufferings that ever were or shall be,
and at the last he died. And when it was finished and he had born us to bliss,
even this could not fully satisfy his marvellous love; and that he showed in
these high surpassing words of love, "If I could suffer more, I would suffer
more."

He could not die any more, but he would not stop working. So next he had to feed us, for a mother's dear love has made him our debtor. The mother can give her child her milk to suck, but our dear mother Jesus can feed us with himself, and he does so most generously and most tenderly with the holy sacrament which is the precious food of life itself. And with all the sweet sacraments he sustains us most mercifully and most graciously. And this is what he meant in those blessed words when he said, "It is I that Holy Church preaches and teaches to you"; that is to say, "All the health and life of the sacraments, all the power and grace of my word, all the goodness which is ordained in Holy Church for you, it is I."

The mother can lay the child tenderly to her breast, but our tender mother Jesus, he can familiarly lead us into his blessed breast through his sweet open side, and show within part of the Godhead and the joys of heaven, with spiritual certainty of endless bliss; and that was shown in the tenth revelation, giving the same understanding in the sweet words where he says, "Look how I love you," looking into his side and rejoicing. This fair, lovely word "mother," it is so sweet and so tender in itself that it cannot truly be said of any but of him, and of her who is the true mother of him and of everyone. To the nature of motherhood belong tender love, wisdom and knowledge, and it is good, for although the birth of our body is only low, humble and modest compared with the birth of our soul, yet it is he who does it in the beings by whom it is done. The kind, loving mother who knows and recognizes the need of her child, she watches over it most tenderly, as the nature and condition of motherhood demands. And as it grows in age her actions change, although her love does not. And as it grows older still, she allows it to be beaten to break down vices so that the child may gain in virtue and grace. These actions, with all that is fair and good, our Lord performs them through those by whom they are done. Thus he is our natural mother through the work of grace in the lower part, for love of the higher part. And he wants us to know it; for he wants all our love to be bound to him. And in this I saw that all the debt we owe, at God's bidding, for his fatherhood and motherhood, is fulfilled by loving God truly; a blessed love which Christ arouses in us. And this was shown in everything, and especially in the great, generous words where he says, "It is I that you love."

6

Hagiography

The Life and Conduct of the Blessed Mary Who Changed Her Name to Marinos
Author unknown

Hagiographies are biographies or lives (*vitae*) of saints. The following, which is the life of St. Mary, is one of several hagiographies about transvestite nuns. These types of hagiographies were popular in Byzantium between the fifth and ninth centuries. This particular hagiography, however, has been found written in Latin, Coptic, Armenian, Arabic, German, and French. The story may have been written in Greek some time between the early sixth century and the middle of the seventh century, probably in Syria. Although the church condemned men dressing as women and women dressing as men (Deuteronomy 22:5), women who dressed as monks elicited great sympathy and admiration for the trials they endured, their patience, and holiness.

Source: *Holy Women of Byzantium: Ten Saints' Lives in English Translation*, edited by Alice-Mary Talbot (Washington D.C.: Dumbarton Oaks Research Library and Collection, 1996), pp. 7-12. Reprinted with permission.

There was a certain man named Eugenios who lived in purity, piety, and in the fear of God. He had an honorable and devout wife, who bore him a daughter whom he named Mary. When his wife died, the father raised the child with much teaching and in [the ways of] a pious life.

When the young girl grew up, her father said to her, "My child, behold, all that I own I place in your hands, for I am departing in order to save my soul." Hearing these things [said] by her father, the young girl said to him, "Father, do you wish to save your own soul and see mine destroyed? Do you not know what the Lord says? That the *good shepherd giveth his life for his sheep?*[1] And again she said [to him], "The one who saves the soul is like the one who created it."

Hearing these things, her father was moved to compunction at her

1. Jn. 10:11.

words, for she was weeping and lamenting. He therefore began to speak to her and said, "Child, what am I to do with you? You are a female, and I desire to enter a monastery. How then can you remain with me? For it is through the members of your sex that the devil wages war on the servants of God." To which his daughter responded, "Not so, my lord, for I shall not enter [the monastery] as you say, but I shall first cut off the hair of my head, and clothe myself like a man, and then enter the monastery with you."

The [father], after distributing all his possessions among the poor, followed the advice of his daughter and cut off the hair of her head, dressed her in the clothing of a man, and changed her name to Marinos. And he charged her saying, "Child, take heed how you conduct yourself, for you are about to enter into the midst of fire, for a woman in no way enters a [male] monastery. Preserve yourself therefore blameless before God, so that we may fulfill our vows." And taking his daughter, he entered the cenobitic monastery.

Day by day, the child advanced in all the virtues, in obedience, in humility, and in much asceticism. After she lived thus for a few years in the monastery, [some of the monks] considered her to be a eunuch, for she was beardless and of delicate voice. Others considered that [this condition] was instead the result of her great asceticism, for she partook of food only every second day.

Eventually it came to pass that her father died, but [Mary, remaining in the monastery], [continued] to progress in asceticism and in obedience, so that she received from God the gift of healing those who were troubled by demons. For if she placed her hand upon any of the sick, they were immediately healed.

Living together within the cenobitic monastery were forty men. Now once a month four of the brethren were officially sent forth to minister to the needs of the monastery, because they were responsible for looking after other monks as well, the solitaries, [who lived] outside [the community]. Midway on their journey was an inn, where both those going and those coming were, on account of the great distance, accustomed to [stop and] rest. Moreover, the innkeeper provided [the monks] with many courtesies, accommodating them each with particular solicitude.

One day, the superior, summoning *abba* (Abbas or abba was a term of respect for monks in general, not limited to abbots) Marinos, said to him, "Brother, I know your conduct, how in all things you are perfect and unwavering in your obedience. Be willing then to go forth and attend to the needs of the monastery, for the brethren are annoyed that you do not go forth unto service. For in doing this you will obtain a greater reward from God." At these words, Marinos fell down at his feet and said, "Father, pray for me, and wherever you direct me, there I shall go."

One day, therefore, when Marinos had gone forth unto service along with three other brethren, and while they were all lodging at the inn, it came to pass that a certain soldier deflowered the innkeeper's daughter, who thereupon became pregnant. The soldier said to her, "If your father should learn of this, say that 'It was the young monk who slept with me.'" Her father, upon realizing that she was pregnant, questioned her closely, saying, "How did this happen to you?" And she placed the blamed on Marinos, saying, "The young monk from the monastery, the attractive one called Marinos, he made me pregnant."

Thoroughly outraged, the innkeeper made his way to the monastery, shouting accusations and saying, "Where is that charlatan, that pseudo-Christian, whom you call a Christian?" When one of the stewards came to meet him, he said, "Welcome." But the [innkeeper] replied, "The hour was an evil one in which I made your acquaintance." In like manner he said to the father superior, "May I never see another monk," and other such things. When he was asked why he was saying these things, he answered, "I had but a single daughter, who I hoped would support me in my old age, but look at what Marinos has done to her, he whom you call a Christian — he has deflowered her and she is pregnant." The superior said to him, "What can I do for you, brother, since [Marinos] is not here at the moment? When he returns from his duties, however, I will have no recourse but to expel him from the monastery."

When Marinos returned with the three other monks, the superior said to him, "Is this your conduct, and is this your asceticism, that while lodging at the inn you deflowered the innkeeper's daughter? And now her father, coming here, has made us all a spectacle to the laity." Hearing these things, Marinos fell upon his face, saying, "Forgive me, father, for I have sinned as a man." But the superior, filled with wrath, cast him out saying, "Never again shall you enter this monastery."

Leaving the monastery, [Marinos] immediately sat down outside the monastery gate, and there endured the freezing cold and the burning heat. Thereafter, those entering the monastery used to ask him, "Why are you sitting outdoors?" To which he would reply, "Because I fornicated and have been expelled from the monastery."

When the day arrived for the innkeeper's daughter to give birth, she bore a male child, and the girl's father took the [infant] and brought it to the monastery. Finding Marinos sitting outside the gate, he threw the child down before him and said, "Here is the child which you have wickedly engendered. Take it." And immediately the innkeeper departed.

Marinos, picking up the child, was filled with distress and said, "Yes, I have received the just reward for my sins, but why should this wretched babe perish here with me?" Accordingly he undertook to procure milk from some shepherds, and so nursed the child as its father. But the distress that overwhelmed him was not all, for the child, whimpering and wailing, continually soiled his [Marinos'] garments.

After the passage of three years, the monks entreated the superior saying, "Father, forgive this brother; his punishment is sufficient, for he has confessed his fault to all." But when they saw that the superior remained unmoved, the brethren said, "If you do not receive him back, then we too will leave the monastery. For how can we ask God to forgive our sins, when today marks the third year that he has been sitting in the open air beyond the gate, and we do not forgive him?"

The superior, considering these things, said to them, "For the sake of your love, I accept him." And summoning Marinos he said to him, "On account of the sin which you have committed, you are not worthy to resume your former position here. Nevertheless, on account of the brethren's love, I accept you back into our ranks, but only as the last and least of all." At this Marinos began to weep and said, "Even this is a great thing for me, my lord, for you have deemed me worthy to come inside the gate, so that I might thus be given the honor of serving the holy fathers."

Consequently the superior assigned him the lowliest chores of the monastery, and he performed them [all] scrupulously and with great devotion. But the child was forever following him about, crying and saying, "Dada, Dada," and such things as children say when they wish to eat. Thus, in addition to the [usual] trials and temptations that beset a monk, Marinos was continually anxious about procuring and providing sustenance for the child. When the boy grew up, he remained in the monastery, and having been raised in the practice of virtues he was deemed worthy of the monastic habit.

One day, after a considerable passage of time, the superior inquired of the brethren, "Where is Marinos? Today is the third day that I have not seen him singing in the choir. He was always the first to be found standing there before the start of the service. Go to his cell, and see whether he is lying ill." Going to his cell, they found him dead, and informed the superior, saying, "Brother Marinos has died." But the [superior] said, "In what state did his wretched soul depart? What defense can he make for the sin that he committed?" [Having thus spoken, the superior then] directed that [Marinos] be buried. But as they were preparing to wash him, they discovered that he was a woman, and shrieking, they all began to cry out in a single voice, "Lord, have mercy."

The superior, hearing their cries, asked them, "What troubles you so?" And they said, "Brother Marinos is a woman." Drawing near and seeing [for himself], the [superior] cast himself down at her feet, and with many tears cried out, "Forgive me, for I have sinned against you. I shall lie dead here at your holy feet until such time as I hear forgiveness for all the wrongs that I have done you." And while he was uttering many such lamentations, as well as things yet more remarkable, a voice spoke to him saying, "Had you acted knowingly, this sin would not be forgiven you. But since you acted unknowingly, your sin is forgiven."

The superior thereupon sent [word] to the innkeeper to come and see him. When he arrived, the superior said to him, "Marinos is dead." The innkeeper replied, "May God forgive him, for he has made of my house a desolation." But the superior said to him, "You must repent, brother, for you have sinned before God. You also incited me by your words, and for your sake I also sinned, for Marinos is a woman." Hearing this, the innkeeper was astonished and wondered greatly at his words. And the superior took the innkeeper and showed him that [Marinos] was a woman. At this [the innkeeper] began to lament and to marvel at what had happened.

They buried her holy remains and placed them in blessed caskets, all the while glorifying God with psalms and hymns. When these things were completed, the innkeeper's daughter appeared, possessed by a demon, and confessing the truth that she had been seduced by the soldier. And she was immediately healed at the tomb of the blessed Mary, and everyone glorified God because of this sign, and because of [Mary's] patient endurance, for she vigorously endured [her trials] until death, refusing to make herself known. Let us then, beloved, zealously emulate the blessed Mary and her patient endurance, so that on the day of judgment we may find mercy from our Lord Jesus Christ, to Whom belongs glory and dominion to the ages of ages. Amen.

III

CHRONICLES

7

Early Church and Germanic Peoples

Germania
Tacitus (55–117)

Cornelius Tacitus was a Roman historian who viewed Roman society as mired in decadence. His *Germania* described the customs of the Germanic people of the first century, who were gradually coming into contact with Rome. Tacitus depicted them as morally superior to the Romans. In the following excerpt he idealizes the importance to the Germans of family and the chastity and practical-mindedness of German women.

Source: *The Agricola and Germania: Tacitus*, translated by R.B. Townshend (London: Methuen, 1894) pp. 70–72.

For all that, the marriage bond is strict, and no feature in their mode of life is more creditable to them than this. Unlike the great majority of barbarians, they are content with one wife: very few of them have more than one, and these few exceptions are not due to wantonness; they are cases of men of high rank, to whom several matrimonial alliances have been offered from motives of policy. The wife does not bring a dowry to her husband; on the contrary, he offers one to her. This part of the affair is arranged by her parents and kinsmen, and they pass judgment on the wedding gifts, which are no toys collected to suit feminine frivolities or adorn a bride; instead of that, they consist of oxen, and a bridled horse, and shield and spear and sword. These are the presents that await her as a wife, and her own wedding present to her husband in return is a gift of arms. This is the strongest bond of union – this the mystery of marriage; these are their gods of wedded life. Lest the woman should think that masculine courage and the perils of war lie beyond her sphere, these tokens remind her upon the threshold of marriage that she comes as the man's partner in toils and dangers; and that in peace and in war she must expect to suffer and to dare the same. This is the signification of the oxen in the yoke, of the harnessed horse, of the offering of arms. Thus is she bound to live and thus to die. She receives what she is to hand on to her sons, inviolate and unprofaned; what her sons' wives are to receive after her, and they in their turn, to hand on to her children's children.

So they guard the chastity of their lives, with no shows to entice them nor orgies to excite their evil passions. To men and women alike such a thing as secret correspondence is unknown. Amongst all this immense population adultery is extremely rare: its penalty is instant, and is left to the husband; he cuts off the hair of the unfaithful wife, strips her, turns her out of his house in the presence of the kinsmen, and scourges her through the whole village. For there is no pardon for the fallen woman; not by her beauty, not by her youth, not by her wealth, will she succeed in finding a husband. For no one there makes a jest of vice, or says that seducing and being seduced is the style of the period.

Better still, to be sure, is the practice of those states in which none but maidens marry, and a woman becomes a wife with a wife's hopes and wishes once and once only. Thus it becomes as much as a matter of course for her to have only one husband as to have only one body or one life, to the end that she may not look beyond him nor let her desires stray further, and that she may not so much cherish her husband as her status as a wife. To limit the number of the family or to put to death any of the later-born infants is held to be an abomination, and with the Germans good customs have more authority than good laws elsewhere.

In every household the naked, dirty children develop the mighty limbs and frames that we see with so much admiration. Every mother suckles her own babes, and does not give them over into the charge of handmaids and nurses. No one could distinguish the young master from the slave by any luxury in his bringing up. Out among cattle, at home on the earthen floor, they live just alike until approaching manhood separates them, and the freeborn youth proves his breeding by his valour.

The youths do not early indulge the passion of love, and hence come to manhood unexhausted. Nor are the maidens hurried into marriage: in their case the same maturity and the same full growth is required; they enter upon marriage equally strong and vigorous, and the children inherit the robust frames of their parents.

Church History
Eusebius (260–before 341)

Eusebius Pamphili, Bishop of Caesarea, has been called the father of Church history. In his *Church History* he sought to detail the historical development of the church from the times of the Apostles up until his own time. In the following passage, he describes his hero Origen, a theologian from the early part of the third century. Origen's strong piety led him to take drastic steps, putting into practice the sentiments found in Matthew 19:12: "For there are eunuchs who have been so from birth, and there are eunuchs who have been made eunuchs by others, and there are eunuchs who have made themselves eunuchs for the sake of the kingdom of heaven. Let anyone accept this who can."

Source: *A Select Library of Nicene and Post-Nicene Fathers of the Christian Church. Second Series. Vol. I. Eusebius: Church History from A.D. 1–324, Life of Constantine the Great, Oration in Praise of Constantine,* under the editorial supervision of Philip Schaff and Henry Wace, (Grand Rapids, MI: WM.B. Eerdmans, second printing 1961), pp. 254–255.

[BOOK VI, CHAPTER VIII:] ORIGEN'S DARING DEED

1. At this time while Origen was conducting catechetical instruction at Alexandria, a deed was done by him which evidenced an immature and youthful mind, but at the same time gave the highest proof of faith and continence. For he took the words, "There are eunuchs who have made themselves eunuchs for the kingdom of heaven's sake,"[1] in too literal and extreme a sense. And in order to fulfill the Saviour's word, and at the same time to take away from the unbelievers all opportunity for scandal,— for, although young, he met for the study of divine things with women as well as men,— he carried out in action the word of the Saviour.

2. He thought that this would not be known by many of his acquaintances. But it was impossible for him, though desiring to do so, to keep such an action secret.

3. When Demetrius, who presided over that parish, at last learned of this, he admired greatly the daring nature of the act, and as he perceived his zeal and the genuineness of his faith, he immediately exhorted him to courage, and urged him the more to continue his work of catechetical instruction.

4. Such was he at that time. But soon afterward, seeing that he was prospering, and becoming great and distinguished among all men, the same Demetrius, overcome by human weakness, wrote of his deed as most foolish to the bishops throughout the world. But the bishops of Cesarea and Jerusalem, who were especially notable and distinguished among the bishops of Palestine, considering

5. Origen worthy in the highest degree of the honor, ordained him a presbyter. Thereupon his fame increased greatly, and his name became renowned everywhere, and he obtained no small reputation for virtue and

---

1. Matthew 19:12.

wisdom. But Demetrius, having nothing else that he could say against him, save this deed of his boyhood, accused him bitterly, and dared to include with him in these accusations those who had raised him to the presbyterate.

6. These things, however, took place a little later. But at this time Origen continued fearlessly the instruction in divine things at Alexandria by day and night to all who came to him; devoting his entire leisure without cessation to divine studies and to his pupils.

History of the Franks
Gregory of Tours (539–594)

The bishop of Tours wrote a universal history entitled *History of the Franks*, which is an important source of Merovingian history. In this work, he detailed the lives of royals, nobility and churchmen. His history is heavily imbued with signs from God and accounts of miracles. In the following excerpt he writes of the precarious situation of Frankish queens, whose status was wholly dependent on the whim of their husbands. As a result, they had to use their sexuality and manipulative techniques in order to gain power and protect their position. As seen below, their efforts met with varying degrees of success.

Source: *The History of the Franks* by Gregory of Tours, translated by Lewis Thorpe (Harmondsworth, Middlesex, England: Penguin Classics, 1974), copyright © Lewis Thorpe, 1974, pp. 218–223. Reprinted with permission.

[BOOK IV]

25. The good King Guntram first made Veneranda his mistress and took her to bed with him. She was the servant of one of his subjects, By her he had a son called Gundobad. Later on Guntram married Marcatrude, the daughter of Magnachar. He packed his son Gundobad off to Orleans. Marcatrude had a son of her own. She was jealous of Gundobad and encompassed his death. She sent him poison in a drink, so they say, and killed him. Soon after Gundobad's death she lost her own son by the judgement of God. As a result the King was estranged from her and he dismissed her. She died not long afterwards. Then Guntram married Austrechild, also called Bobilla. He had two sons by her, the elder called Lothar and the younger Chlodomer.

26. King Charibert married a woman called Ingoberg. He had by her a daughter, who eventually married a man from Kent and went to live there. At that time Ingoberg had among her servants two young women who were the daughters of a poor man. The first of these, who wore the habits of a religious, was called Marcovefa, and the other Merofled. The King fell violently

in love with the two of them. As I have implied, they were the daughters of a wool-worker. Ingoberg was jealous because of the love which the King bore them. She made a secret plan to set their father to work, in the hope that when Charibert saw this he would come to despise the two girls. When the man was working away Ingoberg summoned the King. Charibert came, hoping to see something interesting, and, without approaching too near, watched the man preparing wool for the royal household. He was so angry at what he saw that he dismissed Ingoberg and took Merofled in her place. He had another woman, the daughter of a shepherd who looked after his flocks. Her name was Theudechild and he is said to have had a son by her, but the child was buried immediately after his birth....

Next King Charibert married Marcovefa, the sister of Merofled. They were both excommunicated as a result by Saint Germanus the Bishop. The King refused to give up Marcovefa: but she was struck by the judgement of God and died. Not long afterwards the King himself died in his turn. After his death Theudechild, one of his queens, sent messengers to King Guntram, offering her hand in marriage. The King replied in these terms: "She may come to me and bring her treasure with her. I will receive her and I will give her an honourable place among my people. She will hold a higher position at my side than she ever did with my brother, who has died recently." Theudechild was delighted when she heard this. She collected all her possessions together and set out to join Guntram. When he saw her, Guntram said: "It is better that this treasure should fall into my hands than that it should remain in the control of this woman who was unworthy of my brother's bed." He seized most of her goods, left her a small portion and packed her off to a nunnery at Arles. Theudechild bore ill the fasts and vigils to which she was subjected. She sent messengers in secret to a certain Goth, promising him that, if he would carry her off to Spain and marry her there, she would escape from the nunnery with what wealth remained to her and set off with him without the slightest hesitation. He immediately promised to do what she asked. She once more collected her possessions together and made them into bundles. As she was about to make her escape from the nunnery, she was surprised by the vigilant abbess. The abbess, who had caught her red-handed, had her beaten mercilessly and locked her up in her cell. There she remained until her dying day, suffering awful anguish.

27. King Sigibert observed that his brothers were taking wives who were completely unworthy of them and were so far degrading themselves as to marry their own servants. He therefore sent messengers loaded with gifts to Spain and asked for the hand of Brunhild, the daughter of King Athanagild. This young woman was elegant in all that she did, lovely to look at, chaste and decorous in her behaviour, wise in her generation and of good address. Her

father did not refuse to give her to Sigibert, but sent her off with a large dowry. Sigibert assembled the leading men of his kingdom, ordered a banquet to be prepared and married Brunhild with every appearance of joy and happiness. She was, of course, an Arian, but she was converted by the bishops sent to reason with her and by the King who begged her to accept conversion. She accepted the unity of the blessed Trinity and was baptized with the chrism. In the name of Christ she remains a Catholic.

28. When he saw this, King Chilperic sent to ask for the hand of Galswinth, the sister of Brunhild, although he already had a number of wives. He told the messengers to say that he promised to dismiss all the others, if only he were considered worthy of marrying a King's daughter of a rank equal to his own. Galswinth's father believed what he said and sent his daughter to him with a large dowry, just as he had sent Brunhild to Sigibert. Galswinth was older than Brunhild. When she reached the court of King Chilperic, he welcomed her with great honour and made her his wife. He loved her very dearly, for she had brought a large dowry with her. A great quarrel soon ensued between the two of them, however, because he also loved Fredegund, whom he had married before he married Galswinth. Galswinth was converted to the Catholic faith and baptized with the chrism. She never stopped complaining to the King about the insults which she had to endure. According to her he showed no respect for her at all, and she begged that she might be permitted to go back home, even if it meant leaving behind all the treasures which she had brought with her. Chilperic did his best to pacify her with smooth excuses and by denying the truth as convincingly as he could. In the end he had her garrotted by one of his servants and so found her dead in bed. After her death God performed a great miracle. A lamp suspended on a cord burned in front of her tomb. One day, without anyone touching it, the cord broke and the lamp fell to the stone floor. The hard stone withdrew at the point of impact and the lamp penetrated it just as if it had been made of soft material, and there it stood embedded up to its middle without anything being broken. Everyone who saw this knew that a miracle had occurred. King Chilperic wept for the death of Galswinth, but within a few days he had asked Fredegund to sleep with him again. His brothers had a strong suspicion that he had connived at the murder of the Queen and they drove him out of his kingdom.

History of the Lombards
Paul the Deacon (725–799)

Paul the Deacon was an historian descended from a noble Lombard family. His *History of the Lombards,* an unfinished work which spans 568–744, is important because it preserves the early history, myths, and customs of these Germanic people (also known as the *Langobards* or "Long Beards") who settled in Italy. The following excerpt depicts the treachery of Romilda, the wife of the duke of Forum Julii (Friuli) during the Avar attacks.

Source: *History of the Lombards of Paul the Deacon*, translated by William Dudley Foulke, edited by Edward Peters (Philadelphia: University of Pennsylvania Press, 1974), pp. 181, 183–184.

...While their king, that is the Cagan,[2] was ranging around the walls in full armor with a great company of horsemen to find out from what side he might more easily capture the city, Romilda gazed upon him from the walls, and when she beheld him in the bloom of his youth, the abominable harlot was seized with desire for him and straightway sent word to him by a messenger that if he would take her in marriage she would deliver to him the city with all who were in it. The barbarian king, hearing this, promised her with wicked cunning that he would do what she had enjoined and vowed to take her in marriage. She then without delay opened the gates of the fortress of Forum Julii and let in the enemy to her own ruin and that of all who were there.

...the Avars now killed by the sword all the Langobards who were already of the age of manhood, but the women and children they consigned to the yoke of captivity. Romilda indeed, who had been the head of all this evildoing, the king of the Avars, on account of his oath, kept for one night as if in marriage as he had promised her, but upon the next he turned her over to twelve Avars, who abused her through the whole night with their lust, succeeding each other by turns. Afterwards too, ordering a stake to be fixed in the midst of a field, he commanded her to be impaled upon the point of it, uttering these words, moreover, in reproach: "it is fit you should have such a husband." Therefore the detestable betrayer of her country who looked out for her own lust more than for the preservation of her fellow citizens and kindred, perished by such a death. Her daughters, indeed, did not follow the sensual inclination of their mother, but striving from love of chastity not to be contaminated by the barbarians, they put the flesh of raw chickens under the band between their breasts, and this, when putrefied by the heat, gave out an evil smell. And the Avars, when they wanted to touch them, could not endure the stench that they thought was natural to them, but moved far away from them with cursing, saying that all the Langobard women had a bad smell. By this stratagem then the noble girls, escaping from the lust of the Avars, not only kept themselves chaste, but handed down a

[2.] King of the Avars.

useful example for preserving chastity if any such thing should happen to women hereafter. And they were afterwards sold throughout various regions and secured worthy marriages on account of their noble birth; for one of them is said to have wedded a king of the Alamanni, and another a prince of the Bavarians.

8

Continental Europe, the British Isles and Ireland

Risala
Ibn Fadlan (early tenth century)

Ibn Fadlan was sent by the Caliph of Baghdad as ambassador to the Volga Bulgars, and he recorded the experiences of his travels in *Risala*. Ibn Fadlan described the various peoples he encountered during his travels, such as Turkic tribes like the Oghuz, Pechenegs, and Bashkirs. He also met with a tribe of Rus Vikings. The following is the most detailed account of an elaborate pre–Christian ship burial in which the dead man is placed in a boat and burned.

Source: "Ibn Fadlan's Account of the Rus with Some Commentary and Some Allusions to Beowulf," by H.M. Smyser in *Franciplegius: Medieval and Linguistic Studies in Honor of Francis Peabody Magoun, Jr.*, edited by Jess B. Bessinger, Jr. and Robert P. Creed (New York: New York University Press, 1965), pp. 96, 98–100. Reprinted with permission.

Each woman wears on either breast a box of iron, silver, copper, or gold; the value of the box indicates the wealth of the husband. Each box has a ring from which depends a knife. The women wear neck rings of gold and silver, one for each 10,000 *dirhems* which her husband is worth; some women have many. Their most prized ornaments are green glass beads (corals) of clay, which are found on the ships. They trade beads among themselves and pay a *dirhem* for a bead. They string them as necklaces for their women....

When they have come from their land and anchored on, or tied up at the shore of, the Atil [Volga], which is a great river, they build big houses of wood on the shore, each holding ten to twenty persons more or less. Each man has a couch on which he sits. With them are pretty slave girls destined for sale to merchants; a man will have sexual intercourse with his slave girl while his companion looks on. Sometimes whole groups will come together in this fashion, each in the presence of the others. A merchant who arrives to buy a slave girl from them may have to wait and look on while a Rus completes the act of intercourse with a slave girl....

When the man [great personage] of whom I have spoken died, his girl slaves were asked, "Who will die with him?" One answered, "I." She was then put in the care of two young women, who watched over her and accompanied her everywhere, to the point that they occasionally washed her feet with their own hands. Garments were being made for the deceased and all else was being readied of which he had need. Meanwhile the slave drinks every day and sings, giving herself over to pleasure.

When the day arrived on which the man was to be cremated and the girl with him, I went to the river on which was his ship. I saw that they had drawn the ship onto the shore, that they had erected four posts of birch wood and other wood, and that around it [the ship] was made a structure like great ships'-tent out of wood.... Then they brought a couch and put it on the ship and covered it with a mattress of Greek brocade. Then came an old woman whom they call the Angel of Death, and she spread upon the couch the furnishings mentioned. It is she who has charge of the clothes-making and arranging all things, and it is she who kills the girl slave. I saw that she was a strapping old woman, fat and louring.

When they came to the grave they removed the earth from above the wood, then the wood, and took out the dead man clad in the garments in which he had died. I saw that he had grown black from the cold of the country. They had put *nabid*, fruit, and a pandora in the grave with him. They removed all that. The dead man did not smell bad and only his color had changed. They dressed him in trousers, stockings (?), boots, a tunic [*qurtaq*], and caftan of brocade with gold buttons. They put a hat of brocade and fur on him. Then they carried him into the pavilion [*qubba*] on the ship. They seated him on the mattress and propped him up with cushions. They brought *nabid*, fruits, and fragrant plants, which they put with him, then brought a dog, which they cut in two and put in the ship. Then they brought his weapons and placed them by his side. Then they took two horses, ran them until they sweated, then cut them to pieces with a sword and put them into the ship. They took two cows, which they likewise cut to pieces and put in the ship. Next they killed a rooster and a hen and threw them in. The girl slave who wished to be killed went here and there and into each of their tents, and the master of each tent had sexual intercourse with her and said, "Tell your lord I have done this out of love for him."

Friday afternoon they led the slave girl to a thing that they had made which resembled a door frame. She placed her feet on the palms of the men and they raised her up to overlook this frame. She spoke some words and they lowered her again. A second time they raised her up and she did again what she had done; then they lowered her. They raised her a third time and she did as she had done the two times before. Then they brought her a hen;

she cut off the head, which she threw away, and then they took the hen and put it in the ship. I asked the interpreter what she had done. He answered, "The first time they raised her she said, 'Behold, I see my father and mother.' The second time she said, 'I see all my dead relatives seated.' The third time she said, 'I see my master seated in Paradise and Paradise is beautiful and green; with him are men and boy servants. He calls me. Take me to him.'" Now they took her to the ship. She took off the two bracelets which she was wearing and gave them both to the old woman called the Angel of Death, who was to kill her; then she took off the two finger rings which she was wearing and gave them to the two girls who served her and were the daughters of the woman called the Angel of Death. Then they raised her onto the ship but they did not make her enter into the pavilion.

Then men came with shields and sticks. She was given a cup of *nabid*; she sang at taking it and drank. The interpreter told them that she in this fashion bade farewell to all her girl companions. Then she was given another cup; she took it and sang for a long time while the old woman incited her to drink up and go into the pavilion where her master lay. I saw that she was distracted; she wanted to enter the pavilion but put her head between it and the boat. Then the old woman seized her head and made her enter the pavilion and entered with her. Thereupon the men began to strike with the sticks on the shields so that her cries could not be heard and the other slave girls would not be frightened and seek to escape death with their masters. Then six men went into the pavilion and each had intercourse with the girl. Then they laid her at the side of her master; two held her feet and two her hands; the old woman known as the Angel of Death re-entered and looped a cord around her neck and gave the crossed ends to the two men for them to pull. Then she approached her with a broad-bladed dagger, which she plunged between her ribs repeatedly, and the men strangled her with the cord until she was dead.

Chronicon
Thietmar of Merseburg (975–1018)

He was a German chronicler, Bishop of Merseburg, and distant relative of Emperor Otto the Great. Thietmar took part in many political events of his day, including the battles of the Germans against the neighboring Poles. Thietmar wrote his *Chronicon* in eight books, covering the period between 908 and 1018. The following account describes the recently Christianized Polish society, which was still riddled with pagan customs. Despite being a churchman, Thietmar praised the severity of pagan punishments against sexual transgressions.

Source: *Kronika Thietmara*, translated into Polish by Marian Zygmunt Jedlicki (Poznań: Instytut Zachodni, 1953), pp. 582, 584. Translated from Polish by Martha A. Brożyna.

In the land of her husband[1] there exist many different customs, and although many of them are cruel, they nevertheless are deserving of praise. His people need to be watched like cattle and flogged like a stubborn donkey; for they do not allow themselves to be led in accordance with the interests of the ruler unless they fear harsh penalties. If anyone among these people musters enough audacity to seduce another man's wife or behave lecherously, he is met immediately with the following punishment: he is brought to the market bridge and a spike is nailed through his scrotum. Then, a sharp knife is placed next [to him] and he is given a difficult choice: either he dies on the spot or he cuts off that part of the body.

During pagan times of his father,[2] after the funeral of every man who was burnt on the pyre, his wife was beheaded and in this way, both shared the same fate. And if they found any concubine, they would cut off her pudendum in order to punish her in this ugly and cruel way, then — if it is agreed that I may speak of this — this shameful scrap was hung above the doorway of [her] home, so that every person who entered saw it, and thus remembered in the future and was warned. God's law orders the stoning of such a woman, and in the customs of our ancestors these types of women would be beheaded. In our times, however, wherein debaucherous customs spread everywhere in an excessive and unusual way, not only are there many lusty unmarried women, but there are also a number of married women who behave licentiously during the lives of husbands, ruinously giving in to their lustful tendencies. And even this is not enough for them, not a few secretly incited her lover to kill her husband, and then — O what a terrible example for others!— they would openly take the lover and live in sin — O the horror! They scorn their lawful husbands and they turn him away and they place his vassal above him, comparing him to an affable Habron or Jason.[3] Because there are no harsh punishments these days for this crime, there are many who will practice it day after day as a new custom. O you men of God, be brave, there are no obstacles standing in your way, tear out with a sharp plow the roots of this newly-burgeoning weed! And you lay persons, do not help in this direction. Let those who have entered the holy bonds of matrimony live in peace and innocence and after the adulterers are rooted out let married people live in mutual respect.

1. Oda, the fourth wife of Bolesław Chrobry of Poland.
2. Mieszko I, father of Bolesław Chrobry
3. David Warner refers to *Paulys Realencyclopädie der classischen Altertumswissenschaft* in his translation of Thietmar, which states that Abro or Habron symbolize "high living." David Warner, *Ottonian, Germany: The Chronicon of Thietmar of Merseberg*, Manchester, UK; New York: Manchester University Press; New York: Distributed exclusively in the USA by Palgrave, 2001.

Ecclesiastical History
Orderic Vitalis (1075–ca. 1142)

This monk and historian wrote an important account of Anglo-Norman society in his *Ecclesiastical History*, made up of thirteen books and beginning with the birth of Christ. Up to the eleventh century, Orderic's work was derived from other sources, particularly the ecclesiastical history of Bede the Venerable. After 1050, Orderic based his chronicles on oral history and copied extensively from the history of William of Poitiers, which included an important account of the first stage of the Norman conquest of England. The following excerpt discusses the Norman conquests and some of the difficulties faced by the conquerors.

Source: *The Ecclesiastical History of Orderic Vitalis, vol. 3,* translated by Marjorie Chibnall (Oxford: Clarendon Press, 1969), pp. 219, 221. Reprinted by permission of Oxford University Press.

At this time certain Norman women, consumed by fierce lust, sent message after message to their husbands urging them to return at once, and adding that unless they did so with all speed they would take other husbands for themselves. For they dared not join their men themselves, being unaccustomed to the sea crossing and afraid of seeking them out in England, where they were engaging in armed forays every day and blood flowed freely on both sides. The king, with so much fighting on his hands, was most anxious to keep all his knights about him, and made them a friendly offer of lands and revenues and great authority, promising them more when he had completely rid the kingdom of all his enemies. His loyal barons and stalwart fighting men were gravely perturbed, for they saw that continual risings threatened the king and their brothers, friends, and allies and feared that if they abandoned him they would be openly branded as traitors and cowardly deserters. On the other hand, what could honorable men do if their lascivious wives polluted their beds with adultery and brought indelible shame and dishonor on their offspring? As a result Hugh of Grandmesnil, who was governor of the Gewissae — that is, the region round Winchester — and his brother-in-law Humphrey of Tilleul, who had held the castle of Hastings from the day of its foundation, and many others departed from the country heavy at heart, and unwilling to go because they were deserting the king whilst he was struggling in a foreign land. They returned to Normandy to oblige their wanton wives; but neither they nor their heirs were ever able to recover the fiefs which they had held and chosen to abandon.

The History of the Tyrants of Sicily
"Hugo Falcandus" (mid-twelfth century)

The identity of the author of *The History of the Tyrants of Sicily* is unknown. It is an important source for the history of the Kingdom of Sicily following the death of its founder, King Roger II, in 1154. In it is chronicled the reign of William I of Sicily and the minority of his son William II. The entire narrative focuses on events within Sicily with little attention paid to chronology. The writer is a partisan witness to the events and does not write favorably about most of the people he is describing. The following account shows how a churchman adjudicated unfairly in a divorce case because he was friendly with one of the litigants.

Source: *The History of the Tyrants of Sicily by "Hugo Falcandus,"* 1154–69, translated by Graham A. Loud and Thomas Wiedemann (Manchester, New York: Manchester University Press, 1998), pp. 153–155. Reprinted with permission.

THE FICKLENESS OF WOMEN

...Richard de Say arrived at Palermo, bringing with him his wife, the sister of Bartholomew de Parisio. He wished to divorce her in order to enter into matrimony with the niece of the archbishop of Capua, a whore of high birth with whom he had long ago fallen in love. As Captain and Master Constable for Apulia, this man had remained unshakeably loyal and never deserted the king, while others had rebelled so many times. The queen received him favourably, and invested him with the county of Richard of Aquila, Count of Fondi, who was in exile in Roman territory with no hope of being allowed to return. On the matter of the divorce, she told the *familiares* that the bishops and other clergy should be summoned to listen to what both sides had to say, and reach the decision which fairness demanded. They asked the cardinals to take part in the investigation of this affair on the grounds that they were very familiar with such matters, since the Roman Curia frequently heard cases of this kind. John of Naples was quick to assent to their request. When the Bishop of Ostia, a man of undoubted integrity, saw that his colleague had been prejudiced by bribery and favouritism and that his freedom to come to a correct judgement had thus been taken away, he could not be persuaded by any plea to take part in the proceedings.

The ground on which Richard thought that his marriage ought to be dissolved was this: he claimed to have had an affair with a cousin of his wife long before the marriage had been contracted. Two knights appeared as witnesses of this who stated categorically that they had seen it. The other party denied this, and asserted that there were persons who would prove that they were giving false testimony — not that they thought that a reason this kind, even if were true, would be sufficient cause for divorce, but to counter the insult of the accusation levelled against their cousin. The cardinal thought it best to deal with the matter briefly, and ordered the said witnesses to take an oath. So he dissolved the marriage, made both parties swear not to have intercourse in future, enabled Richard to proceed legitimately to a second marriage, and ordered her to remain without hope of a husband.

THE CARDINAL'S PARTIALLY UNJUST JUDGEMENT

The clerics who were present had no doubts that in this matter he had acted out of favour to Richard de Say and his friends, but they were rather more surprised that while the man who had acted wrongly had been acquitted, he had ordered the woman who had done nothing wrong to live in perpetual chastity. After criticising his disgraceful judgement among themselves, they tried to test him by asking whether they should consistently apply this precedent in cases of a similar kind; he replied that he was allowed to do what they were not, and he had not acted in this case in order to create a precedent.

The Topography of Ireland
Gerald of Wales (1147– 1223)

Gerald was a half–Welsh, half–Norman teacher and later court chaplain to King Henry II of England. In 1185 Henry ordered Gerald to accompany Prince John to Ireland. Gerald wrote about this trip and his experiences in *The Topography of Ireland* and *The History of the Conquest of Ireland*. The following account, from *The Topography of Ireland*, is a typically hostile outsider's view of an unfamiliar culture.

Source: *The Historical Works of Giraldus Cambrensis, Containing: The Topography of Ireland, and The History of the Conquest of Ireland*, translated by Thomas Forester (New York: AMS Press, 1968), pp. 84, 86–87, 134–135. Reprinted courtesy of AMS Press, from its 1968 edition.

OF A WOMAN WHO HAD A BEARD, AND A HAIRY CREST AND MANE ON HER BACK

Duvenald, king of Limerick, had a woman with a beard down to her navel, and, also, a crest like a colt of a year old, which reached from the top of her neck down her backbone, and was covered with hair. The woman, thus remarkable for two monstrous deformities, was, however, not a hermaphrodite, but in other respects had the parts of a woman; and she constantly attended the court, an object of ridicule as well as of wonder. The fact of her spine being covered with hair neither determined her gender to be male or female; and in wearing a long beard she followed the customs of her country, though it was unnatural in her. Also, within our time, a woman was seen attending the court in Connaught, who partook of the nature of both sexes, and was a hermaphrodite. On the right side of her face she had a long and thick beard, which covered both sides of her lips to the middle of her chin, like a man; on the left, her lips and chin were smooth and hairless, like a woman.

OF A GOAT WHICH HAD INTERCOURSE WITH A WOMAN

Roderic, king of Connaught, had a white tame goat, remarkable for its flowing hair and the length of its horns. This goat had intercourse, bestially, with the woman to whose care it had been committed; the wretched creature having seduced it to become the instrument of gratifying her unnatural lust, rather than that the animal was the guilty actor. O foul and disgraceful deed! How dreadfully has reason given the reins to sensuality! How brutally does the lord of brutes, discarding his natural privileges, descend to the level of brutes, when he, rational animal, submits to such intercourse with a beast! For although on both sides it is detestable and abominable, it is by far the least that brutes should be entirely submissive to rational creatures. But though brutes are destined by nature for the service of men, they were created for use, not abuse.

HOW THE IRISH ARE VERY IGNORANT OF THE RUDIMENTS
OF THE FAITH

The faith having been planted in the island from the time of St. Patrick, so many ages ago, and propagated almost ever since, it is wonderful that this nation should remain to this day so very ignorant of the rudiments of Christianity. It is indeed a most filthy race, a race sunk in vice, a race more ignorant than all other nations of the first principles of faith. Hitherto they neither pay tithes nor first fruits; they do not contract marriages, nor shun incestuous connections; they frequent not the church of God with proper reverence. Nay, what is most detestable, and not only contrary to the Gospel, but to every thing that is right, in many parts of Ireland brothers (I will not say marry) seduce and debauch the wives of their brothers deceased, and have incestuous intercourse with them; adhering in this to the letter, and not to the spirit, of the Old Testament;[4] and following the example of men of old in their vices more willingly than in their virtues.

Annals of Roger de Hoveden
Roger de Hoveden (d. 1201)

Roger was an English chronicler who probably came from Howden in Yorkshire. Nothing is known of him until 1174, when he started to work as a

---

4. Deuteronomy 30:5.

clerk for King Henry II with assignments that included secret missions to France. His *Annals* start in 732 and end abruptly in 1201, perhaps indicating his death. Most of the chronicle is borrowed from other sources except the years 1192–1201 that are his own. Roger's strong religiosity is apparent from the following excerpt, with discourses on celibacy and the priesthood.

Source: *The Annals of Roger de Hoveden. Comprising the History of England and of Other Countries of Europe from A.D. 732 to A.D. 1201,* translated by Henry T. Riley (London: H.G. Bohn, 1853), pp. 201–202, 204.

These are the provisions relative to archdeacons, priests, deacons, subdeacons, and secular clergy of whatever degree, which, in the year of our Lord's Incarnation 1108, Anselm, archbishop of Canterbury, and Thomas, archbishop elect of York, and all the other bishops of England, in the presence of the glorious king Henry, with the assent of his earls and barons, enacted:—"it is hereby decreed, that priests, deacons, and subdeacons shall live in chastity, and shall have no women in their houses save only those who are connected with them by close relationship, according to the rule which the holy Synod of Nice has laid down. But those priests, deacons, and subdeacons who have, since the prohibition pronounced by the synod held in London, either retained their wives or married others, if they wish any longer to celebrate the mass, let them so entirely put them away from themselves as not to let them enter their houses; nor are they themselves to go into the houses of such women, or knowingly to meet them in any house; nor are any women of this description to live upon lands belonging to the church. But if for any proper reason it is necessary for either party to communicate with the other, having two lawful witnesses, let them converse together outside of the house. And if, upon the testimony of two or three lawful witnesses, or by the public report of the people of the parish, any one of them shall be accused of having violated this enactment, he shall clear himself, if he is a priest, by bringing six proper witnesses of his own order; if a deacon, four; if a subdeacon, two. But as for him, who shall not thus clear himself, he shall be deemed to be a transgressor of this holy enactment. And as for those priests who, despising the divine altar and the holy canons, have preferred to live with women, let them be removed from the holy office, deprived of all ecclesiastical benefices, and placed without the choir, being pronounced infamous; and he who, being a rebel and contumacious, shall not leave the women, and shall presume to celebrate mass, if, when called upon to make satisfaction, he shall neglect to do so, is to be excommunicated. The same sentence embraces the archdeacons and all the secular clergy, both as to leaving these women and avoiding cohabitation with them, and the severity of the punishment if they shall transgress these statutes. All archdeacons shall also swear that they will not receive money for tolerating the transgression of this enactment, nor suffer priests whom they know to be keeping women to chaunt the mass, or to have substitutes; deans also shall swear to the same effect. The archdeacon, or deacon, or dean, who shall refuse to take oath to this effect, is to lose his archdeaconry or deanery. As to those priests, who, leaving the women, shall make choice to serve God and the holy altars, let them cease during forty days from the performance of their duties, and in the meantime employ substitutes in their places, such penance being imposed on them as to their bishops shall seem fit." ...

In the year 1114, ... on the sixth day before the calends of March, being the third day of the week, Thomas the Younger, archbishop of York, departed this life. When he was first taken ill, his medical men told him that he could not recover, except by means of carnal knowledge of a woman; on which he made answer, "Shame upon a malady which requires sensuality for its cure!" and being thus chosen by the Lord while of virgin purity closed his temporal life.

The Chronicle of Salimbene de Adam
Salimbene de Adam (1221–1288)

Salimbene was a Franciscan monk and historian born in Parma and well traveled throughout Italy. His chronicle covering the years 1167 to 1287 is a useful source for both political and social history and the history of the Franciscan Order in the thirteenth century. In the following passage, Salimbene describes the loose morality of the clergy at the time as well as the criticisms levelled at it.

Source: *The Chronicle of Salimbene de Adam*, translated by Joseph L. Baird, Giuseppe Baglivi, and John Robert Kane (Binghamton, N.Y.: Medieval & Renaissance Texts & Studies, 1986), pp. 430–431. Reprinted by permission of the Center for Medieval and Renaissance Studies.

...I have seen some priests who were devoting themselves wholly to usury and gaining property, so that they could give it to their bastards [*spuriis suis*]. And I have seen some others who were running a tavern selling wine at the sign of the circle with the whole house filled with bastard children, and they sleep with their whore [*focaria*] during the night and rise up to say Mass the next day. And if after Mass, some Hosts are left, that is to say, the body of the Lord himself, they stuff them in the cracks in the walls. And they commit many other shameful and unheard of horrors, which I will not repeat for the sake of brevity. Yet in their churches these priests have indecent missals, parchments, and ecclesiastical vestments which are crude, stained, and filthy; and they have small rusty tin chalices filled with bitter wine or vinegar for the Mass. And their holy wafers are so small that they can scarcely be seen between their fingers, and they are not round but square, and moreover, are befouled with fly specks. Furthermore, many women have better strings in their shoes than the holy vestments of these priests. Once, a certain Friar Minor whom I know well was celebrating Mass on a feast day in one of these churches, and he was forced to make use of the girdle of the priest's whore to which was attached a large number of keys. Thus whenever he turned about in the service to say *Dominus vobiscum,* the congregation heard the keys clanking.... And it is for priests like this that I am supposed to preach on tithing!

"To the ... criticism that we are ladies men, that is, that we love to look on women and talk familiarly with them, we say that this is the malicious slander of those who seek to put 'a blot on the elect.'[5] They are like the jongleurs, minstrels, and the so-called 'court-knight,' who think to excuse their own vanity and lasciviousness by defaming others."

...We Minorites and Preachers are poor mendicants, who necessarily live by alms, and women are among those who treat us well, in accordance with the passage in Ecclesiasticus 36:27: "where there is no wife, he mourneth that is in want." This was written because women are more merciful in giving to the poor and more compassionate toward the afflicted than men are, whose hearts are harder. Thus when women send for us, we are obliged to go in order to do some good for them in their distress or tribulation, lest we are found ungrateful, because the Apostle says, Colossians 3:15: "Be ye thankful." And we do not talk with any woman while drinking wine, for our rules forbid us to drink in the cities, save with members of religious orders, prelates, or lords of the land.

The Chronicles of Jean Froissart
Jean Froissart (1337?–1404?)

Little is known of Froissart's background. He was a poet and historian who traveled all over Europe and met and associated with crowned heads such as Queen Philippa of England and David II of Scotland. He wrote lyric poetry and romances in the courtly love tradition. However, he also wrote history, and his *Chronicles* are an excellent source for a picture of fourteenth century Europe and the Hundred Years' War. Up to the year 1361, Froissart's work leans heavily on Jean la Bel's *Les Vrayes Chroniques,* but later he began to use his own observations, interviews, and source documents. The following recounts the execution of the lover of England's King Edward II.

Source: *Froissart's Chronicles,* by John Jolliffe, editor and translator, copyright © 1967 John Jolliffe. Maps and geological tables drawn by Joan Emerson. Used by permission of Random House, Inc., p. 20.

5. Ecclesiasticus 11:33.

[BOOK I]

13. When the feast was over, Sir Hugh, who was not popular in that district, was brought before the Queen and all the barons and knights in full assembly. A list of all his misdeeds were read out to him, to which he made no reply, and the barons and knights passed sentence on him which was carried out as follows: first, he was dragged on a conveyance through all the streets of Hereford, to the sound of trumpets and clarions; then he was taken to the market-place where all the people were assembled. Then he was tied on a tall ladder in full view of all the people both high and low, and a large fire was lit. Then his private parts were cut off, because he was held to be a heretic, and guilty of unnatural practices, even with the King, whose affections he had alienated from the Queen. When his private parts were cut off they were thrown into the fire and burned. Then his heart and entrails were cut out and thrown on the fire to burn, because his heart had been false and treacherous and he had given treasonable advice to the King, so as to bring shame and disgrace on the country, and had caused the greatest barons in England to be beheaded, by whom the kingdom should have been supported and defended; and he had encouraged the King not to see his wife or his son, who was to be their future king; indeed, both of them had had to leave the country to save their lives. When the other parts of his body had been disposed of, Sir Hugh's head was cut off and sent to London. His body was then divided into quarters, which were sent to the four next largest cities in England.

Annals of the Kingdom of Poland
Jan Długosz (1415–1480)

A Polish historian, diplomat, and tutor to the sons of King Kazimierz Jagiellończyk, Długosz authored a twelve-volume history of Poland covering the years 965 to 1480 modeled on Livy's *History of Rome*. Aside from its extensive treatment of early Polish history, the *Annals of the Kingdom of Poland* also provides information about Belarus, Bohemia, Hungary, Lithuania, and the Ukraine during this period.

Source: *Jana Długosza Roczniki Czyli Kronika Sławnego Królestwa Polskiego*, vols. 7–8 (Warszawa: Państwowe Wydawnictwo Naukowe, 1974). Translated from the Polish by Martha A. Brożyna.

1271

Princess Gryfina, daughter of the Russian prince Roscislaw, was the wife of Leszek the Black, Prince of Sieradz. She called together a group of nobles, knights, and ladies of Sieradz and told them that although she had been living with her husband Leszek the Black for almost six years, to the present day she remained a virgin untouched by her husband, thereby accusing him of impotence and frigidity. Leszek agreed to this accusation silently. She removed her hood, with which as a married woman she used to cover her head, before the Franciscan monastery in Kraków in the presence of many people, and then walked around with her head uncovered, avoiding the company of Leszek and making it clear for all to see that she wished to dissolve the marriage.

1275

Bolesław the Bashful, Prince of Kraków and Sandomierz, was saddened by the four-year separation of Gryfina and Leszek and the shameful circumstances and damage to the reputation of his brother that had characterized it. He went personally to Sieradz and he and his noble friends of Kraków entered into negotiations that resulted in the reconciliation of Princess Gryfina with Prince Leszek the Black on the sixth of August. These discussions put an end to the misunderstandings and dispute between the couple and caused them to return to a state of marital love, which continued from that point on genuinely until their deaths.

9

Russia and the Byzantine Empire

Secret History
Procopius of Caesarea (d. 562)

Procopius was a legal secretary to the Byzantine general Belisarius and an historian. He wrote *History in Eight Books*, describing the Persian, Vandal, and Gothic wars of Emperor Justinian. He also wrote a shorter work, *Anekdota* or *Secret History*, in 550 as a supplement to his *History*. In the *Secret History*, Procopius detailed court intrigue, viciously attacking Justinian and his wife Theodora as well as his former employer Belisarius and his wife. The excerpt below illustrates how Procopius sought to denigrate Theodora's humble background as a former actress and prostitute.

Source: *Procopius: Secret History*, translated by Richard Atwater (Ann Arbor, MI: University of Michigan Press, 1963). The first edition as an Ann Arbor paperback 1963. Foreword copyright © by the University of Michigan 1961, p. 46–48, 51–52.

But as soon as she arrived at the age of youth, and was now ready for the world, her mother put her on the stage. Forthwith, she became a courtesan, and such as the ancient Greeks used to a call a common one, at that: for she was not a flute or harp player, nor was she even trained to dance, but only gave her youth to anyone she met, in utter abandonment. Her general favors included, of course, the actors in the theater; and in their productions she took part in the low comedy scenes. For she was very funny and a good mimic, and immediately became popular in this art. There was no shame in the girl, and no one ever saw her dismayed: no role was too scandalous for her to accept without a blush.

She was the kind of comedienne who delights the audience by letting herself be cuffed and slapped on the cheeks, and makes them guffaw by raising her skirts to reveal to the spectators those feminine secrets here and there which custom veils from the eyes of the opposite sex. With pretended laziness she mocked her lovers, and coquettishly adopting ever new ways of embracing, was able to keep in constant turmoil the hearts of the sophisticated. And she did not wait to be asked by anyone she met, but on the contrary, with inviting jests and a comic flaunting of her skirts herself tempted all men who passed by, especially those who were adolescent.

On the field of pleasure she was never defeated. Often she would go picnicking with ten young men or more, in the flower of their strength and virility, and dallied with them all, the whole night through. When they wearied of the sport, she would approach their servants, perhaps thirty in number, and fight a duel with each of these; and even thus found no allayment of her craving. Once, visiting the house of an illustrious gentleman, they say she mounted the projecting corner of her dining couch, pulled up the front of her dress, without a blush, and thus carelessly showed her wantonness. And though she flung wide three gates to the ambassadors of Cupid, she lamented that nature had not similarly unlocked the straits of her bosom, that she might there have contrived a further welcome to his emissaries.

Frequently, she conceived, but as she employed every artifice immediately, a miscarriage was straightway effected. Often, even in the theater, in the sight of all the people, she removed her costume and stood nude in their midst, except for a girdle about the groin: not that she was abashed at revealing that, too, to the audience, but because there was a law against appearing altogether naked on the stage, without a least this much of a fig-leaf. Covered thus with a ribbon, she would sink down to the stage floor and recline on her back. Slaves to whom the duty was entrusted would then scatter grains of barley from above into the calyx of this passion flower, whence geese, trained for the purpose, would next pick the grains one by one with their bills and eat. When she rose, it was not with a blush, but she seemed rather to glory in the performance. For she was not only impudent herself, but endeavored to make everybody else as audacious. Often when she was alone with other actors, she would undress in their midst and arch her back provocatively, advertising like a peacock both to those who had experience of her and to those who had not yet had that privilege her trained suppleness.

Now as long as the former Empress was alive, Justinian was unable to find a way to make Theodora his wedded wife. In this one matter she opposed him as in nothing else; for the lay abhorred vice, being a rustic and of barbarian descent as I have shown. She was never able to do any real good, because of her continued ignorance of the affairs of state. She dropped her original name for fear people would think it ridiculous, and adopted the name of Euphemia when she came to the palace. But finally her death removed this obstacle to Justinian's desire.

Justin, doting and utterly senile, was now the laughing stock of his subjects; he was disregarded by everyone because of his inability to oversee state affairs; but Justinian they all served with considerable awe. His hand was in everything, and his passion for turmoil created universal consternation.

It was then that he undertook to complete his marriage with Theodora. But as it was impossible for a man of senatorial rank to make a courtesan his wife, this being forbidden by ancient law, he made the Emperor nullify this ordinance by creating a new one, permitting him to wed Theodora, and consequently making it possible for anyone else to marry a courtesan. Immediately after this he seized the power of the Emperor, veiling his usurpation with a transparent pretext: for he was proclaimed colleague of his uncle as Emperor of the Romans by questionable legality of an election inspired by terror.

The Russian Primary Chronicle
Authors unknown

This details the history of the early Russian state, which was centered around Kievan Rus. It covers the years 852–1116. Traditionally, it had been ascribed to the monk Nestor, but modern scholars conclude that it was in fact written by several authors. It is an important source for the history of the eastern Slavs (Belarussians, Russians, and Ukrainians). It shows how Slavic tribes were bound by a common language and origin, but points out their differing cultures and mores. The chronicle uses a number of varied sources such as hagiography, documents, and legends. The most prominent sources are Byzantine chronicles, particularly that of Georgious Hamartolus, who is mentioned in the text below.

Source: *The Russian Primary Chronicle: Laurentian Text* edited by Samuel Hazzard Cross and Olgard P. Sherbowitz-Wetzor (Cambridge, MA: Medieval Academy of America, 1953), pp. 55–58. Reprinted with permission.

Now while the Slavs dwelt along the Danube, as we have said, there came from among the Scythians, that is, from the Khazars, a people called Bulgars who settled on the Danube and oppressed the Slavs. Afterward came the White Ugrians, who inherited the Slavic country. These Ugrians appeared under the Emperor Heraclius, warring on Chosroes, King of Persia. The Avars, who attacked Heraclius the Emperor, nearly capturing him, also lived at this time. They made war upon the Slavs, and harassed the Dulebians, who were themselves Slavs. They even did violence to the Dulebian women. When an Avar made a journey, he did not cause either a horse or a steer to be harnessed, but gave command instead that three of four or five women should be yoked to his cart and be made to draw him. Even thus they harassed the Dulebians. The Avars were large of stature and proud of spirit, and God destroyed them. They all perished, and not one Avar survived. There is to this day a proverb in Rus' which runs, "They perished like the Avars." Neither race nor heir of them remains. The Pechenegs came after them, and the Magyars passed by Kiev later during the time of Oleg....

These Slavic tribes preserved their own customs, the law of their forefathers, and their traditions, each observing its own usages. For the Polyanians retained the mild and peaceful customs of their ancestors, and showed respect for their daughters-in-law and their sisters, as well as for their mothers and fathers. For their mothers-in-law and their brothers-in-law they also entertained great reverence. They observed a fixed custom, under which the groom's brother did not fetch the bride, but she was brought to the bridegroom in the evening, and on the next morning her dowry was turned over.

The Derevlians, on the other hand, existed in bestial fashion, and lived like cattle. They killed one another, ate every impure thing, and there was no marriage among them, but instead they seized upon maidens by capture. The Radimichians, the Vyatichians, and the Severians had the same customs. They lived in the forest like any wild beast, and ate every unclean thing. They spoke obscenely before their fathers and their daughters-in-law. There were no marriages among them, but simply festivals among the villages. When the people gathered together for games, for dancing, and for all other devilish amusements, the men on these occasions carried off wives for themselves, and each took any woman with whom he had arrived at an understanding. In fact, they even had two or three wives apiece. Whenever a death occurred, a feast was held over the corpse, and then a great pyre was constructed, on which the deceased was laid and burned. After the bones were collected, they were placed in a small urn and set upon a post by the roadside, even as the Vyatichians do to this day. Such customs were observed by the Krivichians and the other pagans, since they did not know the law of God, but made a law unto themselves.

Georgius says in his *Chronicle*:

"Among all the nations, there are some that possess a written law, while others simply observe certain fixed customs, for, among those devoid of law, their ancestral usage is accepted in its stead. To this class belong the Seres, who live at the end of the world, and apply as law the customs of their ancestors, which forbid them to commit adultery or incest, to steal, to bear false witness, to kill, or do any wrong whatsoever.

"The law of the Bactrians, called Brahmans or Islanders, which is derived from the forefatherly prescription, prohibits them for reasons of piety from eating meat, drinking wine, committing adultery, or doing any sort of wrong, solely in consequence of religious scruple. But among the Indians, who dwell beside them, are found murderers, criminals and doers of violence beyond all nature. In the most remote portion of their country, they practice cannibalism and kill travelers and, what is worse still, they devour them like dogs.

"The Chaldeans and the Babylonians have a different code, which allows them to marry their mothers, to commit a carnal sin with their nieces, and to commit murder. They regard every shameless deed as a virtue when they commit it, even when they are far from their own country.

"The Gelaeans maintain other customs: among them, the women plough, build houses, and perform men's work. But they indulge in vice to the extent of their desire, for they are by no means restrained by their husbands, nor do the latter at all concern themselves about the matter. There are among them bold women who are capable of capturing wild beasts by virtue of their strength. The women have control over the husbands, and rule them.

"In Britain, many men sleep with one woman, and likewise many women have intercourse with one man. The people carry on without jealousy or restraint the vicious customs of their ancestors.

"The Amazons have no husbands, but like the brute beasts they are filled with desire once each year in the springtime, and come together with the neighboring men. This season seems to them, as it were, a time of celebration and great festival. When they give birth to children and a male is born, they kill it, but if the child is of the female sex, then they nurse it and bring it up carefully."

Just so, even in our own day, the Polovcians maintain the customs of their ancestors in the shedding of blood and in glorifying themselves for such deeds, as well as in eating every dead or unclean thing, even hamsters and marmots. They marry their mothers-in-law and their sisters-in-law, and observe other usages of their ancestors. But in all countries we Christians who believe in the Holy Trinity, in one baptism, and in one faith, have but one law, as many of us have been baptized into Christ Lord and have put on Christ.

Annals of Niketas Choniates
Niketas Choniates (1155–1215/16)

This Greek historian chronicled Byzantine history from 1118 to 1207, including the sack of Constantinople by the Crusaders in 1204. The following account depicts the power struggle immediately after the death of Emperor Alexius Komnenos between his son and successor Emperor John Komnenos and his sister Anna Komnena, who wished to see her husband, Nikephoros Bryennios, ascend to the throne.

Source: *O City of Byzantium, Annals of Niketas Choniates*, translated by Harry J. Magoulias (Detroit, MI: Wayne State University Press, 1984), p. 8. Reprinted by permission.

The first year of the emperor's reign had not yet run its course when his relatives – how, one cannot say – stitched up a plot against him, ranting and raving and casting the evil eye. A band of evil-working men, pledging good faith, rallied around Bryennios; because he had been educated in the liberal arts, displayed royal bearing, and was the most outstanding of those connected to the imperial family by marriage, they handed over the royal power to him. (As we have said elsewhere, he was married to the emperor's sister, Kaisarissa Anna, who was ardently devoted to philosophy, the queen of all the sciences, and was educated in every field of learning.) They probably would have struck quickly at night with murderous weapons while the emperor was encamped at Philopation, a place well suited for running horses and situated a little distance from the gates of the land walls, since they had previously plied the keeper of the gates with lavish bribes, had not Bryennios' customary sluggishness and languor forestalled any attempt to gain the throne and compelled him to remain immobilized, ignoring his compacts, and thus extinguishing the zeal of his partisans. It is said that Kaisarissa Anna, disgusted with her husband's frivolous behavior and distraught in her anger, and being a shrew by nature, felt justified in strongly contracting her vagina when Bryennios' penis entered deep inside her, thus causing him great pain.

Notes Upon Russia
Sigmund Herberstein (1486–1566)

Herberstein was a diplomat and ambassador of the Holy Roman Empire to Russia between 1517 and 1526. He was a witness to Russian social customs during the reign of Basil III. In the following passage he describes social customs in Russia, including the practice of secluding women from public view in the *terem* or women's quarters. It was primarily the upper classes that could afford this practice.

Source: *Sigismund von Herberstein: Notes Upon Russia; Being a Translation of the Earliest Account of that Country, Entitled Rerum Moscoviticarum Commentarii*, vol. 1, translated by R.H. Major (New York: B. Franklin, 1967). The Hakluyt Society. First Series No. 101851, pp. 93–95. Reprinted with the permission of David Higham Associates.

They do not call it adultery unless one have the wife of another. Love between those that are married is for the most part lukewarm, especially among the nobles and princes, because they marry girls whom they have never seen before; and being engaged in the service of the prince, they are compelled to desert them, and become corrupted with disgraceful connexions with others.

The condition of the women is most miserable; for they consider no woman virtuous unless she live shut up at home, and be so closely guarded that she go out nowhere. They give a woman, I say, little credit for modesty, if she be seen by strangers or people out of doors. But shut up at home they do nothing but spin and sew, and have literally no authority or influence in the house. All the domestic work is done by the servants. Whatever is strangled by the hands of a woman, whether it be a fowl, or any other kind of animal, they abominate as unclean. The wives, however, of the poorer classes do the household work and cook. But if their husbands and the menservants happen to be away, and they wish to strangle a fowl, they stand at the door holding the fowl, or whatever animal it may be, and a knife, and generally beg the men that pass by to kill it. They are very seldom admitted into the churches, and still less frequently to friendly meetings, unless they be very old and free from all suspicion. On certain holidays, however, men allow their wives and daughters, as a special gratification, to meet in very pleasant meadows, where they seat themselves on a sort of wheel of fortune, and are moved alternately up and down, or they fasten a rope somewhere, with a seat to it, in which they sit, and are swung backwards and forwards; or they otherwise make merry with clapping their hands and singing songs, but they have no dances whatever.

There is at Moscow a certain German, a blacksmith, named Jordan, who married a Russian woman. After she had lived some time with her husband, she one day thus lovingly addressed him: "Why is it, my dearest husband, that you do not love me?" The husband replied, "I do love you passionately." "I have as yet," said she, "received no proofs of your love." The husband inquired what proofs she desired. Her reply was: "You have never beaten me." "Really," said the husband, "I did not think that blows were proofs of love; but, however, I will not fail even in this respect." And so not long after he beat her most cruelly; and confessed to me that after that process his wife showed much greater affection towards him. So he repeated the exercise frequently; and finally, while I was still at Moscow, cut off her head and her legs.

The Travels of Olearius
Adam Olearius (1603–1671)

Olearius was a scholar who traveled with the embassy of Duke Frederick of Holstein to Muscovy on two separate trips (1633–1635 and 1635–1639) in an attempt to obtain Tsar Michael's permission for travel through Russia to Persia. Although the diplomatic mission failed, Olearius managed to write a fascinating account of his travels, which was first published in 1647. Within a decade the work had become popular throughout Europe. In the excerpt below, he describes Russian behaviors, which he views as shameless.

Source: *The Travels of Olearius in Seventeenth-Century Russia*, translated and edited by Samuel H. Baron. Copyright © 1967 by the Board of Trustees of the Leland Stanford Jr. University, pp. 142–143. Used with the permission of Stanford University Press, www.sup.org.

...they speak of debauchery, of vile depravity, of lasciviousness, and of immoral conduct committed by themselves and by others. They tell all sorts of shameless fables, and he who can relate the coarsest obscenities and indecencies, accompanied by the most wanton mimicry, is accounted the best companion and is the most sought after. Their dances have the same character, often including voluptuous movements of the body. They say that roving comedians bare their backsides, and I know not what else. The Danish ambassador [Ulfeldt] was entertained by such shameless dances when he was there. He tells in his *Hodoeporicon* of seeing Russian women assume strange poses and make strange signs at the windows of their houses.

So given are they to the lusts of the flesh and fornication that some are addicted to the vile depravity we call sodomy; and not only with boys (as Curtius [*De Rebus Gestis*] tells) but also with men and horses. Such antics provide matter for conversation at their carouses. People caught in such obscene acts are not severely punished. Tavern musicians often sing of such loathsome things, too, in the open streets, while some show them to young people in puppet shows. Their dancing-bear impresarios have comedians with them, who, among other things, arrange farces employing puppets. These comedians tie a blanket around their bodies and spread it above their heads, thus creating a portable theater or stage with which they can run about the streets, and on top of which they can give puppet shows.

"They have divested themselves of every trace of shame and restraint," says Jakob [Ulfeldt]. In Moscow we ourselves several times saw men and women come out of public baths to cool off, and, as naked as God created them, approach us and call obscenely in broken German to our young people. Idleness strongly prompts them to this kind of dissolute behavior. Daily you can see hundreds of idlers standing about or strolling in the market place or in the Kremlin. And they are more addicted to drunkenness than any nation in the world. Hieronymus [St. Jerome] said, "A stomach filled with wine craves immediate sexual satisfaction." After drinking wine to excess they are like unbridled animals, following wherever their passions lead. I recall in this connection what the Grand Prince's interpreter told me at Great Novgorod: "Every year there is a great pilgrimage to Novgorod [to the Khutynskii Monastery]. At that time a tavern keeper, for a consideration given the Metropolitan, is permitted to set up several tents around the tavern;

beginning at daybreak, the pilgrim brothers and sisters, as well as the local people, gather to toss off several cups of vodka before the service of worship. Many of them stay all day and drown their pilgrim devotion in wine. On one such day it happened that a drunken woman came out of the tavern, collapsed in the street nearby, and fell asleep. Another drunken Russian came by, and seeing the partly exposed woman lying there, was inflamed with passion, and lay down with her to quench it, caring not that it was broad daylight and on a well-peopled street. He remained lying by her and fell asleep there. Many youngsters gathered in a circle around this bestial pair and laughed and joked about them for a long time, until an old man came up and threw a robe over them to cover their shame."

Part IV

LAW

10

Secular Law

Byzantine Law: The Ecloga

In the early eighth century, Emperor Leo III of Isauria and his son and co-emperor Constantine V revised sixth-century laws compiled under Emperor Justinian (*Corpus Iuris Civilis*). Their goal was to summarize the essential laws into a short legal code and to alter certain laws for the "greater humanity." This revision, published in 726, is known as the Ecloga. It focused on family law and featured increased rights for women. Yet it also shows oriental influences, especially punishments involving mutilation, which were nonexistent under Justinian. This law code remained in place for about 150 years.

Source: *A Manual of Roman law, the Ecloga, Published by the Emperors Leo III and Constantine V of Isauria at Constantinople A.D. 726*, translated by Edwin Hanson Freshfield (Cambridge: Cambridge University Press, 1926), pp. 72, 108–112, 126–127, 134, 135–137.

CONCERNING THE CONTRACT OF CHRISTIAN MARRIAGE

1. The marriage of Christians, man and woman, who have reached years of discretion, that is for a man at fifteen and for a woman at thirteen years of age, both being desirous, and having obtained the consent of their parents, shall be contracted either by deed or by parol.

OFFENCES AND PUNISHMENTS

19. A married man who commits adultery shall by way of correction be flogged with twelve lashes; and whether rich or poor he shall pay a fine.

20. An unmarried man who commits fornication shall be flogged with six lashes.

21. If a married man consorts with his wife's maidservant and has carnal knowledge of her, the maid shall be taken before the local magistrates and shall be sold into slavery on behalf of the State and the price of her shall inure to the State.

22. Anyone who has carnal knowledge of another person's servant shall, if he is a person of means, pay for the offence thirty nomismata to the master

of the servant. If he is poor he shall be whipped and shall pay as much as he can in proportion to the thirty nomismata.

23. A person who has carnal knowledge of a nun shall, upon the footing that he is debauching the Church of God, have his nose slit, because he committed wicked adultery with her who belonged to the Church; and she on her side must take heed lest similar punishment be reserved to her.

24. Anyone who carries away forcibly a nun or any virgin woman in any place, shall, if he corrupts her, have his nose slit. Abettors of the rape shall be exiled.

25. Anyone who, intending to take in marriage a woman who is his goddaughter in Salvation-bringing baptism, had carnal knowledge of her without marrying her, and being found guilty of the offence, shall, after being exiled, be condemned to the same punishment meted out for other adultery, that is to say both the man and the woman shall have their noses slit.

26. If anyone should be found doing the same thing to his stepdaughter both shall have their noses slit and be severely flogged.

27. A man who commits adultery with a woman under coverture shall have his nose slit. And also the adulteress; since thenceforward she becomes a whore and is parted from her husband and lost to her children, disregarding the word of the Lord who teaches us that He has made one flesh of man and wife. And after their noses have been slit the adulteress shall take the things which she brought in to her husband and nothing more. But the adulterer shall not be separated from his own wife though his nose be slit. And the beginning of the adultery shall be enquired into with much care, and the Court shall interrogate the accusers of the intrigue; and if the accuser is the father, husband, mother, brother or the like, the ground for the charge shall be the more credible. And if the accusers are strangers, they must satisfy the Court concerning their legal citizenship; and they shall be examined for proof of the facts. And if they prove the adultery the adulterer and the adulteress shall have their noses slit. And if they do not prove the adultery but have made the accusation maliciously they shall, as slanderers, suffer the like punishment.

28. The husband who is cognizant of, and condones, his wife's adultery shall be flogged and exiled, and the adulterer and the adulteress shall have their noses slit.

PUNISHMENTS APPLICABLE TO SOLDIERS
18. Those who have been condemned for adultery or some other public crime shall not be eligible for military service if they wish to enlist.

30. Anyone who by means of intoxicant, wine, or other debauchery makes a soldier fall and commit crime, shall be forgiven capital punishment, but shall be degraded from his own rank.

CONCERNING PERSONS OF EMINENCE WHO ARE NOT TO CONSORT WITH LOW CLASS WOMEN

4. If a woman, through lust, has carnal intercourse with her slave she shall be separated from him and the slave shall be burned. And the status of such person shall be registered as of a slave honoured by emancipation. But the children born to them shall not enjoy any rank or honour. It is sufficient for them to be free.

ORDINANCE CONCERNING MURDERERS AND SORCERERS

3. Adulterers, procurers, and abettors of those abominations shall suffer capital punishment.

6. Anyone who commits adultery with a woman who, for gain, has been debauched by many, shall not suffer the punishment inflicted for adultery, since the adulterer did not suborn the woman into the evil business.

8. Those who provide potions to procure abortion, whether love philtres or not, commit a sin. And as the example is of the worst kind, the offender shall, if he is a poor person, be sent to the mines; those who are affluent shall be exiled to the islands and they shall suffer a partial confiscation of their means. If in consequence of the offence the woman should happen to die, the offender, whether man or woman, shall suffer capital punishment.

18. Anyone who gives a potion as a philtre, or to cause miscarriage without evil intent, shall, if he is of mean estate, be sent to the mines. If he is a person of substance he shall be banished and suitably fined. And if the person treated should die in consequence the offender shall suffer capital punishment.

Alamannic Laws

Alamans were one of the many Germanic tribes that started to invade the Roman Empire in the third century. Ultimately, they settled in the territory of the former Roman Empire in what is now Switzerland. Each tribe had its own set of laws based on custom and passed down orally. The first version of the laws was codified and circulated in the seventh century. Because of the fear of feuds among kin groups, a system of monetary payments called *wergeld* was established to punish crimes. The amount of the wergeld was determined according to social status, injury and sex.

Source: *Laws of the Alamans and Bavarians*, translated by Theodore John Rivers (Philadelphia: University of Pennsylvania Press, 1977). Copyright © 1977 by the University of

Pennsylvania Press, pp. 83, 85, 89, 98. Reprinted by permission of the University of
Pennsylvania Press.

50. IF ANYONE ABDUCTS ANOTHER'S WIFE
If any freeman abducts another's wife contrary to law, let him return her and
compensate with eighty solidi. If, however, he does not wish to return her,
let him pay for her with 400 solidi, if the previous husband agrees to receive
this payment. And if she dies before her husband sought her, let him [the
abductor] compensate with 400 solidi.

If, however, that abductor, who took her for himself as a wife, has sons and
daughters by her before he pays for her, and a son or daughter dies, let him
pay for that child to the former husband with the wergeld. If, however, the
children are living, they do not belong to him who begot them, but remain
under the guardianship [*mundium*] of the former husband.

51. IF ANYONE TAKES ANOTHER'S BETROTHED
If anyone takes another's betrothed contrary to law, let him return her and
compensate with 200 solidi. If, however, he does not wish to return her, let
him pay for her with 400 solidi, even if she dies under his [custody].

52. IF ANYONE DISMISSES ANOTHER'S BETROTHED DAUGHTER
If anyone dismisses another's betrothed daughter and takes another, let him
compensate for her whom he betrothed and dismissed with forty solidi, and
let him swear with twelve oathtakers, five designated and six selected [him-
self as the twelfth], that he rejects her through no vice or contempt, nor does
he find any fault in her, but love of another led him to dismiss her and take
another as a wife.

53. IF ANYONE TAKES AN UNBETROTHED DAUGHTER
If anyone takes another's unbetrothed daughter for himself as a wife, let him
return her and compensate for her with forty solidi, if her father demands
her back.

If, however, this woman dies under his [custody], before he acquired the
guardianship [*mundium*] from her father, let him pay 400 solidi for her to
her father. And if he begets sons and daughters before [he acquires the
mundium], and all their children die, let him compensate to the woman's
father with the wergeld for each child.

56. IF ANYONE UNCOVERS A WOMAN'S HEAD
If any free virgin woman [maiden] goes on a journey between two estates,
and anyone meets her [and] uncovers her head, let him compensate with six
solidi. And if he raises her clothing to the knee, let him compensate with
six solidi. And if he exposes her so that her genitalia or posterior appears,

let him compensate with twelve solidi. If, however, he fornicates with her against her will, let him compensate with forty solidi.

If, however, this happens to an adult woman, let him compensate all things twice what we said above concerning the virgin.

88. CONCERNING AN ABORTION IN A WOMAN

If anyone causes an abortion in a pregnant woman so that you can immediately recognize whether [the offspring] would have been a boy or a girl: if it was to be a boy, let him compensate with twelve solidi; however, if a girl, [let him compensate] with twenty-four [solidi].

If whether [the fetus is male or female] cannot be immediately recognized, and [the fetus] has not changed the shape of the mother's body, let him compensate with twelve solidi. If he seeks more, let him clear himself with oath-takers.

Norwegian Laws

The following come from two different sets of laws covering personal rights. The first comes from the Gulathing, the region found in the southwestern part of Norway. The second comes from the Frostathing, the area around Trondheim. Both are believed to date back to the reign of King Hakon the Good (935–61). In many ways, these laws are comparable to continental Germanic laws before the introduction of the *wergeld*. They stress the honor of freemen, and they show the right accorded an injured party or his kin to avenge a crime that had been committed.

Source: *The Earliest Norwegian Laws, Being the Gulathing Law and the Frostathing Law,* translated by Laurence M. Larson, copyright © 1935, Columbia University Press, pp. 141, 143, 271–275. Reprinted with the permission of the publisher.

The Law of Personal Rights — Gulathing

190. IF A MAN STRIKES A WOMAN

If a man strikes a woman or a woman [strikes] a man, the offender shall pay such compensation as the injured person has a right to claim, and a baug to the king. If women come to blows no man can claim any atonement, only the women themselves [can claim it]. A minor shall neither receive nor pay atonement [for injury] till he is twelve winters old; then he is a man in the half-atonement class in either respect till he is fifteen winters old.

196. CONCERNING INSULTING REMARKS THAT CALL FOR ATONEMENT

These are the [kinds of] insulting remarks that call for full atonement. The first is when a man says of another that he has given birth to a child. The second is when he says that the man has been used as a woman. The third is when he likens him to a mare or calls him a slut or a whore or likens him to any kind of a female beast. For these [remarks] he shall pay the man a full atonement; but the man may also seek satisfaction in blood and outlawry for the sayings that I have now enumerated, if he has asked witnesses to take note of them. Men may repent of their utterances and withdraw them if they wish, and acknowledge that they know nothing worse about the man than about [any] good man. It is an insult that calls for a full atonement for a man to call a free man a thrall or a monster or a malefactor. It is also an insult that calls for a full atonement to accuse a woman of being a whore and to call her a whore, if she is without guilt.

The Law of Personal Rights — Frostathing

33. If a Woman Slays a Man
If a woman slays a man, his kinsmen have the right to kill her if they wish, if she does not leave the land within five days in the summer and half a month in the winter.

35. If a Woman Kills Her Husband
If a woman kills her husband or contrives [his death], being impelled by the wickedness of lying with another man or intending [to lie with him], the kinsmen of the slain man shall take no atonement in her case. Let them do as they prefer, maim her or kill her; and full wergeld shall be taken out of her possessions if she did the killing and half a wergeld if she contrived it. And out of the property of him who did the killing the kinsmen of the dead man shall have a full wergeld; and the king shall have what remains both in land and in movables; and the man shall go into permanent outlawry. If she denies doing or having contrived the deed, let her clear herself with a hot iron. If a husband uses his wife ill without cause and the facts are known to eyewitnesses, and if anger overcomes her [to such a degree] that she does him injury, let her leave the land and abide abroad according as the archbishop shall advise and the circumstances of the case [shall demand]. And the husband's kinsmen shall have such compensation out of her property as seems right to good men. And if she returns on the advice of the archbishop, the king shall have payment for the release from the outlawry.[1]

39. Concerning the Seven Women on Whose Account a Man May Fight and Kill
Now, there are seven women on whose account a man may fight and kill without fear of [action either by] king or kinsmen and with right to bring

---

1. *Skogarkaup*: payment for security outside the woods to which an outlaw would naturally flee.

suit against the dead man. The first is the man's wife, the second his mother, the third his daughter, the fourth his sister, the fifth his stepdaughter, the sixth his daughter-in-law, the seventh his brother's wife. He shall send forth the arrow with this message that he found the man in carnal union with the woman, whoever is named. As testimony [let him offer] the upper or the lower bed sheet or bloody clothes or such witnesses as were present, men or women.

43. CONCERNING THE MAIMING OF A MAN

If a man castrates another who is free and entitled to peace and security, or cuts out his tongue, he is an outlaw and shall never be allowed in the land again. The arrow shall be sent forth and those who were maimed shall come to the thing. Three men shall suffer outlawry in such a case, the one who removed [the member] and the two who held [the man]. The one whose tongue was cut away shall come forward at the thing to see if he can point out the man who did him ill; and if he recognizes him, he shall thrust his ax handle at the man, and the man shall be outlawed. But if he is not at the thing, the maimed one shall write his name, if he knows runes; if he does not know them, let him make such signs as will tell men what the truth is. Then the three who did the deed shall go into outlawry, the two who held the man and the one who did the cutting. But if he [the maimed one] accuses others of having shared in the deed, let them defend themselves with a three-fold oath.

Serbo-Croatian Laws

The first law code excerpted below comes from the coastal region in northern Croatia called Vinodol (wine valley) and is one of the oldest law codes in a Slavic language. Established in 1288 when the Croats had already been under the rule of the Hungarians for almost two centuries, it shows how Croatian autonomy had withered away. Crimes under this code were considered as having been perpetrated against the count rather than the victims themselves because the count was the recipient of most of the fines.

The second law code dates to the middle of the fourteenth century when Serbia was at the peak of its power. Emperor Stefan Dušan had expanded Serbia's control to Albania, Macedonia, and parts of Greece, and he had ambitions to conquer Constantinople. He revised the legal system established by his grandfather King Milutin, and borrowed heavily from Byzantine legal sources.

Source: *Monumenta Serbocroatica: A Bilingual Anthology of Serbian and Croatian Texts from the 12th to the 19th Century*, translated by Thomas Butler (Ann Arbor: Michigan Slavic Publications, 1980), pp. 61, 63, 195, 197. Reprinted with permission.

Vinodol Law Code

18. ...a good woman of good reputation, brought forward as a witness when there are no other witnesses, is to be believed when there is a dispute between women, whether it be for cursing, beating, or wounding.

27. Further, if a man should pull the kerchief or covering from a woman's head with evil intent, and this can be proven by three good men or women, he has to pay fifty libras if a complaint has been filed because of that. Of these fifty libras his Lordship the Prince receives forty soldin, and the woman who has been shamed — forty eight libras.

If a woman pulls the above-mentioned head covering from a woman, she pays two libras to the court, and two sheep to that woman.

56. Further, if someone should use force on a woman and have intercourse with her or intend to have intercourse with her, he has to pay the Prince fifty libras and the same amount to the woman, if he cannot straighten the matter out with her in some way.

And if the said rape should have no witnesses, she is to be believed; but by the same token only twenty five character witnesses have to swear, putting their hands on the book, concerning the rape and against the accused.

Let the woman find witnesses as best she can. If there are none, or if she cannot find enough, that woman must swear for those whom she lacks. Those who swear with her, but with her in first place, have to touch the book with their hands and say the oath. And all her witnesses have to be women. And when a woman is being sworn in her respondent has to answer: "Yes, I too will swear by this oath." And she has to swear as is stated above.

And if that same woman or any of her character witnesses should make a mistake in any of the above, let the one against whom she is speaking be cleared of the above mentioned crime.

59. Further, if a woman should be found to be a sorceress, and if this can be proven by reliable testimony, the first time she has to pay the Prince 100 libras, or let her be burned if she has nothing with which to pay.

And from then on if she does it, let his Lordship the Prince punish her as he wishes.

And let a man likewise be punished with the same punishment if he be found guilty of that sin.

Law Code of Emperor Stefan Dušan

2. CONCERNING MARRIAGE:

Noblemen and other people should not get married without having been blessed by their archpriest, or else they should be blessed by those whom the archpriests have appointed, when they chose them for priests.

3. CONCERNING THE WEDDING:

No wedding should be made without a marriage ceremony, and if it is done without the blessing, and without an inquiry by the Church, let such people be separated.

53. CONCERNING RAPE:

If some lord takes a noble woman by force, let both his hands be cut off, and his nose slit; if a freeman takes a noble woman by force, let him be hung; if he takes one of his own kind by force, let both his hands be cut off and his nose slit.

London City Archives

The following two sources come from the London city archives. The first group consists of various city laws, rights, observances, and penalties from between 1276 and 1419. The second group comes from a compilation called the *Liber Albus* (The White Book) by John Carpenter, a London town clerk. In 1419, he brought together the same sources mentioned above from the London archive and compiled them into one volume. Both these works provide a fascinating look into late medieval urban life.

Memorials of London and London Life

Source: *Memorials of London and London Life*, by Henry Thomas Riley (London, Longmans, Green and Co., 1868), pp. 458–459, 484–486, 534–535.

WOMEN OF BAD REPUTE RESTRICTED TO A CERTAIN GARB [REIGN OF RICHARD II—1382]

On the 13th day of February, in the 5th year etc., it was ordered by the Mayor, and Aldermen, and Common Council, that all common harlots, and all women commonly reputed as such, should have and use hoods of ray[2] only; and should not wear any manner of budge, or *perreie*,[3] or *revers*,[4] within the franchise of the City. And if any one should be found doing to the contrary thereof, she was to be taken and brought to the Compter, and the Sheriffs were to have the coloured hood, brudge, *perreie*, or *revers*, to the contrary of this Ordinance upon her found.

PUNISHMENT OF THE PILLORY, INFLICTED UPON A PROCURESS [REIGN OF RICHARD II—1385]

On the 27th day of July, in the 9th year etc., Elizabeth, the wife of Henry Moring, was brought before Nicholas Brembre, Knight, the Mayor, the

---

2. Striped cloth.
3. Probably the same as the fur called *puree*, cleansed minever.
4. Some kind of fur, especially used for trimmings and linings.

Aldermen, and the Sheriffs of London, in the Guildhall, for that, as well at the information of divers persons, as upon the acknowledgment and confession of one Johanna, her serving-woman, the same Mayor, Aldermen, and Sheriffs, were given to understand that the said Elizabeth, under colour of the craft of broidery, which she pretended to follow, took in and retained the same Johanna and divers other women, as her apprentices, and bound them to serve her after the manner of apprentices in such art; whereas the truth of the matter was, that she did not follow that craft, but that, after so retaining them, she incited the same Johanna and the other women who were with her, and in her service, to live a lewd life, and to consort with friars, chaplains, and all other such men as desired to have their company, as well in her own house, in the Parish of All Hallows near the Wall, in the Ward of Bradstret, in London, as elsewhere; and used to hire them out to the same friars, chaplains, and other men, for such stipulated sum as they might agree upon, as well in her own house as elsewhere, she retaining in her own possession the sum so agreed upon.

And in particular, on Thursday the 4th day of May last past, by the compassing and procuring of the said Elizabeth, and of a certain chaplain, whose name is unknown, she sent the same Johanna, and ordered her to accompany the same chaplain at night, that she might carry a lantern before him to his chamber — but in what Parish is likewise unknown; — it being her intention that the said Johanna should stay the night there with the chaplain; of their own contriving, while the said Johanna herself, as she says, knew nothing about it. Still, she remained there with such chaplain the whole of that night; and when she returned home to her mistress on the morrow, this Elizabeth asked her if she had brought anything with her for her trouble that night; to which she made answer that she had not. Whereupon, the same Elizabeth used words of reproof to her, and ordered her to go back again to the chaplain on the following night, and whatever she should be able to lay hold of, to take the same for her trouble, and bring it to her. Accordingly, Johanna by her command went back on the following night to the said chaplain, at his chamber aforesaid, and again passed the night there: and on the morrow she rose very early in the morning, and bearing in mind the words of her mistress, and being afraid to go back without carrying something to her said mistress, she took a Portifory that belonged to the chaplain, and carried it off, the chaplain himself knowing nothing about it; which Portifory she delivered to the said Elizabeth, who took it, well knowing how and in what manner the same Johanna had come by it. And after this, the said Elizabeth pledged this Portifory for eight pence, to a man whose name is unknown.

And many other times this Elizabeth received the like base gains from the same Johanna, and her other serving-women, and retained the same for her own use; living thus abominably and damnably, and inciting other women to live in the like manner; she herself being a common harlot and a procuress.

Whereupon, on the same day, the said Elizabeth was asked by the Court, how she would acquit herself thereof; to which she made answer, that she was in no way guilty, and put herself upon the country as to the same. Therefore, the Sheriffs were instructed to summon twelve good men of the venue aforesaid to appear here on the 28th day of the same month, to make a Jury thereon; and the said Elizabeth was in the meantime committed to prison.

Upon which day the good men of the venue aforesaid appeared, by Robert Tawyere and eleven others etc.; who declared upon their oath, the same Elizabeth to be guilty of all the things above imputed to her; and that she was a common harlot, and a common procuress. And because that through such women and the like deeds many scandals had befallen the said city, and great peril might through such transactions in future arise; therefore, according to the custom of the City of London in such and the like cases provided, and in order that other women might beware of doing the like; it was judged that the said Elizabeth should be taken from the Guildhall aforesaid to Corn-hulle, and be put upon the *thewe*[5], there to remain for one hour of the day, the cause thereof being publicly proclaimed. And afterwards, she was to be taken to some Gate of the City, and there be made to forswear the City, and the liberty thereof, to the effect that she would never again enter the same; on pain of imprisonment for three years, and the said punishment of the *thewe*, at the discretion of the Mayor and Aldermen for the time being, so often as it should please them that she should suffer such punishment.

REGULATION AS TO STREET-WALKERS BY NIGHT, AND WOMEN OF BAD REPUTE [REIGN OF RICHARD II—1393]

Let proclamation be made, that no man, freeman or foreigner, shall be so daring as to go about by night in the City of London, or the suburbs thereof, after nine of the clock, on pain of imprisonment, and of making fine to the Chamber for the offence; unless he be a lawful man, and of good repute, or the servant of such, for some real cause, and that, with a light. And that no man who is an alien, shall go about by night in the same city, or in the suburbs thereof, after eight of the clock, on pain of imprisonment and of fine, as aforesaid; unless he be a lawful man, and of good repute, or the servant of such, for some real cause, and that, with light. And that no man, of whatsoever condition he be, shall go about the said city, or in the suburbs thereof, with visor or false face, during this solemn Feast of Christmas, on pain of imprisonment, and of making fine, for such contempt.

5. A type of pillory.

Also,—whereas many and divers affrays, broils, and dissensions, have arisen in times past, and many men have been slain and murdered, by reason of the frequent resort of, and consorting with, common harlots, at taverns, brewhouses of *huksters*, and other places of ill-fame, within the said city, and the suburbs thereof; and more especially through Flemish women, who profess and follow such shameful and dolorous life:—we do by our command forbid, on behalf of our Lord the King, and the Mayor and Aldermen of the City of London, that any such women shall go about or lodge in the said city, or in the suburbs thereof, by night or by day; but they are to keep themselves to the places thereunto assigned, that is to say, the Stews on the other side of Thames, and Cokkeslane; on pain of losing and forfeiting the upper garment that she shall be wearing, together with her hood, every time that any one of them shall be found doing to the contrary of this proclamation. And every officer and serjeant of the said city shall have power to take such garments and hoods, in manner and form aforesaid: the which they shall bring to the Guildhall, and shall have the half thereof for their trouble.

Liber Albus

Source: *Liber Albus: The White Book of the City of London. Comp. A.D. 1419, by John Carpenter*, translated by Henry Thomas Riley (London, R. Griffin and Company, 1861), pp. 246–247, 394–396.

OF THIEVES AND COURTESANS

And whereas thieves and other persons of light and bad repute are often, and more commonly, received and harboured in the houses of women of evil life within the City than elsewhere, through whom evil deeds and murders, by reason of such harbouring, do often happen, and great evils and scandals to the people of the City.—The King doth will and command, that from henceforth no common woman shall dwell within the walls of the City. And if any such shall hereafter be found within the City residing and dwelling, he shall be imprisoned forty days. And let the Warden cause search to be made throughout the City in the best manner that he shall see fit, where such women are received, and who they are; and then, when they shall be found, let their limits be assigned unto them. And let no [such person] from henceforth wear minever[6] [or cendal[7]] on her dress or on her hood; and if any one shall do so, let her lose the minever and the cendal. And as to such minever and cendal, let the same be forfeited unto the serjeant who shall have found such woman and have taken her in such guise.

6. A costly fur.
7. A kind of thin silk.

OF THE PUNISHMENT OF COURTESANS AND BAWDS

Whereas in divers Wardmotes holden before the Aldermen in their Wards, there are indicted by the good folks of the Ward certain men as common whoremongers, common adulterers, and common bawds; as also, certain women, as common courtesans, common adulteresses, common bawds, and scolds; for the purpose of removing them out of the City, or for making them cease so to offend, to the pleasing of God, the salvation of their souls, and the cleanness and honesty of the said city; of whom no correction has heretofore been made, because no Ordinance thereupon has been made, but rather, they have been suffered and allowed, to the great displeasing of God and to the dishonour of the City:— It is ordained and agreed by the Mayor, and Aldermen, and Common Council of the said City, that from henceforth each Alderman, forthwith after his Wardmote is held and the verdict unto him returned, shall, if any such of evil and wicked life be indicted before him, cause the same to be taken and carried to prison, there to remain until they shall be cleared by Inquisition, or confronted [?], or otherwise attainted, by their own acquaintance; he making return unto the Mayor the day of the verdict given, or within the next two days, of the names of the persons so indicted, and the cause. And well and lawfully to do the same, without tardiness therein, all the Aldermen are strictly bound by their oaths.

OF A MAN WHO IS FOUND TO BE A WHOREMONGER OR BAWD, AND OF HIS PUNISHMENT

In the first place, if any man shall be found to be a common whoremonger or bawd, and shall of the same be attainted, first, let all his head and beard be shaved, except a fringe on the head, two inches in breadth; and let him be taken unto the pillory, with minstrels, and set thereon for a certain time, at the discretion of the Mayor and Aldermen. And if he shall be a second time attainted thereof, let him have the same punishment, and in the same manner for a certain time, at the discretion of the Mayor and Aldermen; and besides this, let him have ten days' imprisonment, without ransom. And the third time, let him have the same punishment, and in the same manner for a certain time, at the discretion of the Mayor and Aldermen; and afterwards let him be taken to one of the City Gates, and there let him forswear the City forever.

Item, if any woman shall be found to be a common receiver of courtesans or bawd, and of the same shall be attainted, first, let her be openly brought, with minstrels, from prison unto the thew, and set thereon for a certain time, at the discretion of the Mayor and Aldermen, and there let her hair be cut round about her head. And if she shall be a second time attainted thereof, let her have the same punishment, and in the same manner for a certain time, at the discretion of the Mayor and Aldermen; and besides this, let her have ten days' imprisonment, without ransom. And the third time, let her have the same punishment, and in the same manner for a certain time, at the discretion of the Mayor and Aldermen; and after this, let her be taken to one of the Gates of the said city, [and let her there forswear the City] for ever.

Item, if any woman shall be found to be a common courtesan, and of the same shall be attainted, let her be taken from the prison unto Algate, with a hood of ray, and a white wand in her hand; and from thence, with minstrels, unto the thew, and there let the cause be proclaimed; and from thence, through Chepe and Newgate to Cokkeslane, there to take up her abode. And if she shall be a second time attainted thereof, let her be openly brought, with minstrels, from prison unto the thew, with a hood of ray, and set thereon for a certain time, at the discretion of the Mayor and Aldermen. And the third time, let her have the same punishment, at the discretion of the Mayor and Aldermen, and let her hair be cut round about her head while upon the thew, and, after that, let her be taken to one of the City Gates, and let her [there] forswear the City for ever.

Item, if any man or woman shall be attainted of being a brawler or scold, let such person be taken unto the thew, with a distaff dressed with flax [called *"dystaf with towen"*] in his or her hand, with minstrels, and be set thereon for a certain time, at the discretion of the Mayor and Aldermen.

Item, if any priest shall be found with a woman, let him be taken unto the Tun on Cornhulle, with minstrels. And if he shall be so found three times, let him forswear the City for ever.

Item, if any person shall be impeached of adultery, and be thereof lawfully attainted, let him be taken unto Newgate, and from thence, with minstrelsy, through Chepe, to the Tun on Cornhulle, there to remain at the will of the Mayor and Aldermen.

Item, if any adulteress shall be found with a priest or with a married man, let them both be taken unto the Compter of one of the Sheriffs, or unto Newgate, and from thence to the Guildhall, before the Mayor and Aldermen, and there arraigned; and if they shall then be lawfully attainted thereof, let them be taken to Newgate; and there let the said adulterer and adulteress be shaved, like an appealer;[8] and from thence, with minstrelsy, let them be brought through Chepe unto the same Tun, there to remain at the will of the Mayor and Aldermen.

Item, if a single woman shall be found in company with a priest, let them both be taken unto the Compter of one of the Sheriffs, and from thence unto the said Tun, there to remain at the will of the Mayor and Aldermen.

8. A false informer.

11

Canon Law

Penitentials

Penitentials were guides used by priests when a person confessed his sins. They were first written by Irish and English churchmen beginning in the sixth century and then brought to continental Europe. Penitentials provided lists of sins and the types of acts the sinner had to undertake in order to atone for them. They focused heavily on sexual sins, many of which cannot be found in other types of legislation, either ecclesiastical or secular.

The following excerpts are taken from two penitentials. The first was compiled by an Irish monk, Cummean, in 650 and later circulated in the Frankish Empire during the ninth century. The second excerpt is attributed to Theodore Tarsus, the Archbishop of Canterbury (668–690). However, it is not believed to be a work written directly by him, but rather answers given by him to a presbyter named Eoda.

Source: *Medieval Handbooks of Penance: A Translation of the Principal Libri Poenitentiales and Selections from Related Documents*, by John T. McNeill and Helena M. Gamer, copyright © 1938 Columbia University Press, pp. 112–113, 184–186, 195–197, 208–211. Reprinted with the permission of the publisher.

The Penitential of Cummean

1. Boys talking alone and transgressing the regulations of the elders, shall be corrected by three special fasts.

2. Those who kiss simply shall be corrected with six special fasts; those who kiss licentiously without pollution, with eight special fasts; if with pollution or embrace, with ten special fasts.

3. But after the twentieth year (that is, adults) they shall live at a separate table (that is, in continence) and excluded from the church, on bread and water.

4. Children who imitate acts of fornication, twenty days; if frequently, forty.

5. A boy who takes communion in the sacrament although he sins with a beast, one hundred days.

6. But boys of twenty years who practice masturbation together and confess [shall do penance] twenty or forty days before they take communion.

7. If they repeat it after penance, one hundred days; if frequently, they shall be separated and shall do penance for a year.

8. [One of] the above-mentioned age who practices femoral masturbation, one hundred days; if he does it again, a year.

9. A small boy misused by an older one, if he is ten years of age, shall fast for a week; if he consented, for twenty days.

13. A man who practices masturbation by himself, for the first offense, one hundred days; if he repeats it, a year.

14. Men guilty of homosexual practices, for the first offense, a year; if they repeat it, two years.

15. If they are boys, two years, if men, three or four years; but if it has become a habit, seven years, and a method of penance shall be added according to the judgment of this priest.

17. A boy coming from the world who has recently sought to commit fornication with some girl but who was not polluted, shall do penance for twenty days; but if he was polluted, one hundred days; if indeed, as is the usual thing, he fulfills his intention, for a year.

The Penitential of Theodore

OF FORNICATION

1. If anyone commits fornication with a virgin he shall do penance for one year. If with a married woman, he shall do penance for four years, two of these entire, and in the other two during the three forty-day periods and three days a week.

2. He judged that he who often commits fornication with a man or with a beast should do penance for ten years.

3. Another judgment is that he who is joined to beasts shall do penance for fifteen years.

5. A male who commits fornication with a male shall do penance for ten years.

6. Sodomites shall do penance for seven years, and the effeminate man as an adulteress.

12. If a woman practices vice with a woman, she shall do penance for three years.

13. If she practices solitary vice, she shall do penance for the same period.

15. "Qui semen in os miserit"[1] shall do penance for seven years: this is the worst of evils. Elsewhere it was his judgment that both [participants in this offense] shall do penance to the end of life; or twelve years; or as above seven.

16. If one commits fornication with his mother, he shall do penance for fifteen years and never change except on Sundays. But this so impious incest is likewise spoken of by him in another way — that he shall do penance for seven years, with perpetual pilgrimage.

17. He who commits fornication with his sister shall do penance for fifteen years in the way in which it is stated above of his mother. But this [penalty] he also elsewhere established in a canon as twelve years. Whence it is not unreasonable that the fifteen years that are written apply to the mother.

19. If a brother commits fornication with a natural brother, he shall abstain from all kinds of flesh for fifteen years.

20. If a mother imitates acts of fornication with her little son, she shall abstain from flesh for three years and fast one day in the week, that is until vespers.

21. He who amuses himself with libidinous imagination shall do penance until the imagination is overcome.

OF THE PENANCE FOR SPECIAL IRREGULARITIES IN MARRIAGE

1. In a first marriage the presbyter ought to perform Mass and bless them both, and afterward they shall absent themselves from church for thirty days. Having done this, they shall do penance for forty days, and absent themselves from the prayer; and afterwards they shall communicate with the oblation.

2. One who is twice married shall do penance for a year; on Wednesdays and Fridays and during the three forty-day periods he shall abstain from flesh; however, he shall not put away his wife.

3. He that is married three times, or more, that is in a fourth or fifth marriage, or beyond that number, for seven years on Wednesdays and Fridays and during the three forty-day periods they shall abstain from flesh; yet they shall not be separated. Basil so determined, but in the canon four years [are indicated].

4. If anyone finds his wife to be an adulteress and does not wish to put her away but has had her in the matrimonial relation to that time, he shall

---

1. "He who releases semen into the mouth."

do penance for two years on two days in the week and [shall perform] the fasts of religion; or as long as she herself does penance he shall avoid the matrimonial relation with her, because she has committed adultery.

5. If any man or woman who has taken the vow of virginity is joined in marriage, he shall not set aside the marriage but shall do penance for three years.

6. Foolish vows and those incapable of being performed are to be set aside.

8. He who puts away his wife and marries another shall do penance with tribulation for seven years or a lighter penance for fifteen years.

9. He who defiles his neighbor's wife, deprived of his own wife, shall fast for three years two days a week and in the three forty-day periods.

10. If [the woman] is a virgin, he shall do penance for one year without meat and wine and mead.

11. If he defiles a vowed virgin, he shall do penance for three years, as we said above, whether a child is born of her or not.

12. If she is his slave, he shall set her free and fast for six months.

13. If the wife of anyone deserts him and returns to him undishonored, she shall do penance for one year; otherwise for three years. If he takes another wife he shall do penance for one year.

14. An adulterous woman shall do penance for seven years. And this matter is stated in the same way in the canon.

15. A woman who commits adultery shall do penance for three years as a fornicator. So also shall she do penance who makes an unclean mixture of food for the increase of love.

16. A wife who tastes her husband's blood as a remedy shall fast for forty days, more or less.

24. Women who commit abortion before [the foetus] has life, shall do penance for one year or for the three forty-day periods or for forty days, according to the nature of the offense; and if later, that is, more than forty days after conception, they shall do penance as murderesses, that is for three years on Wednesdays and Fridays and in the three forty-day periods. This according to the canons is judged [punishable by] ten years.

25. If a mother slays her child, if she commits homicide, she shall do penance for fifteen years, and never change except on Sunday.

26. If a poor woman slays her child, she shall do penance for seven years. In the canon it is said that if it is a case of homicide, she shall do penance for ten years.

27. A woman who conceives and slays her child in the womb within forty days shall do penance for one year; but if later than forty days, she shall do penance as a murderess.

OF THE USE OR REJECTION OF ANIMALS

9. Animals that are polluted by intercourse with men shall be killed, and their flesh thrown to dogs, but their offspring shall be for use, and their hides shall be taken. However, when there is uncertainty, they shall not be killed.

OF MATTERS RELATING TO MARRIAGE

1. Those who are married shall abstain from intercourse for three nights before they communicate.

2. A man shall abstain from his wife for forty days before Easter, until the week of Easter. On this account the Apostle says: "That ye may give yourselves to prayer."

3. When she has conceived a woman ought to abstain from her husband for three months before the birth, and afterward in the time of purgation, that is, for forty days and nights, whether she has borne a male or a female child.

5. If the wife of anyone commits fornication, he may put her away and take another; that is, if a man puts away his wife on account of fornication, if she was his first, he is permitted to take another; but if she wishes to do penance for her sins, she may take another husband after five years.

6. A woman may not put away her husband, even if he is a fornicator, unless, perchance, for [the purpose of his entering] a monastery. Basil so decided.

7. A legal marriage may not be broken without the consent of both parties.

10. When his wife is dead, a man may take another wife after a month. If her husband is dead, the woman may take another husband after a year.

30. A husband who sleeps with his wife shall wash himself before he goes into a church.

31. A husband ought not to see his wife nude.

33. If a man and a woman have united in marriage, and afterward the woman says of the man that he is impotent, if anyone can prove that this is true, she may take another [husband].

Church Councils

From the fourth century onwards, Church councils were called together to work out common policies and correct abuses. Their decisions were binding for all

Christians. The following examples come from ecumenical councils in which bishops from all over the Christian world convened under the aegis of the pope.

Source: *Decrees of the Ecumenical Councils*, Vol. 1, edited by Norman P. Tanner (copyright © 1980 Sheed & Ward Ltd. and Georgetown University Press, 1990), pp. 6–7, 153–155, 242, 257–258, 266. Reprinted with the permission of the Continuum International publishing Group.

First Council of Nicaea

CONCERNING THOSE WHO MAKE THEMSELVES EUNUCHS AND OTHERS WHO SUFFER THE SAME LOSS AT THE HANDS OF OTHERS

1. If anyone in sickness has undergone surgery at the hands of physicians or has been castrated by barbarians, let him remain among the clergy. But if anyone in good health has castrated himself, if he is enrolled among the clergy he should be suspended, and in future no such man should be promoted. But, as it is evident that this refers to those who are responsible for the condition and presume to castrate themselves, so too if any have been made eunuchs by barbarians or by their masters, but have been found worthy, the canon admits such men to the clergy.

CONCERNING WOMEN WHO HAVE BEEN BROUGHT IN TO LIVE WITH THE CLERGY

3. This great synod absolutely forbids a bishop, presbyter, deacon or any of the clergy to keep a woman who has been brought in to live with him, with the exception of course of his mother or sister or aunt, or of any person who is above suspicion.

Second Council of Nicaea

FROM NOW ON IT IS NOT RIGHT THAT DOUBLE MONASTERIES BE STARTED, AND ON THE SUBJECT OF DOUBLE MONASTERIES

20. We decree that from now on no more double monasteries are to be started, because this becomes a cause of scandal and a stumbling block for ordinary folk. If there are persons who wish to renounce the world and follow the monastic life along with their relatives, the men should go off to a male monastery and their wives enter a female monastery; for God is surely pleased with this.

The double monasteries that have existed up to now should continue to exist according to the rule of our holy father Basil, and their constitutions should follow his ordinances. Monks and nuns should not live in one monastic building, because adultery takes advantage of such cohabitation. No monk should have the licence to speak in private with a nun, nor any nun with a monk. A monk should not sleep in a female monastery, nor should he eat alone with a nun. When the necessary nourishment is being carried from the male area for the nuns, the female superior, accompanied by one of the older nuns, should receive it outside the door. And if it should happen that a monk wishes to pay a visit to one of his female relatives, let him speak with her in the presence of the female superior, but briefly and rapidly, and let him leave her quickly.

It Is the Duty of Monks to Say Grace and to Eat with Great Parsimony and Propriety When Occasion Arises to Eat in the Company of Women

22. It is very important to dedicate everything to God and not to become slaves of our own desires; for *whether you eat or drink* (1 Corinthians 10:31), the divine apostle says, *do all for the glory of God.* Now Christ our God has instructed us in his gospels to eradicate the beginnings of sins. So not only adultery is rebuked by him, but also the movement of one's intention towards the performance of adultery, when he says: *He who looks on a woman lustfully has already committed adultery with her in his heart.* (Matthew 5:28)

Thus instructed we should purify our intentions: *For if all things are lawful, not all things are expedient* (1 Corinthians 6:12, 10:23), as we learn from the words of the apostle. Now everybody is certainly obliged to eat in order to live, and in the case of those whose life includes marriage and children and the conditions proper to layfolk it is not reprehensible that men and women should eat in one another's company; though they should at least say grace to thank the giver of their nourishment, and they should avoid certain theatrical entertainments, diabolical songs, the strumming of lyres and the dancing fit for harlots; against all such there is the curse of the prophet which says, *Woe on those who drink their wine to the sound of lyre and harp, those who pay no attention to the deeds of the Lord and have never a thought for the works of his hands.* (Isaiah 5:12) If ever such people are found among Christians, they should reform, and if they do not, let the canonical sanctions established by our predecessors be imposed on them.

Fourth Lateran Council

On Punishing Clerical Incontinence

14. In order that the morals and conduct of clerics may be reformed for the better, let all of them strive to live in a continent and chaste way, especially those in holy orders. Let them beware of every vice involving lust, especially that on account of which *the wrath of God came down* from heaven...

On the Restriction of Prohibitions to Matrimony

50. It should not be judged reprehensible if human decrees are sometimes changed according to changing circumstances, especially when urgent necessity or evident advantage demands it, since God himself changed in the new

Testament some of the things which he had commanded in the old Testament. Since the prohibitions against contracting marriage in the second and third degree of affinity, and against uniting the offspring of a second marriage with the kindred of the first husband, often lead to difficulty and sometimes endanger souls ... we decree, by this present constitution, that henceforth contracting parties connected in these ways may freely be joined together. Moreover the prohibition against marriage shall not in future go beyond the fourth degree of consanguinity and of affinity, since the prohibition cannot now generally be observed to further degrees without grave harm. The number four agrees well with the prohibition concerning bodily union about which the Apostle says, that *the husband does not rule over his body, but the wife does; and the wife does not rule over her body, but the husband does*; for there are four humours in the body, which is composed of the four elements. Although the prohibition of marriage is now restricted to the fourth degree, we wish the prohibition to be perpetual, notwithstanding earlier decrees on this subject issued either by others or by us. If any persons dare to marry contrary to this prohibition, they shall not be protected by length of years, since the passage of time does not diminish sin but increases it, and the longer that faults hold the unfortunate soul in bondage the graver they are.

ON THE PUNISHMENT OF THOSE WHO CONTRACT CLANDESTINE MARRIAGES

51. Since the prohibition against marriage in the three remotest degrees has been revoked, we wish it to be strictly observed in the other degrees. Following in the footsteps of our predecessors, we altogether forbid clandestine marriages and we forbid any priest to presume to be present at such a marriage. Extending the special custom of certain regions to other regions generally, we decree that when marriages are to be contracted they shall be publicly announced in the churches by priests, with a suitable time being fixed beforehand within which whoever wishes and is able to may adduce a lawful impediment. The priests themselves shall also investigate whether there is any impediment. When there appears a credible reason why the marriage should not be contracted, the contract shall be expressly forbidden until there has been established from clear documents what ought to be done in the matter. If any persons presume to enter into clandestine marriages of this kind, or forbidden marriages within a prohibited degree, even if done in ignorance, the offspring of the union shall be deemed illegitimate and shall have no help from their parents' ignorance, since the parents in contracting the marriage could be considered as not devoid of knowledge, or even as affecters of ignorance. Likewise the offspring shall be deemed illegitimate if both parents know of a legitimate impediment and yet dare to contract a

marriage in the presence of the church, contrary to every prohibition. Moreover the parish priest who refuses to forbid such unions, or even any member of the regular clergy who dares to attend them, shall be suspended from office for three years and shall be punished even more severely if the nature of the fault requires it. Those who presume to be united in this way, even if it is within a permitted degree, are to be given a suitable penance. Anybody who maliciously proposes an impediment, to prevent a legitimate marriage, will not escape the church's vengeance.

The Register of Eudes of Rouen
Eudes Rigaud (d. 1275)

Eudes Rigaud of Rouen was a Franciscan who became archbishop in 1248. He was a reformer, living as a churchman only several years after the reigns of reforming popes such as Innocent III, Honorius III, and Gregory IX. As part of his reform program, Eudes visited monasteries and parish houses throughout his archdiocese for twenty-two years in order to make sure that clerics, monks, and nuns as well as laypersons under his spiritual guidance were keeping to the precepts of canon law. During his visits, he kept a journal recording all the abuses he discovered.

Source: *The Register of Eudes of Rouen*, translated by Sydney M. Brown, edited by Jeremiah O'Sullivan, (copyright © 1964 Columbia University Press) pp. 33–34, 383–384, 443, 588. Reprinted with permission of the publisher.

January 29, 1248: At St-Just, where we visited the deanery of Brachy. We found the priest at Royville to be ill famed of incontinence with a stonecutter's wife, who is said to have borne him a child; item, it is said that he has many other children; he is nonresident, plays ball, is nonresident [*sic*], and rides about clad in an open cape. We have a letter from him which is entered on folio 125. Item, the priest at Gonnetot is ill famed of two women; he went to see the Pope because of this, and it is said that he fell into sin again after his return; item, concerning a certain woman from Waltot. Item, the priest at Venestanville is ill famed of incontinence with one of his parishioners, whose husband, as a result, has gone overseas; he has kept this woman for eight years and she is now pregnant; item, he plays dice and drinks too much; he haunts the taverns, does not keep adequate residence in his parish and rides his horse at will about the country. The penalty which we have imposed upon him is entered on folio 125. Item, the priest at Brachy is [ill famed] of a certain woman, and since she has foresworn his house he goes to eat with her and has his provisions and grain carried there. The chaplain at Brachy frequents taverns. Simon, priest at St-Just, is quarrelsome and argumentative. Item, the priest at Vibeuf frequents taverns and drinks up to the gullet. Item, the priest at Rainfreville drinks too much. The priest at Offranville does not keep satisfactory residence and went to England without permission. Item, the priest at Ouville has his daughter at home despite the synodal prohibition. Item, the priest at Bourville is a drunkard and is quarrelsome and belligerent. Item, Henry of Avremesnil is ill famed of incontinence. Item, Walter, parson of St-Just, is ill famed of Matilda of Caletot. Item, the priest at Gruchet, being incontinent and disciplined there for, is said to have sinned again. He had a child by a certain woman; the child was sent to be baptized at Luneray. Item, Ralph priest at Essarts, is seriously ill famed of incontinence. Item, the parson of Reuville does not reside in his church. Item, the priest at Gueures is ill famed of a certain woman. Item, Lawrence, priest at Longueil, is keeping Beatrice Valeran, the wife of a man who is outside the country, and has had a child by her.

July 9, 1259: We visited the nuns at St-Saëns and preached there. Fifteen nuns were in residence; two were at Ste-Austreberte. They frequently omitted singing their Hours with modulation. Some of them remained away too long when they received permission from the prioress to go out; we gave orders that an earlier time for returning be imposed upon such as these. They owed about one hundred pounds. Joan Martel was rebellious and disobedient and quarreled with the prioress; she rode out on horseback to see her relatives, clad in a sleeved gown made of dark material; she had her own messenger whom she often sent to her relatives. Nichola gave birth to a child in the priory on Ash Wednesday, and it is said that the father is Master Simon, the parson at St- Saëns. The child was baptized at their monastery and then sent away to one of the mother's sisters; the mother lay there and was churched at the monastery; at the time of the delivery she had two midwives from the village. Item, she bore another child once before and of the same Simon. A portion of food was given to each, but they did not hand in the fragments for alms; indeed, they sold or gave what remained to whomsoever they wished. The prioress was under suspicion because of Richard of Maucomble; she was also reported to handle the goods and affairs of the house very badly, and to conceal some of the fruits and rents. This same Richard slept at the house with the brother and relatives of the prioress, and had often eaten there. The community promised and agreed to receive and veil four nieces of some of the nuns, provided that we would agree; each of the nuns had letters from the community covering this concession. We, in full chapter, broke and tore to pieces these letters, being highly annoyed at a concession of this kind. Once again we expressly forbade them to receive or veil anyone without our special permission. Indeed, having heard that the prioress had been inefficient in business deals and in handling affairs, and was still incompetent, we desired to get an audit from her, and to assist at this audit we deputed the Priors of Salle-aux-Puelles and of Bellencombre.

February 1, 1260: We celebrated the feast of the Purification of the Blessed Virgin Mary, preached, with God's grace, a sermon in the church at Les Andelys, and spent the night at our new residence.

This day Walter of Courcelles, knight, paid us a fine for having contracted a marriage without publishing the banns in church. The fines for this sort of thing should be imposed and exacted by us. Sir Robert of Croisy, knight, and Sir John of St-Clair, knight, presented themselves as his sureties.

April 23, 1265: We convoked all the priests of the deanery of Bourgtheroulde before us at Thuit-Herbert. We found that the chaplain of the leper house at Orival seldom resides in his chapel; he had performed a clandestine marriage, was excommunicate, and was also defamed of incontinence.

Consistory Courts

The territory that the Church watched over spiritually was divided into administrative divisions called dioceses. Every diocese had a consistory court under the direction of a bishop, who appointed an official to run it. By the late twelfth century, the church courts had jurisdiction over questions regarding the validity of a marriage and issues of precontract (one party stating that he or she had contracted a legitimate marriage with another party), impotence, bigamy, and consanguinity and affinity. Furthermore, these courts also claimed authority to judge cases involving sin, so they also dealt with matters of adultery and fornication.

There are two sets of consistory records in the following excerpts. The first two cases come from England and pertain to defamation. The second group, from the Kraków ecclesiastical archives, contain cases from both the Kraków and Lublin consistory courts.

Cases from English Records

Source: *Select Cases on Defamation to 1600*, edited for the Selden Society by R.H. Helmholz (London: Selden Society, 1985), pp. 21, 24. Reprinted with permission.

DIOCESE OF BATH AND WELLS, CONSISTORY COURT, 1464. EX OFFICIO
    CONTRA HANCOKE

Item on the same day Margaret Hancoke wife of M. Edward Hancoke proctor of the consistory of Wells appeared before the aforesaid official and asserted that she was defamed of that M. Richard Gautier, rector of the parish church of Stoke Gifford, did often commit the grievous crime of adultery with her. And this article having been put before her she denied it and

canonically purged herself upon the same article by honest women neighbours of hers, namely Agnes Sholer, Joan Smyth, Agnes Grype, Alice Adam,
Joan Foliot, Agnes Broke, Christine Bowgell, Rose Hicks, and Joan Bridde
and many others. And the official declared her legitimately purged and
wrongfully defamed and restored her to her good fame etc.

DIOCESE OF LINCOLN, COMMISSARY COURT, 1514,

JAMES CONTRA HARMON

Harmon is charged *ex officio* that she did defame Margaret James by
calling her in English "strong priest's whore" and "bawdy whore" on the 1st
of July. She was cited for the Wednesday following, on which day Harmon
appeared. In the presence of James she confesses saying publicly of her that
she keeps an ill governance in her house, and she denies the other article.
His lordship assigned [a day] for proof to her on the Saturday following on
which day James appeared in the presence of Harmon and produced Thomas
Aspring, in whose presence Harmon confessed the article, that she said of
the same [James] that she went among the gypsies to learn her fortune and
one gypsy said publicly to her, "You know your fortune, for he that stands
beside you should jape you three times before you go to your bed [and] to
your husband." And she offers to prove this. And his lordship assigned [a
day] for proof to her on the Monday next and ordered James to purge herself four-handed the same day. On which day the parties appeared and James
failing in purgation, his lordship declared her convicted and caused her to
swear to abide etc. And Harmon failing to prove in the production of witnesses, his lordship ordered James to march before the procession on the
Sunday following with a wax candle and a rosary in her right hand, dressed
in honest garb, and at the time of the priest's offertory to declare publicly
to the congregation the cause for which she was undergoing penance. And
to Harmon his lordship ordered this similar penance and to seek the pardon
of the aforesaid James and to make certification the Monday following. (The
parties are agreed and the penance is set aside.)

Kraków Archives

Source: "Praktyka w Sprawach Małżenskich w Sądach Duchownych Dyjecezyi
Krakowskiej w Wieku XV," edited by Bolesław Ulanowski in *Archiwum Komisyi Histo-
rycznej*, vol. 5 (1885), pp. 104, 106, 111, 122, 133, 155. Translated from the Latin by Martha
A. Brożyna and Jarosław Suproniuk.

[KRAKÓW CONSISTORY, JULY 4, 1446]

42. Stanisław of Herbolthouicze [Harbutowice], a layperson now staying in
Kazimierz, testified verbally against his lawful wife, Katherine, before the
court. [It is] stated that ten years ago she left her husband, Stanisław, and
tramped around, gallivanting with others, and through adultery had a child

by another man. Stanisław is asking [for permission] to leave her, because, as he reminds [the court], she left him having children with others even though Stanisław was her husband. The above-mentioned woman admits to giving birth to a child by a man other than her husband and that she strayed with others. Stanisław testified that he is not trying to show bad intent or intrigue, he is seeking that they be separated. The court decided that they are to be separated and they are forbidden to remain in a union or to initiate a new one, and the woman must go to confession for penance; [the decision is given] in the presence of Thomas of Lapscziczo, a priest, and Stanisław Swyradsky.

[KRAKÓW CONSISTORY, FEBRUARY 16, 1452]
51. Stachna, a woman from Krzyssowicz [Skrzeszowice], daughter of John Wawrethko of Scholmpnyky [Słomniki] brought an action accusing her husband Martin Nyewczawicz of Krzyssowicz of impotence stating that she dealt with it for ten years wanting to have a sexual relationship with him, but realizing that she will never be able to know him [sexually] and as she wants to be the mother of children, she is seeking separation from him. [Martin] admitting to the accusation was examined and found impotent because of his inept member. The woman will present proof within fifteen days that for the last three of those ten years she was continuously expending all efforts to make their union work.

[KRAKÓW CONSISTORY, JUNE 27, 1453]
64. The judge decided and recognized that Stanisław of Morsko and Margaret of Barczkow [Barczków], a married couple, have lived together for three years as a test of the impediment of impotence Margaret brings against Stanisław. An examination reveals him to have a lively and functioning member; the blister [which it had] has drained and it is apparent that they can now seek to have children or suffer the penalty of excommunication and incarceration, this [case] being presented before John of Morsko, Paul of Jezewo, notary, Matthew of Odalino, proctor, and Stanisław, the cleric of Grzibow and others.

[LUBLIN CONSISTORY DECEMBER 4, 1454]
95. Stanisław, proctor of Jadwiga Vaskonis of Skoki brought Stanisław of Naszuthow [Nasutów] to court stating that in accordance with the solemnity of marriage and its consecration in the church, he took as his wife the woman with whom he was in a relationship for one and a half years, but being a lame and castrated man, he could not fulfill his marital debt and could not open the gates of her virginity, and her body remains intact. She is seeking to be divorced and to have the right to remarry a healthy man and wishes

to be free of any canonical harm. In the event of this being denied, she will seek proof [of virginity] through a lawful, visual examination by honest women appointed by the court. She is seeking reimbursement of court costs as well as the restitution of her dowry, and satisfactory [compensation] for the labor done in his house, together with damages and harm she estimates at thirty florins.

Stanisław himself confessed to being a castrate. Nevertheless he said that he knew her superficially, but could not have sexual relations with her. This case will be decided in two weeks.

[LUBLIN CONSISTORY, SEPTEMBER 1, 1456]
126. Jacob of Vidow, from the diocese of Płock, who is suspected of bigamy brought suit against Margaret, the [daughter of] John Nowak from Gyelczuya [Giełczew], widow of Peter Spoth of Pyasek [Piaski], that while she was in an existing, legal marriage with the said Peter, she was with Jacob carnally and had him in an adulterous relationship. He did not know that [John] died, and that with the help of the devil, she had poisoned him. Then while he was ignorant of the impediment of adultery that is punishable by the Church, she cohabited with him in a state of marital affection, giving and demanding from him the marital debt. [Jacob] claimed ... she threatened him with the same death stating, "one went down the path of death through my hand, and you should be prepared to go the same way." Because of this, Jacob is seeking separation from her because their marriage contract is nonexistent, and in the event this is denied then he will prove the justice of his case.

Margaret confessed that she did poison her first husband, but that she did it with his consent.

The case will be resolved in two weeks.

[LUBLIN CONSISTORY, OCTOBER 24, 1470]
168. Peter, a priest from Lublin, proctor of Margaret, widow of Snopkow [Snopków] brought against Jacob also of Snopkow, a peasant, [claiming] that the said Jacob came one night without [her] knowledge into Margaret's room and climbed into bed with her there; also, that he proposed to marry Margaret and personally swore an oath and had carnal relations with her, [thereby] consummating matrimony and impregnating her. Now he is resisting union in the church with her, and because of this she is seeking to compel him to accept church union and continuance of their relationship as a true marriage; should this be denied, she will provide proof of her claim only at a convenient time and place. The peasant Jacob of Snopkow will respond to the accusation within eight days.

12

A University Record

University of Kraków

The earliest universities began emerging in the twelfth and thirteenth centuries. Students and faculty organized themselves into corporations in order to maintain certain economic, social, and legal privileges and protections from the local townspeople. One of these privileges included exemption from secular authority. Therefore, students and faculty were tried by their own courts and before judges who were usually university rectors. The following cases come from the University of Kraków (present-day Jagiellonian University), originally founded in 1370. The court entries provide insight into university life, an elite, male-dominated world, against a backdrop of frequent clashes between students and local townspeople.

Source: *Acta rectoralia almae Universitatis Studii Cracoviensis, vol.1 1469 –1537*, edited by Władysław Wisłocki (Cracoviae: Sumptibus Academiae Litterarum Cracoviensis, 1893-1897), pp. 129, 169, 393-394, 614. Translated from the Latin by Martha A. Brożyna and Jarosław Suproniuk.

608. Monday, the tenth of November 1477. Margaret of Vythkowycze [Witkowice], servant of Michael the knife-maker, personally testified before the judge against the student Nicholas of Rawa that on the eve of the feast of St. Martin, upon arriving at the home of the above-mentioned Michael, Nicholas said to her "you are a disreputable person and your habits are ones that would be found in a brothel." She believes that such slander is deserving of ten marks and the student should be publicly exposed for having unjustly slandered her person. In his defense, Nicholas denies everything and wishes the matter to be reexamined next time the court convenes.

797. Wednesday, twenty-eighth of July 1479. Fabian of Heilsberg [Lidzbark Warmiński], a student living in the philosophy dormitory, is charged by the office of the rector-judge for a certain abominable deed, which he committed publicly in the presence of many students and laypersons. While he was

taking a woman to the Vistula River, he touched and held her shamelessly and undressed her; once in the river he fondled the [already] nude woman, thus scandalizing many students and laypersons. For this reason, Fabian is brought to the rector and university council. In accordance with university statutes, the rector fines him one quarter of a mark, which he should pay within the next eight days or be fined double.

1733. Thursday, eighth of January 1495. Student Valentine of Piscaria [Rybitwy] brought to court the venerable John of Głogów because on the feast day of St. John the Evangelist (December 27, 1494) [John] slandered him before the members of the canon law dormitory by calling him a sodomite and a traitor[1] who does not have the right to call himself a good and honest person. The above-mentioned master defends himself against the "traitor" saying that he did accuse him of sodomy because he [the master] was informed about this. The master is also filing a complaint against Valentine for disrespecting a man of such high status as himself through his accusation of slander. The next time the court convenes, the master must prove that Valentine is a sodomite. The rector will look at the evidence and if there is no proof, he will render a decision in compliance with university statutes.

1735. Saturday, tenth of January 1495. Master John of Głogów stands before the court in a traveler's garb as if on a foreign pilgrimage and testifies that he had made no allegation of sodomy against the student Valentine, the accusation having come from Valentine's own self-incrimination, and states that he [the master] knows nothing about him [the student], other than that he is a good and just person. Valentine counters that this is insufficient and seeks the intervention of the court to convict this master. The rector and his advisors give their reasoned decision and end the case by invoking the name of Christ, and order that Master John of Głogów spend one hour before the members of the canon law dormitory retracting the slanderous words and accusations of the crime against Valentine and recognize him as an innocent and cleared person and admit that he knows nothing bad about him — under the penalty of excommunication. Furthermore, he must pay three florins to the university between today and March 4 or he will be excommunicated.

2609. Nicholas Iaskmanczyczky, John Zkyersky, John Schumsky, and John Obiedzynsky are fined one florin each because of violence they committed in a public and infamous brothel by beating the women, robbing some of the women's things such as their purses, etc., and they must return this [stolen] money within eight days.

---

1. By "traitor" is here meant a betrayer of the Christian faith and morals.

V

BIOLOGY,
MEDICINE,
AND SCIENCE

13

Understanding Male and Female

On the Usefulness of the Parts of the Body
Galen (c. 130-200)

One of the most famous physicians living in the Roman Empire, Galen attended to the emperors Marcus Aurelius and Lucius Verus. He was the author of a large number of medical and philosophical writings, of which more than eighty still survive. Like Aristotle five centuries before him Galen promulgated the view that a woman's anatomy is physically the imperfect inversion of a man's (as discussed in the excerpt below). Although Galen's work *On the Usefulness of the Parts of the Body* was not translated until the first half of the fourteenth century, his ideas were drawn on in the fourth century work *De natura hominis (On the nature of man)* by Nemesius of Emesa.

Source: *Galen on the Usefulness of the Parts of the Body*, translated by Margaret Tallmadge May. Copyright © 1968, Cornell University Press. Used by permission of the publisher, Cornell University Press.

The female is less perfect than the male for one, principal reason — because she is colder; for if among animals the warm one is the more active, a colder animal would be less perfect than a warmer. A second reason is one that appears in dissecting.

All the parts, then, that men have, women have too, the difference between them lying in only one thing, which must be kept in mind throughout the discussion, namely that in women the parts are within [the body], whereas in men they are outside, in the region called the perineum. Consider first whichever ones you please, turn outward the woman's, turn inward, so to speak and fold double the man's, and you will find them the same in both in every respect. Then think first, please, of the man's turned in and extending inward between the rectum and the bladder. If this should happen, the scrotum would necessarily take the place of the uteri, with the testes lying outside, next to it on either side; the penis of the male would become the neck of the cavity that had been formed; and the skin at the end of the penis, now called the prepuce, would become the female pudendum [the vagina] itself. Think too, please of the converse, the uterus turned outward and projecting. Would not the testes[the ovaries] then necessarily be inside it? Would it not contain them like a scrotum? Would not the neck [the cervix], hitherto concealed inside the perineum but now pendent, be made into the male member? And would not the female pudendum, being a skin-like growth upon this neck, be changed into the part called the prepuce? It is also clear that in consequence the position of the arteries, veins, and spermatic vessels [the ductus deferentes and Fallopian tubes] would be changed too. In fact, you could not find a single male part left over that had not simply changed its position; for the parts that are inside in woman are outside in man. You can see something like this in the eyes of the mole, which have vitreous and crystalline humors and the tunics that surround these and grow out from the meninges, as I have said, and they have these just as much as animals do that make use of their eyes. The mole's eyes, however, do not open, nor do they project but are left there imperfect and remain like the eyes of other animals when these are still in the uterus...

Forthwith, of course, the female must have smaller, less perfect testes, and the semen generated in them must be scantier, colder, and wetter (for these things too follow of necessity from the deficient heat). Certainly such semen would be incapable of generating an animal, and, since it too has not been made in vain, I shall explain in the course of my discussion what its use is: the testes of the male are as much larger as he is the warmer animal. The semen generated in them, having received the peak of concoction, becomes the efficient principle of the animal. Thus, from one principle devised by the creator in his wisdom, that principle in accordance with which the female has been made less perfect than the male, have stemmed all these things useful for the generation of the animal: that the parts of the female cannot escape to the outside; that she accumulates an excess of useful nutriment and has imperfect semen and a hollow instrument to receive the perfect semen; that since everything in the male is the opposite [of what it is in the female], the male member has been elongated to be most suitable for coitus and the excretion of semen; and that his semen itself has been made thick, abundant, and warm....

Etymologia
Isidore of Seville (560-636)

Isidore was a bishop and encyclopedist whose most famous work is *Etymologia (Etymologies)*, a twenty-volume work intended to compile all the

Explanation in terms of final purpose /
function that God intended it
to serve

13. Understanding Male and Female   143

existing knowledge of his time. The Etymologia was widely used throughout the Middle Ages. When discussing matters of anatomy and biology, Isidore's descriptions were teleological and based on etymology rather than actual observation. In this regard he followed popular practice among medical writers throughout the Middle Ages.

Source: *Isidore of Seville: The Medical Writings*, translated by William D. Sharpe. Transactions of the American Philosophical Society, Vol. 54. Part 2, 1964, pp. 45, 47-48, 50. Reprinted with permission of the American Philosophical Society.

The *genitalia* are parts of the body, as the name itself shows, which have taken a name from the generation of offspring, procreated and given birth by these parts. They are also called *pudenda* from "modesty," *verecundia*, or because of the hair which appears on the body at the age of puberty: we cover these parts with clothing for the same reason. Those some [parts] are also called the "unchaste parts" since they lack the same decent appearance as the members placed before the eyes.

The penis, *veretrum*, is so named because it is "proper to a man," *viri est tantum*, or because semen, *virus*, is emitted from it; for *virus*, properly speaking, is the fluid which comes from the male organs of generation.

The testis, *testiculus*, is named by diminution from "witness," *testis*, and their number commences at two. These supply semen which comes from the spinal cord, kidneys, and loins to the penis, *calamus*, for the purpose of procreation. The scrotum, *fiscus*, is the skin within which the testes are located.

It is called the *uterus* because it is double and divides itself into two parts which spread in differing directions opposite each other and bend around very much like a ram's horn, or because inside it is filled with the fetus. Hence also [it is called] the "pouch," *uter*, because it has something inside, members and viscera.

…It is called the *matrix* since the fetus arises therein: it carefully cherishes the semen which it has received, and fashions what it has warmed into a body, drawing this embodied mass out into members.

The *vulva* is named by analogy to a folding door, *valva*, that is, the door of the belly, because it receives the semen or because the fetus proceeds from it.

Seed, *semen*, is that which once sown, is taken up either by the earth or by the womb for the generation of fruit or fetus. It is liquid made through a decoction of food and of the body and spread through the veins and spinal cord whence, sweated out in the manner of bilge-water, it condenses in the kidneys. Ejaculated during coitus and taken up in the woman's womb, it is shaped in the body of a certain visceral heat and the humidity of the menstrual blood.

The menstrual flow is a woman's superfluous blood: it is termed "menstrual," *menstrua*, because of the phase of the light of the moon by which this flow comes about. The moon is called *MENE* in Greek. These are also called the "womanlies," *muliebria*, for woman is the only menstrual animal. On contact with this gore, crops do not germinate, wine goes sour, grasses die, trees lose their fruit, iron is corrupted by rust, copper is blackened. Should dogs eat any of it, they go mad. Even bituminous glue, which is dissolved neither by iron nor by [strong] waters, polluted by this gore, falls apart by itself.

A man, *vir*, is named because there is greater force, *vis*, in him than in women, whence also "strength," *virtus*, takes its name, or because he rules over woman by force.

Woman, *mulier*, is named from "softness," *mollities*, as though "softer," *mollier*, with a letter changed and one taken away were "woman," *mulier*.

Both differ in bodily strength and weakness, the man's strength being greater, the woman's less, so that she may be subject to the man lest, women having repelled a man, lust may not drive him to strive after another woman, or to fall upon his own sex.

Woman is named according to her feminine sex, not according to a corruption of integrity, and this is clear from the language of Sacred Scripture, since Eve was made directly from her husband's side, and was forthwith named "woman," as Scripture says, without yet having been touched by a man [Genesis 2:23]: *et formavit eam in mulierem*, "And he formed her into a woman."

A virgin, *virgo*, is named from the green freshness, *viridior*, of her age, as is also a sapling, *virga*, or a calf, *vitula*. Others hold that it is from "incorruption," as a virago, since she does not yet know womanly passion.

A *virago* is so named because she does manly things, *virum agere*, that is, she does a man's work, and her strength is masculine. The ancients thus named strong women. But a virgin is not properly called a *virago* if she does not exercise the office of a man, although if a woman really does a man's work, as an Amazon, she is rightly called a *virago*.

The word *femina* is derived from those parts of the thighs by which this sex is distinguished from men. Others think that *femina* is derived by a Greek etymology from "fiery force," because she lusts so strongly, for the female is much more sensual than the male, among women just as among animals. Hence, love beyond measure among the ancients was called "womanly love," *femineus amor*.

Medieval Woman's Guide to Health (late fourteenth/early fifteenth centuries)
Author unknown

This anonymous manuscript from England is not a medical treatise of great intellectual magnitude, but a practical guide directed at women and unlicensed practitioners. It was therefore written in Middle English rather than Latin. The guide's format first introduces a topic by stating the complaint; it then describes the symptoms, provides reasons for the complaint, and offers a cure. The following excerpt deals with the medieval belief of the "wandering womb"— the concept that a woman becomes hysterical and irrational because her uterus has left its place and moved around the body.

Source: *Medieval Woman's Guide to Health*, translated by Beryl Rowland (Kent, OH: Kent State University Press, 1981), pp. 87, 89, 91, 93. Reprinted with permission of The Kent State University Press.

Suffocation of the uterus is when a woman's heart and lungs are thrust together by the uterus so that the woman seems dead except for her breathing, and some call it a heart attack because it is a malady of the heart. For when an evil fume comes from the uterus and goes up to the head, either by the backbone into the back part of the head or by the breast into the front part of the head, because a woman's brain is larger than her heart, the fume cannot stay in the head but strikes down into the heart, troubling it very much and making it tighten more than it naturally should. And in this sickness women fall to the ground as though they had the falling sickness and lie as though in a faint. And this pain lasts either two or three days. And this sickness is due to various reasons, such as the retaining of blood or of corrupt and venomous uterine humors that should be purged in the same way that men are purged of seed that comes from their testicles next to the penis. And just as men fall into various illnesses through retaining their seed within them, so do women. But when women have this sickness or when they fall down, they have great pain and discomfort from the navel downward, and they bow their heads to their knees for distress, and hold their womb and clasp it hard together with their hands, and sometimes make other people thrust their womb together, and they hold their teeth together and afterward they fall down to the ground as though they were dead; and sometimes they beat the earth with their hands and feet because of the great pain that they have. And if this sickness comes from the retention of blood previously mentioned, one can best determine from what the patient says, for she knows best whether she was purged of her blood as she should be, or not. And if it is from corrupt humors that are in the uterus, these may be of two kinds, either hot or cold. If the humors be hot, she feels pricking and burning in the cavity of the uterus, and loosening hot vapors that are dispersed throughout the entire body, making her have an unnatural heat, like a fever, in her body. But if the humor is cold, then she has much heaviness in the cavity of her uterus, loosening a cold vapor that strikes up to the head by the backbone and by the stomach also. And she feels at times great pain about the spleen on the left side. But if it comes from corrupt seed previously, then the pain is without these signs mentioned earlier. Even so, the uterus seems full of such moistness.

The cure for this: To help women with this sickness one must purge the uterus of blood, if it is of the first kind; or of the corrupt humors that are in the uterus, if it is of the second or third kind. Nevertheless, if the ailment is of the third kind, it is helpful to have relations with a man. But understand what I have to say: the relations must be lawful, such as with her husband and no other; for certainly it is better for man or woman to have the greatest physical illness while they live than to be healed through a deed of lechery or any other deed against God's commands....

...And let the patient smell stinking things that are exceptionally odorous, such as burnt felt, dog's hair, goat's hair, or horse's bone set alight and then extinguished, or hartshorn, old shoes, burnt feathers, a wick, moistened in oil, ignited and then extinguished, a woollen rag, or a live smoking coal.

...And from the navel down to the privy member anoint her with fragrant things such as ointment and oils, and make a fumigation underneath of pleasant, sweet-smelling things and draw the matter down from the heart. And such things that are good for this are French muscat, mush, cassia wood, ambergris, frankincense, storax resin, sweet calamus, wood aloes, balm, and such things as have a fragrant smell. And also, at the time of her attack, bind her legs and thighs together and rub the soles of her feet well with vinegar and salt. And make her a fumigation underneath of sweet-smelling things so that neither the smoke nor the smell reaches her nose. But let her smell asafetida and other evil-smelling things as I said before.

14

Sexual Activity and Reproduction

Gynaecia
Soranus (first century)

Soranus was a Greek physician who practiced medicine in Alexandria and in Rome. He wrote around twenty works, but his *Gynaecia* (*Gynecology*) was the best known in the Middle Ages. The following excerpts concern themselves with a number of different issues: choosing a midwife, conception, and the difference between contraception and abortion. While suggestions for treatment are offered, Soranus also moralizes about issues such as the importance of a midwife's character and the preference of contraception over abortion.

Source: *Soranus' Gynecology*, translated by Owsei Temkin. Copyright © 1991 Johns Hopkins University Press, pp. 5, 32-33, 62-64, 66-68. Reprinted with permission of The Johns Hopkins University Press.

WHAT PERSONS ARE FIT TO BECOME MIDWIVES?

This paragraph is of use to prevent fruitless work and the teaching of unfit persons too accommodatingly. A suitable person will be literate, with her wits about her, possessed of a good memory, loving work, respectable and generally not unduly handicapped as regards her senses, sound of limb, robust, and, according to some people, endowed with long slim fingers and short nails at her fingertips. She must be literate in order to be able to comprehend the art through theory too; she must have her wits about her so that she may easily follow what is said and what is happening; she must have a good memory to retain the imparted instructions (for knowledge arises from memory of what has been grasped). She must love work in order to persevere through all vicissitudes (for a woman who wishes to acquire such vast knowledge needs manly patience). She must be respectable since people will have to trust their household and the secrets of their lives to her and because to women of bad character the semblance of medical instruction is a cover for evil scheming. She must not be handicapped as regards her senses since there are things which she must see, answers which she must hear when questioning, and objects which she must grasp by her sense of touch. She needs sound limbs so as not to be handicapped in the performances of her work and she must be robust, for she takes a double task upon herself during the hardship of her professional visits. Long and slim fingers and short nails are necessary to touch a deep lying inflammation without causing too much pain. This skill, however, can also be acquired through zealous endeavor and practice in her work.

HOW TO RECOGNIZE THOSE CAPABLE OF CONCEPTION
    Since women usually are married for the sake of children and succession, and not for mere enjoyment, and since it is utterly absurd to make inquiries about the excellence of their lineage and the abundance of their means but to leave unexamined whether they can conceive or not, and whether they are fit for childbearing or not, it is only right for us to give an account of the matter in question. One must judge the majority from the ages of 15 to 40 to be fit for conception, if they are not mannish, compact, and oversturdy, or too flabby and very moist. Since the uterus is similar to the whole [body], it will, in these cases, either be unable, on account of its pronounced hardness, easily to accept the attachment of the seed [in the beginning], or by reason of its extreme laxity and atony [let it fall again]....
    But some people have included those women who [show] neither joy nor sorrow in their expression while considering as less fitted those who quickly change color, especially if the color deepens. For, they maintain, there is much heat in their desire causing the change and the darkening; by this heat the seed, dried up in some fashion, is destroyed. But it is a more reliable [and] fundamental indication [according to] Diocles, that women can conceive if in their loins and flanks they are fleshy, if they are rather broad, freckled, ruddy, and masculine-looking, whereas those with contrary characteristics are sterile, namely: the undernourished, the thin or the very fat, and those who are either too old or too young....

WHETHER ONE OUGHT TO MAKE USE OF ABORTIVES AND
    CONTRACEPTIVES AND HOW?
    A contraceptive differs from an abortive, for the first does not let conception take place, while the latter destroys what has been conceived. Let us, therefore, call the one "abortive" (phthorion) and the other "contraceptive" (atokion). And an "expulsive" (ekbolion) some people say is synonymous with an abortive; others, however, say that there is a difference because an expulsive does not mean drugs but shaking and leaping.... For this reason

they say that Hippocrates, although prohibiting abortives, yet in his book "On the Nature of the Child" employs leaping with the heels to the buttocks for the sake of expulsion. But a controversy has arisen. For one party banishes abortives, citing the testimony of Hippocrates who says: "I will give to no one an abortive"; moreover, because it is the specific task of medicine to guard and preserve what has been engendered by nature. The other party prescribes abortives, but with discrimination, that is, they do not prescribe them when a person wishes to destroy the embryo because of adultery or out of consideration for youthful beauty; but only to prevent subsequent danger in parturition if the uterus is small and not capable of accommodating the complete development, or if the uterus at its orifice has knobby swellings and fissures, or if some similar difficulty is involved. And they say the same about contraceptives as well, and we too agree with them. And since it is safer to prevent conception from taking place than to destroy the fetus, we shall now first discourse upon such prevention.

For if it is much more advantageous not to conceive than to destroy the embryo,...during the sexual act, at the critical moment of coitus when the man is about to discharge the seed, the woman must hold her breath and draw herself away a little, so that the seed may not be hurled too deep into the cavity of the uterus. And getting up immediately and squatting down, she should induce sneezing and carefully wipe the vagina all round; she might even drink something cold....

...in order that the embryo be separated, the woman should have [more violent exercise], walking about energetically and being shaken by means of draught animals; she should also leap energetically and carry things which are heavy beyond her strength. She should use diuretic decoctions which also have the power to bring on menstruation, and empty and purge the abdomen with relatively pungent clysters; sometimes using warm and sweet olive oil as injections, sometimes anointing the whole body thoroughly therewith and rubbing it vigorously, especially around the pubes, the abdomen, and the loins, bathing daily in sweet water which is not too hot, lingering in the baths and drinking first a little wine and living on pungent food. If this is without effect, one must also treat locally by having her sit in a bath of a decoction of linseed, fenugreek, mallow, marsh mallow, and wormwood.

For a woman who intends to have an abortion, it is necessary for two or even three days beforehand to take protracted baths, little food and to use softening vaginal suppositories; also to abstain from wine; then to be bled and a relatively great quantity taken away. For the dictum of Hippocrates in the "Aphorisms," even if not true in a case of constriction, is yet true of a healthy woman: "A pregnant woman if bled, miscarries." For just as sweat, urine or faeces are excreted if the parts containing these substances slacken very much, so the fetus falls out after the uterus dilates. Following the venesection one must shake her by means of draught animals (for now the shaking is more effective on the parts which previously have been relaxed) and one must use softening vaginal suppositories. But if a woman reacts unfavorably to venesection and is languid, one must first relax the parts by means of sitz baths, full baths, softening vaginal suppositories, by keeping her on water and limited food, and by means of aperients and the application of a softening clyster; afterwards one must apply an abortive vaginal suppository.... In addition, many different things have been mentioned by others; one must, however, beware of things that are too powerful and of separating the embryo by means of something sharp-edged, for danger arises that some of the adjacent parts be wounded. After the abortion one must treat as for inflammation.

De Coitu
Constantine the African (1015-1087)

Constantine the African was a writer, professor of medicine at Salerno, and Benedictine monk originally from Carthage in North Africa. Being a Muslim convert to Christianity, he was one of the few scholars in Europe at the time who could read Arabic. His translations into Latin, therefore, brought to the West Arabic medical writings which greatly influenced the study of reproduction and anatomy in the West. The following is a translation from an anonymous Arabic work, *On Coitus*.

Source: "Constantinus Africanus *De Coitu:* A Translation," translated by Paul Delany, in *Chaucer Review* 4 (1970), pp. 57-60.

SEXUAL CHARACTERISTICS OF DIFFERENT MEN
We will first discuss those men who are strong and excel in producing semen. Their testicles must have warmth and moisture in the right proportion; for example, men who are great wine-drinkers will have plenty of desire and of semen. This will also be the case if the season is spring, when warmth and moisture are well-mixed. Warmth increases desire and masculinity, whereas cold reduces desire and renders effeminate. If a man has warm testicles, therefore, he will be very lecherous and will conceive more boys; his pubic hair will appear at the right time and also the hair on the rest of his body. But men with cold testicles will be effeminate and without desire; their hair will appear late and will be scanty around the pubis and groin. If the testicles are dry the man will have little desire, and his semen will be scanty and weak. If they are moist, much semen will be produced and the hair will be flat and soft. So much for testicles of simple quality.

If the organs are warm and moist, the man will be very lusty (from the warmth) and very hairy (from the moisture); he will have plenty of semen, will have intercourse frequently without harm, and will not tolerate abstinence, as Galen says. With warm and dry organs, the semen will be scanty because of the dryness but he will have great pleasure in ejaculation and conceive boys as a rule; he will be very lusty (especially at the onset of puberty) and his hair will spread from the pubis to the navel and halfway across the hips. Such men will also have an excessive desire for intercourse and will finish quickly — for if they linger about the act they will be harmed. With cold and dry testicles, the cold causes lack of desire and the dryness makes the semen scanty. If they are cold and moist, the cold will reduce desire, hair will appear only around the pubis, and mostly daughters will be born; semen will be abundant, because of the moisture, and nocturnal pollutions common — for excessive moisture hastens to an outlet and causes the effusion of semen (though without very much pleasure). This also happens when the sight of women gives pleasure and, remembered in dreams, brings on pollutions — though these are not, like the others, caused by excessive moisture. The clues to the nature of the testicles we have mentioned should be looked for in the entire body.

CONDITIONS FOR INTERCOURSE

...Intercourse is without doubt beneficial and an aid to health; and Galen shows to whom it will do good and to whom it will not, and how it should be performed. For he tells when it should be done and at what intervals, so that no bodily harm ensues. For if a sluggish and weak person has intercourse his body will feel more sprightly afterwards and his mind will be more cheerful. There is, however, a proper hour for intercourse, when the body is in complete outward harmony i.e. neither replete nor fasting, neither cold nor hot, dry nor wet, but well-tempered. However, if a man strays from these precepts and has intercourse while hot, this is better than if he were cold; also full is better than fasting, wet than dry, and before sleep is better than after. For if one sleeps after the act its virtue will be more beneficial, because of the rest. Galen again says that if intercourse is performed as he recommends the conception and the fetus will be healthier if it is a boy, or even a girl. For the woman preserves the semen better if she sleeps afterwards, and they do this by nature without being taught. So it is always better to have intercourse in the way we have explained.

Anyone who has intercourse around midnight makes a mistake, for his dinner will be half-digested; similarly if he does so in the morning before he has eaten and fully-digested his breakfast. Some observant doctors say that if someone has intercourse before fully digesting a meal the fetus so conceived will be mentally defective, even if complete in its limbs — if not hydro-cephalic or otherwise deformed. And so we say: anyone who has intercourse before digesting his meal makes a serious mistake. The morning is also a bad time, for the reason given. Moreover, since weakness must follow intercourse, it is unwise to work at anything afterwards. It is obvious from this that intercourse is better before sleep than after, because sleep gives rest from labor: and if anyone wants to have intercourse in the morning he must strain his body afterwards to make it capable of work.

Causa et Curae
Hildegard of Bingen (1098–1179)

Noble-born and convent-educated, Hildegard was a woman of many identities: theologian, philosopher, music composer, physician, writer, and abbess. She was in correspondence with some of the most important people of her time, including bishops, popes, abbots, and kings. Since childhood she experienced visions, but did not write about them until she was in her forties. She also conducted some important scientific studies that resulted in two works, *Physica* and *Causa et Curae*. The following excerpts show how Hildegard mingled theology with medicine to explain human reproduction.

Source: *Hildegard of Bingen: On Natural Philosophy and Medicine,* translated by Margret Berger. (Woodbridge, Suffolk; Rochester, NY: DS Brewer, 1999), pp. 51–53, 62–63. Reprinted with permission of Boydell and Brewer.

HUMAN SEXUALITY

What the moon indicates ... People sow seed when heat and cold are temperate, and it grows into fruit. For who would be foolish enough to sow seed during the extreme heat of summer or during the extreme cold of winter? It would perish and would not grow.

The time for procreation. The same is true for humans who refuse to take into consideration the time of maturity in their lives and the time of the moon but want to procreate according to their impulses. For that reason their children will suffer with much pain from physical debility. But however much and whenever they are physically debilitated, God gathers his young buds. Therefore a man must be aware of the time of his physical maturity, and he must examine the time of the moon with as much care as someone who offers his pure prayers. He should not behave like someone stuffing himself with food like a glutton who disregards proper mealtimes but, rather, like someone who observes proper mealtimes so that he is not like a glutton. That is how a person should be and how he should seek the appropriate time for procreation. A man should not approach a woman when she is still a girl but when she is a young woman, because then she is mature.

He should not touch a woman before he has grown a beard, but when he has a beard, because then he is mature enough to procreate offspring. A person who is given to excessive eating and drinking will have leprous and tortuous limbs. However someone who eats and drinks with moderation will have good blood and a healthy body. Similarly, someone who, driven by sexual desire and physical energy, always gives in to his impulse and wastes his semen when he is overcome by his urge to procreate will oftentimes be destroyed by his own semen. One who sheds his semen properly will bring forth healthy offspring.

Sperm. Boiling with the ardor and heat of lust, human blood emits foam which we call semen. This is like a pot that, placed over a fire, emits foam from the water because of the fire's fervor.

Conception. When a human being is conceived from the semen of an infirm person or from semen that is thin and unconcocted but intermingled with waste matter and putridity, then often in his life he will be infirm too, and full of decay, so to speak, like a piece of wood that is eaten up by worms and emits decay. Therefore such a person is often full of ulcers and putridity and will quite easily attract waste matter and putridity from foods in addition to the putridity which he already has. A person who is without this is healthier. But if an excessive amount of putridity is in the semen, the person conceived will be intemperate, unrestrained, fragile, and excessive.

Why the human being is not hairy. That human beings are not hairy stems from their rationality. Because in the place of hair and feathers they have rationality with which they cover themselves and fly wherever they want to. But that the male has a beard and more hair on his body than a woman is because the male is formed from earth and has greater strength and warmth and is everywhere more active than woman. Likewise the earth, steeped in rain and the heat of the sun, produces plants and grasses and nourishes on its surface hairy and feathered animals. But woman is without a beard because she is formed from the flesh of man and is subordinate to man and lives in greater quiet. Thus reptiles too, that are born from the earth, are not hairy but they lie in the earth and feel rain and sun less than the other animals that live on the earth....

Diversity in conception. When a man who has intercourse with a woman has an emission of strong semen and feels proper affectionate love for the woman and when the woman at that hour feels proper love for the man, then a male is conceived because it was so ordained by God. It cannot be otherwise than that a male is conceived, since Adam too was formed from clay which is stronger matter than flesh. This male will be intelligent and virtuous because he was conceived from strong semen and with mutual affectionate love. If, however, the woman's love for the man is lacking, so that the man alone at that hour feels proper affectionate love for the woman and the woman does not feel the same for the man, and if the man's semen is strong, then still a male is conceived because the man's affectionate love is predominant. Yet this male child will be weak and not virtuous because the woman's love for the man was lacking. If the man's semen is thin, yet he feels affectionate love for the woman and she feels the same love for him, then a virtuous female is procreated. If, on the other hand, the man feels affectionate love for the woman and the woman does not feel the same for the man, or if the woman feels affectionate love for the man and the man does not feel the same for the woman, and if, further, the man's semen is thin at that hour, then a female is born due to the semen's weakness. But if the man's semen is strong, yet the man feels no affectionate love for the woman and the woman does not feel any for the man, then a male is procreated because the semen was strong, but he will be bitter on account of his parents' bitterness. And if a man's semen is thin and if at that hour neither feels affectionate love for the other, a female of bitter disposition is born. The warmth of women who are obese by nature outweighs the man's semen, such that the child's face often resembles the mother's. But women who are thin by nature often generate a child whose face resembles the father's.

Women's subordination. As woman represents the subjection to man until they become one, so too woman represents the union of man's semen with her blood so that they become one flesh.

More on conception. When man's semen falls into its place, woman's blood receives it with the will of love and draws it into herself, just as breath draws something in. Thus woman's blood mingles with man's semen and becomes one blood, so that woman's flesh too, warmed by this sanguineous mixture, grows and increases. And so, through man, woman is one flesh with the flesh of man. But man's flesh is concocted, inside and out, by woman's warmth and sweat and thus it draws into itself some of the foam and the sweat of the woman. For man's blood liquefies from the very strong force of his will and flows off and goes around like a mill. It receives some of the woman's foam and sweat, and thus his flesh mingles with the woman's so that he becomes one flesh with her and through her. Because man and woman are thus one flesh, a woman easily conceives a child from a man provided she is fertile. But, that man and woman thus become and are one flesh was concealed in man's side when, taken from man's side, woman became his flesh. For that reason, at conception man and woman, through their blood and sweat, flow together into one so much more easily. The power of eternity that draws the child from the mother's womb thus makes man and woman one flesh.

Adultery. If a man and a woman, forgetting their rightful sexual union and with burning lust turn toward another connection so that they enter into a wrongful union with another person, then the man has joined his blood, that is the blood of his rightful wife, with another woman. Similarly a woman has joined her blood, that is the blood of her rightful husband, with another man. Therefore the children, who are born later on from such rightful as well as wrongful husbands or such rightful as well as wrongful wives, will often be unhappy because the origin of their conception derives from diverse attitudes and diverse blood on the part of men as well as of women. For that reason those parents are called, before God, transgressors of the established decree that God instituted with Adam and Eve. As Adam and Eve transgressed God's precept and delivered themselves and all their descendents to death, so those, too, who defile the divine decree in this manner pollute themselves and their descendants and cause them unhappiness, because in them rationality is polluted and they have adopted the habits of cattle. ...

Female pleasure. Pleasure in woman compares to the sun which mildly, gently, and steadily pervades the earth with its warmth so that it will bring forth fruit. For if the sun burned the earth more severely with its steady glow, it might damage rather than produce the fruit born by the earth. Similarly, pleasure in woman has a mild and gentle, yet steady, warmth so that she may conceive and bear children. Because if she remained continuously in the ardor of pleasure she would not be able to conceive and could not procreate. For when pleasure rises in woman it is gentler in her than it is in man because that fire does not burn as strongly in her as it does in man.

Male pleasure. When the storm of lust surges in a male, it turns around in him like a mill. For his loins are like a forge which the marrow provides with fire. This forge then pours the fire into the male's genital area and lets it strongly burn. But when the wind of pleasure comes forth from the female's marrow it falls into her uterus, which is joined to the navel, and it stirs her blood toward pleasure. This wind spreads out in her abdomen because in the area around a woman's navel the uterus has a wide and, as it were, open space. Consequently she will burn there more gently with pleasure, albeit more frequently because of her moisture. Therefore, out of fear or out of shame woman is able to refrain from pleasure more easily than man, so that she emits the foam of semen more seldom than man; it is sparse and scanty compared to man's foam, like a piece of bread compared to a whole [loaf]. Yet when the said foam is not expelled from a woman after she has experienced pleasure, it happens frequently it mingles in the blood vessels of the uterus which are white and fatty, so that it then flows off through menstruation. Any residue is discharged from the uterus. Sometimes it is also dispersed, broken up and reduced to nothing in the uterus when a woman experiences pleasure without being touched by a man. The fertile nature of woman is colder and more sanguineous than man's nature and her forces are weaker than man's. Therefore she burns more gently with pleasure than man, because the female is merely a vessel for conceiving and bearing children. For that reason, her wind is windy, her blood vessels are open and the members of her body loosen more easily than man's. Fertile men who abstain from women are somewhat weakened, but not as much as [fertile] women [who abstain from men], because men discharge more semen than women. Barren women, however, are healthy if they are without men but are weakened when they have men....

The change in the moon and in the humors. When the moon waxes and becomes full, then too the blood in humans increases. And when the moon wanes, then too the blood in humans decreases. It is always like that for woman as well as for man. For if the blood in humans reached its fullness and then would not decrease, they could not withstand it but would completely break asunder.

The time for procreation. When the blood in a human being has increased with the waxing of the moon, then the human being too, whether woman or man, is fertile for bearing fruit, that is, for procreating offspring. For when, as the moon increases, the human's blood also increases, then the human's semen is strong and powerful. And when, as the moon is on the wane, the human's blood also decreases, then the human's semen is weak and without strength, similar to dregs. Consequently it is then highly ineffectual for procreating offspring. If a woman conceives a child at that time, whether male or female, it will be infirm, weak and not virtuous. Accordingly, with the waxing of the moon blood increases in woman as well as in man and, with the waning of the moon, blood decreases in woman as well as in man until the fiftieth year of life.

Dragmaticon
William of Conches (1080–1154)

William of Conches was a philosopher and theologian whose best known work is the *Dragmaticon (Dialogue of Natural Philosophy)*, in which he wrote on topics such as physics, astronomy, geology, optics, and biology. It takes the form of a dialogue between himself and his patron, Geoffrey Plantagenet, the duke of Normandy. The dialogue repeats the widespread medieval belief that if a woman does not experience pleasure during intercourse then she will not emit any seed and so will not be able to conceive. This belief had far-reaching repercussions, not only for propagating the view that a woman needed to attain orgasm during intercourse in order to conceive, but also for its application to rape victims who became pregnant — the suggestion being that even if they had not wanted the sexual encounter to begin with, the body was easily seduced.

The excerpt below concerns the effects of prostitution and rape.

Source: *William of Conches: A Dialogue on Natural Philosophy*, translated by Italo Ronca and Matthew Curr (Notre Dame, IN: University of Notre Dame Press, 1997) pp. 136-138. Reprinted with permission.

6. Duke: Since professional prostitutes have sexual intercourse most often, how is it that they rarely conceive?

Philosopher: Conception cannot take place from the male seed alone; unless the sperm of man and woman is joined, the woman does not conceive. Therefore, prostitutes, who have sexual relations for money alone, taking no pleasure during the act, have no emission and thus do not conceive.

7. Duke: We see prostitutes consumed by love for one man; surely they have no intercourse with him without delight, and yet they do not conceive except rarely.

Philosopher: You will have a better understanding of the reason for this if you become aware of the shape and nature of the womb [*matrix*]. The womb is a receptacle for the sperm and is shaped like an *alchanna*. This is a wine flagon having a sizeable opening at the top, a round large belly below and a long thin neck between mouth and belly.

8. The womb is hairy inside to retain the sperm better. It has seven little cells impressed with a human figure as [wax] with a seal, so a woman can bear up to seven children and no more at one birth. From her frequent coition, therefore, a prostitute's womb is covered with slime, and the hairs by which the womb ought to detain the sperm are wholly covered by slime: thus, her womb immediately releases whatever it receives, as oiled marble would do.

9. Duke: I recall what you just said, that nothing is conceived without seed of the woman, but this is not plausible. For we see that raped women, who have suffered violence despite their protest and weeping, still have conceived. From this it is apparent that they had no pleasure from such an act. But without pleasure the sperm cannot be released.

10. Philosopher: Although raped women dislike the act in the beginning, in the end, however, from the weakness of the flesh, they like it. Furthermore, there are two wills in humans, the rational and natural, which we often feel are warring within us: for often what pleases the flesh displeases reason. Although, therefore, a raped woman does not assent with her rational will, she does have carnal pleasure. And why do you doubt that the

mother's sperm is present at conception when you see sons born like their mothers and contracting their infirmities?

11. Duke: We often see that legitimate wives who have intercourse with great pleasure only with their husbands never conceive. I would like to know the reason for this.

Philosopher: The reason for this lies with the woman as much as with the man. For it sometimes happens that the womb is too fatty, so that the inferior mouth of the womb is blocked by the excessive fattiness and thus the sperm cannot reach the place of conception. Sometimes it is constricted by too much dryness, sometimes it is lined inside by slimy secretions. Sometimes it lacks the retentive force, and the expulsive force prevails. Sometimes the contractive muscles are too weak.

12. Sometimes, although there is no fault in the womb, the woman still does not conceive. This is a result of the quality of the sperm from either partner or both: for if it is too hot, it has a drying and destructive power; if too cold, it congeals; if too moist, it is dispersed; if too dry, it is hard and resists assimilation.

13. Duke: I concede that there are many causes of sterility in the man as well as in the woman. But there is still one thing about the act of sexual intercourse that amazes me: why is that if a leper lies with a woman she is not infected, and yet the next man to lie with her becomes a leper?

Philosopher: The woman's complexion is cold and moist. In fact, Hippocrates says: "the warmest woman is colder than the coldest man." Such a complexion is harsh and resists corruption, especially coming from the man. Nevertheless, the putrid matter coming from the coition with the leper remains in the womb. So when a [second] man enters her, his male member, which consists of nerves, enters the womb and, by virtue of its attractive force, draws the corruption to it and transmits it to the parts adjoining.

14. Duke: I do not venture to inquire any further about sexual intercourse because the subject is not quite decent, but ask instead that you proceed to the other topics.

Philosopher: nothing that is natural is indecent: for it is a gift of the Creator....

On the Secrets of Women
Pseudo–Albertus Magnus (late thirteenth or early fourteenth century)

This work was written by a disciple of Albertus Magnus (St. Albert the Great), the twelfth century scientist, philosopher, and theologian. The "secrets" in its title refer to sexual and reproductive issues, and this work draws from both scientific medicine derived from writers like Avicenna and Averroës and folk remedies. Pseudo-Albertus's intended audience was probably male, and this was reflected in some of the topics addressed, such as how to determine a woman's chastity.

Source: *Women's Secrets: A Translation of Pseudo-Albertus Magnus' 'De Secretis Mulierum'* with commentaries by Helen Rodnite Lemay (Albany, NY: State University of New York, Press, 1992), pp. 123-128. Copyright © 1992 State University of New York. All rights reserved.

ON THE SIGNS OF WHETHER A MALE OR FEMALE IS IN THE UTERUS

Now we shall treat the signs of whether a male or female is in the uterus, and these are as follows. If a male is conceived, the woman's face is of a reddish color, and her movement is light.

Another sign of a male is if the abdomen protrudes on the right, and if it is rounded.

A further sign of a male is when the milk that flows from the woman's breasts is thick and well digested, such that, if placed on a surface that has been well cleaned it does not separate, but rather the parts adhere to one another instead of spreading apart.

Another sign of a male is if the milk of a pregnant woman, or a drop of her blood extracted from the right side, is placed either in a clear fountain or in her urine, and it goes straight down to the bottom. If it floats on the top, this is the sign of a female.

If the right breast is bigger, the child is male; if the left breast is bigger the child is female. If salt is placed on the nipples and does not liquefy, this is the sign of a male.

Another sign of the child's sex is if the woman moves her right foot first; then she is carrying a male.

Other signs of a female child are: the woman is heavy and pale; her abdomen is of an oblong shape; it is round in the left side; the breast on the left side grows black; the milk it produces is black, undigested, bluish and watery; if it is poured on a stationary body it clearly divides into parts; if placed on a fountain or on urine it remains on the top, etc.

Another test is: if there is pain on the left side the child is always female; if it is on the right side the child is a male.

Another test that I know to be tried and true is as follows. If someone should wish to know whether a woman is pregnant, he should give her hydromel to drink. If she has cramps around the umbilicus, she has conceived; and if she does not, she has not conceived.

Hydromel is a drink which is made from water and honey. To prepare it take two spoonfuls of water and one of honey and mix them together. The woman should drink this when she is going to bed or immediately afterwards. Since women who are aware of what is happening might tell you the opposite of what is true, the experimenter should say nothing about impregnation. He should rather wait until the woman complains of pain in the head or somewhere else, as women are accustomed to do, and then give her the drink as a remedy against it. In the morning he should ask if she has pain anywhere, and if she says she feels discomfort around the umbilicus, then a judgment of conception is indicated. If she replies otherwise, then she has not conceived. Some women, however, are so clever and so aware of the trick that they refuse to tell the truth, but rather say something else instead.

ON THE SIGNS OF CORRUPTION OF VIRGINITY

Sometimes virgins are gravely corrupted so that their vagina is greatly enlarged because the male member is exceedingly large and inept. When this happens the woman's vagina becomes so widened that the man can enter there without any pain to his member, and this is a sign that the woman was first corrupted.

This is the reason why when young women first lose their virginity they have pain in the vagina for a time, because it is being enlarged and disposed for coitus. Another reason for this pain is that there is a certain skin in the vagina and the bladder which is broken. But the more they have sex, the more they become accustomed to it.

ON THE SIGNS OF CHASTITY

The signs of chastity are as follows: shame, modesty, fear, a faultless gait and speech, casting eyes down before men and the acts of men. Some women are so clever, however, that they know how to resist detection by these signs, and in this case a man should turn to their urine. The urine of virgins is clear and lucid, sometimes white, sometimes sparkling. If the urine is of a golden color, clear and heavy, this is the sign of a temperament with an appetite for pleasure, however this is found in women who are not corrupted. Corrupted women have a muddy urine because of the rupture of the aforementioned skin, and male sperm appear at the bottom of this urine.

In menstruating women the urine is bloody, and when a woman suffers menstrual pain she has watery eyes, the color of her face is changed, and she has no taste for food. A man should beware of having sex with women in this condition, and prudent women know how to keep themselves apart, and remain separated from men during their monthly flow.

15

Remedies

Writings of Trotula
Trotula of Salerno (eleventh or twelfth century)

Little historical evidence exists about Trotula, but her legend was known throughout Europe in the late Middle Ages. She was said to have been the first female professor of medicine at Salerno, and her writings were the most popular medical works in Europe between the twelfth and fifteenth centuries. Her work reached an even greater audience in the fifteenth century when it began to be translated into the European vernacular languages. The following excerpts from *On the Treatments for Women* and *On Cosmetics* are both attributed to her.

Source: *The Trotula: A Medieval Compendium of Women's Medicine*, edited and translated by Monica H. Green. Copyright © 2001 University of Pennsylvania Press, pp. 145, 147, 167, 171, 189. Reprinted by permission of the University of Pennsylvania Press.

A GOOD CONSTRICTIVE

190. A constrictive for the vagina so that they may appear as if they were virgins. Take the whites of eggs and mix them with water in which pennyroyal and hot herbs of this kind have been cooked, and with a new linen cloth dipped in it, place it in the vagina two or three times a day. And if she urinates at night, put it in again. And note that prior to this the vagina ought to be washed well with the same warm water with which these things were mixed.

191. Take the newly grown bark of a holm oak. Having ground it, dissolve it with rainwater, and with a linen or cotton cloth place it in the vagina in the above-mentioned manner. And remove all these things before the hour of the commencement of intercourse.

192. Likewise take powder of natron or blackberry and put it in; it constricts [the vagina] marvelously.

193. Likewise, there are some dirty and corrupt prostitutes who desire to

seem to be more than virgins and they make a constrictive for this purpose, but they are ill counseled, for they render themselves bloody and they wound the penis of the man. They take powered natron and place it in the vagina.

194. In another fashion, take oak apples, roses, sumac, great plantain, comfrey, Armenian bole, alum, and fuller's earth, of each one ounce. Let them be cooked in rainwater and with this water let the genitals be fomented.

195. What is better is if the following is done one night before she is married: let her place leeches in the vagina (but take care that they do not go in too far) so that blood comes out and is converted into a little clot. And thus the man will be deceived by the effusion of blood.

On Women's Cosmetics

242. In order that a woman might become very soft and smooth and without hairs from her head down, first of all let her go to the baths, and if she is not accustomed to do so, let there be made for her a steam bath in this manner. Take burning hot tiles and stones and with these placed in the steam bath, let the woman sit in it. Or else take hot tiles or hot black stones and place them in the steam bath or a pit made in the earth. Then let hot water be poured in so that steam is produced, and let the woman sit upon it well covered with cloths so that she sweats. And when she has well sweated, let her enter hot water and wash herself very well, and thus let her exit from the bath and wipe herself off well with a linen cloth.

249. ...noblewomen should wear musk in their hair, or clove, or both, but take care that it not be seen by anyone. Also the veil with which the head is tied should be put on with cloves and musk, nutmeg, and other sweet-smelling substances.

305. I saw a certain Saracen woman liberate many people with this medicine. Take a little bit of laurel leaves and a little bit of musk, and let her hold it under the tongue before bad breath is perceived in her. Whence I recommend that day and night and especially when she has to have sexual intercourse with anyone she hold these things under her tongue.

Writings of Moses Maimonides
Moses Maimonides (1135-1204)

Maimonides was a physician and codifier of Jewish law who was born in Cordova, Spain, but settled in North Africa. He was the court physician to Saladin's Vizier and then to Saladin's successor and eldest son. The first excerpt comes from the *Treatise on Cohabitation*, written at the request of the Sultan of Egypt, who desired "increases (in coital activities) because of the multitude of young maidens." The second excerpt comes from *Medical Aphorisms*, a work comprised of 1,500 medical aphorisms based mostly on Greek writers. It contains twenty-five chapters dealing with a variety of medical topics including anatomy, diagnosis, gynecology, phlebotomy, and surgery.

Source: *Sexual Ethics in the Writings of Moses Maimonides,* translated by Fred Rosner (New York, Bloch Pub. Co. 1974), pp. 19-21, 27, 75-77. Reprinted with permission from Dr. Fred Rosner and Jason Aronson, Inc.

Treatise on Cohabitation

[CHAPTER 3]

And it is known that this activity is not purely a natural function; that is, erection is not similar to nutritional or growth activities in which emotion plays no part. Rather it is also an emotional process controlled by the psyche. As a result, various emotions can be greatly detrimental or beneficial (for coitus): i.e., sorrow, anxiety, and mourning, or the repulsiveness of the woman with whom one intends to have sexual intercourse, are among the things that markedly weaken coitus. The converse emotions incite one thereto and produce a powerful stimulation.

Physicians have already mentioned that which especially weakens coitus: sexual intercourse with numerous maidens, elderly women, a young girl who has not reached puberty, or a woman who for many years has not been intimate or a menstruating or ill woman; even more than all this is coitus with a repugnant woman who has passed the menopause and is repulsive for this reason. Indeed, nature teaches and accustoms one to laziness if (a woman's condition) has converted to this (post-menopausal) state. Therefore, whenever the person has the desire (for coitus) but finds his lust insufficient, he should follow the regimen that can be gleaned from this, my treatise which includes that which should be striven for, and that which should be avoided in this regard.

[CHAPTER 9]

They also state that because there are many people who desire to have prolonged erection and who are unable to ejaculate, it seems appropriate that I mention the following remedy. It is a wondrous secret which no person has (heretofore) described: take one liter each of carrot oil, and radish oil, one quarter liter of mustard oil, combine it all and place therein one half liter of live saffron-colored ants. Set the oil in the sun for between four and seven days and afterwards utilize it. Massage the penis therewith for three hours or two hours before sexual intercourse. Then wash it with warm water, and it will remain in erection even after ejaculation. Nothing comparable has yet been prepared for this purpose.

Another (aphrodisiac) which he mentions: one drachm of pyrethrum, one half drachm of euphorbia, and one quarter drachm of musk. All this is pulverized and diluted in an ounce of jasmine oil, and one massages therewith daily near the genitals and the testicles and the penis.

Medical Aphorisms

[CHAPTER 20:72]
Pigeon eggs are good aphrodisiacs. Similarly, all eggs help the libido, especially if they are cooked with onion or turnip.

[CHAPTER 22:50]
If the virile member is rubbed with hedgehog fat, a strong and powerful erection is stimulated, and increased pleasure is derived from sexual intercourse. The hedgehog penis, if dried and pulverized and imbibed, also stimulates a strong erection. The same is accomplished with the penis of a ram, because of this specific property which lies therein.

[CHAPTER 24:18]
One should examine a male at the time he reaches puberty. If his right testicle is larger, he will give rise to male offspring; if it is the left, he will give rise to females. The same situation applies for the breasts of a girl at the time of puberty.

[CHAPTER 24:29]
If one excises the ovaries of a female creature, she will not lust (for coitus), and will not receive a male for pleasure. The "power of femininity" (sex appeal?) will be abolished. Thus, female swine are castrated in the land of *Athens*, and also in other nations. Then their bodies fatten, and their flesh becomes better to eat than the flesh of the other female (noncastrated) swine. If a person wishes to castrate a female, it is obligatory in this situation to remove both ovaries. In this matter the castration of a female is much more dangerous (than that of a male).

[CHAPTER 24:30]
A woman can find sexual satisfaction without a man approaching her, and this is during pollution that occurs to her during the night while she is asleep, just as this occurs to a man (at night), and after masturbation. This is just as we have related it regarding the situation of a certain woman who was a widow (in Galen's De semine, II). This aforementioned woman is the same one whose situation is well described (at the end of Galen "De Locis Affectis"), that is, she derived more satisfaction from illusionary sexual intercourse than actual (coitus).

Thesaurus pauperum
Peter of Spain (1205-1277)

The exact identity of Peter of Spain is not known, but the man responsible for writing the medical tract *Thesaurus pauperum* is believed to be the Portuguese doctor and philosopher Pedro Juliano Rebolo (or Rebello). He was elected pope in 1276 as Pope John XXI, but reigned less than a year before dying in office. The following remedies from his tract are meant to cure various ailments of the reproductive organs. He also provided advice on birth control, which was somewhat surprising given that church doctrine was against contraception even at that time. It is important to note that Peter's work is derivative and he lists the authors from whom he quotes.

Source: *Obras Médicas de Pedro Hispano*, ediçoēs comentadas por Maria Helena da Rocha Pereira (Coimbra: Universidade de Coimbra, 1973), pp. 230, 232, 238, 250, 252, 258. Translated from the Portuguese by Aidan J. McNamara.

ITCHING OF THE PENIS

1. Wash frequently with wine mulled with sage. Macer Floridus. 2. *Item* ash of dried pumpkin quickly cures ulcers on the penis, even if they are putrefied. Dioscorides. 3. *Item* a poultice with olive leaf wine. Experimentator. 4. *Item* if there is <swelling>, mix dried figs and wheat flour with ordinary olive oil and apply. *Idem.* 5. *Item* application of extract of lamb's tongue,[1] boiled with a little honey, cures ulcers on the penis. Dioscorides. 6. *Item* litargirium dissolved in rose oil is very good. *Circa instans.* 7. *Item* boil donkey's or goat's milk with plantain juice; this cures ulcers of the kidneys, the bladder, or penis, if taken frequently. Dioscorides. Isaac Judaeus.

SWELLING OF THE TESTICLES

1. If the testicles swell up, fava bean flour dissolved in extract of danewort and olive oil immediately reduces the swelling. Dioscorides. 2. *Item* toasted danewort or eastern pellitory of the wall[2] leaves do the same. 3. *Item* danewort and elder leaves do the same. That is mine. 4. *Item* goat's dung dissolved in wine cures a tumor completely. Cyranides. 5. *Item* a plaster of ground black henbane leaves and seeds with wine cures a tumor completely. Macer Floridus. 6. *Item* application of betony, ground and boiled in wine, takes away the pain and the tumor from the testicles. Dioscorides.

MALADIES OF THE PENIS

1. If the penis swells or hurts, mix wax, olive oil, and extract of purslane and apply; it is a proven thing. Constantine the African. 2. *Item* a poultice

---

1. A plant.
2. Parietaria officinalis.

of barley flour boiled in mead removes the pain and the tumor. Constantine the African. 3. *Item* against cancer in the penis and other parts; ground olive leaves with honey cure it. Constantine the African. 4. *Item* a sprinkling of ground socotrine aloes is an admirable cure for cancerous ulcers. Constantine the African. 5. *Item* carrying root of hop trefoil and centaury cures cancer completely in a few days. Albert the Great. 6. *Item* wash the area with hot vinegar, dry with a linen cloth and sprinkle oak-apple powder on it; do this three times a day; it cures completely. Galen 7. *Item* placing extract of duckweed on the cancer kills it.

ILLNESSES OF THE BREASTS
1. If the breasts swell because of excessive milk, cover them firstly with clay or with split and ground fava bean and egg white, or with lentils boiled in vinegar; should the problem continue, apply egg with rose oil, so that the tumor and hardness of the breasts are removed. 2. *Item* apply a small piece of bread coated in celery juice. Constantine the African. 3. *Item* apply bull dung, fenugreek, and melilot with olive oil. 4. *Item* apply topically linseed mixed with honey. Constantine the African. 5. *Item* cabbage root, mint, fava bean flour; the application of all these things and of each one of them alone frees up and suppresses the milk. *Idem.* 6. *Item* if there is a fistula or a cancer, goat's dung mixed with honey will destroy the fistula and the cancer and remove all the decay. Constantine the African. 7. *Item* smear the nipple with balsam; it removes the pain. *Idem.* 8. apply ground nut worms. It is a sure thing. *Idem.* 9. *Item* ground olive leaves kill the tumor, the cancer and the itching, wherever it may be. *Idem.* 10. *Item* burned human excrement cures cancerous and incurable ulcers. *Idem.* 11. *Item* always carry hop trefoil, because with all certainty it cures cancer. It is a matter of experience. This is mine. 12. *Item* apply hot ground mallows with ordinary olive oil against tumors on the breasts. Dioscorides. 13. *Item* application of black henbane seed ground with wine removes the pain and tumor of the breasts. Macer Floridus. 14. *Item* if a virgin has frequently and since the beginning, smeared her breasts with extract of water hemlock, they will always be small, hard, and firm. Idem. 15. *Item* a fava bean poultice will not allow milk to leak from the breasts and will remove a tumor from them. Dioscorides. 16. *Item* a plaster made of scabwort leaves and of horehound with lard removes the tumor and hardness of the breasts. Experimentator. 17. *Item* a plaster made of mint does the same thing. *Circa instans.* 18. *Item* a plaster of honey, wax, and pigeon's droppings mixed together at the same time and placed on swollen breasts, removes the pain and the tumor and <does not> allow them to grow. Experimentator. 19. *Item* fennel powder ground with lard, and mint remove the tumor. *Idem.* 20. *Item* application of a mixture of goat's dung with vinegar

and barley flour resolves the tumor completely and in admirable fashion. Dioscorides.

DAMPING OF EROTIC DESIRE

1. It can be read in book one of Cyranides that, if you give someone nine ants boiled with extract of asphodelus, in all the days of their life, they will not have sexual potency. 2. *Item* a plaster of hemlock on the testicles keeps intercourse completely at a distance. Macer Floridus. 3. *Item* if you drink root of water-lily with water for thirty days the desire will be extinguished. Petrus Lucrator 4. *Item* if you prepare a mixture of opium, henbane seed, and mandrake with wax and olive oil, made into an ointment, containing the above items; and if you anoint the genital areas with olive oil and place the plaster on the testicles; this eliminates coitus. Experimentator. 5. *Item* anoint the genital areas frequently with extract of black nightshade and of house leeks and vinegar; it does good. This is mine. 6. *Item* all say, and especially Dioscorides, that pepper, rue, agnus castus, calamint, and costus consume the seed of procreation, drying it with its properties and strong heat. 7. *Item* anoint the penis with olive oil in which camphor has been mixed; you will not achieve an erection. Constantine the African. 8. *Item* if someone eats blossom of willow or poplar, they will cool down completely in themselves the heat of desire; but this is for protracted use. Dioscorides. 9. *Item* you can read in Book I of Cyranides that the gladiola has two roots, one above the other; taking the lower one wards off coitus and removes the seed of procreation. 10. *Item* carrying verbena prevents an erection of the penis, until it is taken away. Cyranides. 11. *Item* if you put it under the pillow, there will be no erection of the penis, rather it will stay flaccid. *Idem.* 12. *Item* taking a little verbena prevents erection of the penis during seven days. *Idem.* 13. *Item* if you want to test it give it to a cock with his meal, and he will not climb on top of the hens. *Idem.* 14. *Item* smear extract of verbena on a leather strap and wear it close to the flesh; you will become effeminate; and, if you touch someone with it, this person will be incapable of performing the service of Venus, as the heart of the person it touches will soften. *Idem.* 15. *Item* carrying a stone which can be found on the left side of the jaw of the salpuga [unclear] impedes the erection of the penis. 16. *Item* rhubarb takes away lasciviousness and suppresses the semen. 17. *Item* when a firefly is carried frequently by a man, it turns him inhuman. Gilbertus Anglicus. 18. *Item* applying broad bean flour to the groin of a boy suppresses libido and does not allow the pubic hair to grow or the testicles to develop. Dioscorides and Isaac Judaeus. 19. *Item* anointing the penis with cedar pitch contracts the genitals in such a way that they become useless for coitus or procreation. Dioscorides. 20. *Item* a rooster's testicles with blood of the same,

placed under the bed, prevent coitus for anyone lying in it. Sixtus to Octavian. 21. *Item* taking the seed of the water-lily restrains from sex. Dioscorides. 22. *Item* frequent taking of water-lily diminishes defilement and destroys the desire for coitus, if you drink an ounce of it with syrup of poppy; the semen is congealed along with its properties and its root. Avicenna. 23. *Item* lettuce seed dries semen and quiets down desire for coitus and defilement. *Idem*. 24. *Item* water, in which has been boiled lentils and lettuce seed, extinguishes the impulse to libidinousness with efficacy. Scipio. 25. *Item* the stone of topaz generates chastity and suppresses Venus. Lapidarius. 26. *Item* if you drink three ounces of coriander seed, coitus is prevented. Constantine the African. 27. *Item* anointing the penis with juniper gum prevents your erection. *Idem*.

PREVENTION OF CONCEPTION

1. When a woman does not wish to conceive, perhaps because she fears dying or for some other reason, she should eat bone of the heart of the deer (?) and she will not conceive. Constantine the African. 2. *Item* carry with you close to your skin the womb of a goat that has not given birth and you will not conceive; or carry the stone you find in it. Trotula. 3. *Item* if a woman walks over menstrual blood of another woman and anoints herself with it, she will not conceive. Dioscorides. 4. *Item* a certain experienced woman told me that, annoyed at the frequency of childbirth, she ate a bee and did not conceive again. 5. *Item* if a woman carries with her a piece of a mule's ear or its skin, she will never conceive. Trotula and Cyranides. 6. *Item* testicles of a live, male weasel, castrated by a woman, and wrapped in the skin of a goose or similar, avoids conception. *Idem*. 7. *Item* if a woman carries a jet stone she will not conceive. Trotula. 8. *Item* it is an astonishing thing and its veracity is suspect; when a woman does not wish to give birth again, she places in the placenta as many grains of castor beans or barley as the number of years she wishes to stay sterile, and for that number of years she will not conceive. Trotula 9. *Item* if a woman takes one dram of black ivy shoots after menstruation, procreation is prevented. Dioscorides. 10. *Item* drinking poplar leaves after menstruation prevents conception. *Idem*. 11. *Item* a woman ties around herself grains of peony with hairs from the ear of a mule, and she will not conceive while bearing them. Cyranides. 12. *Item* placing extract of mint on the vulva during coitus, impedes conception. Avicenna. 13. *Item* a woman applies the tentacles of a slug to herself and she will not conceive; these have the ability of preventing conception. Gilbertus Anglicus. 14. *Item* it is believed that attaching root of the pimpernel prevents conception, while a woman wears it. Dioscorides. 15. *Item* hanging bone of heart of deer (?) from the arm prevents conception. Sixtus to Octavian. 16. *Item* if the woman

carries with her the small bone which is found in the vulva of the female donkey she will never conceive. *Idem* 17. *Item* if a woman imbibes or wears ears or testicles of the male donkey, she will not conceive. *Idem* 18. *Item* imbibing or carrying the heart of a mule does the same thing. *Idem* 19. *Item* carrying the stone found in the stomach or the vulva or in the heart of a deer does the same. *Idem*. 20. *Item* take to drink the lining of the stomach of a hare, after you give birth, and you will not conceive again. Avicenna. 21. *Item* taking rust prevents conception in a woman. 22. *Item* taking the root and the leaves of the *epimedium*[3] with wine after it has been cleansed, prevents procreation; this is a herb which has a stalk like ivy, ten or twelve leaves, without a flower, without fruit, with a disagreeable smell and an insipid taste. Dioscorides. 23. *Item* application of menstrual blood down below impedes conception. 24. *Item* hanging a *scolopendria*[4] above the bed avoids pregnancy. 25. *Item* the dog has two testicles, whose effects and properties are contrary one to the other; one stays more on top and the other lower; one is hard and almost dry and the other soft and moist; eating the one that is dry destroys coitus; eating the soft and humid one strengthens and augments it; if the male takes the dry, larger one, the offspring will be of masculine sex and strong; if the woman takes the smaller, she will conceive a female. Hali and Avicenna. 26. *Item* if the woman carries elephant's dung, she will not conceive. Constantine the African.

3. Dioscorides provides a detailed description of the plant, because it appears to be very uncommon and little known, hence in translation it is normally left in the original Latin

4. It is uncertain whether this refers to a myriopod or a plant of the scolopendria group.

VI

LITERATURE

16

Poetry

Lyrics

Lyrics were a form of romantic poetry written and sung by troubadours who were often members of the nobility. Lyrics were often very sexual in nature, but varied in style. Most centered on courtly love, which focused on an idealized, passionate love and the courtesy and loyalty offered to a woman. Other lyrics celebrated love of life and the beauty of the world, while still others could be bawdy. This genre originated in southern France in the twelfth century and then became disseminated to different parts of Europe.

The following lyrics illustrate several different themes. The first one falls into the category of an *alba* or dawn song, telling of lovers who spend their nights together but are separated during the day. They are usually warned by a watchman of the impending daybreak so they can part without risk of discovery. The second one is flirtatious, supposedly sung by a young woman. The third one comes from Germany and tells playfully of a tryst between two young lovers. The last is bawdy and recounts the life of an old prostitute.

"A Knight Was with His Lady Fondly Lying"
(Gaucelm Faidit, 1185–1215)

Source: *An Anthology of Medieval Lyrics* by Angel Flores (New York: Modern Library, 1962), pp. 72–73, 161–163, 435–436. Reprinted with the permission of the Estate of Angel Flores, c/o The Permission Company, High Bridge, N.J.

> A knight was with his lady fondly lying —
> The one he cherished most — and gently sighing
> As he kissed her, complained: My love, the day
> Soon will arrive, chasing this night away.
> Alas!
> Already I can hear the watchman crying:
> Begone!
> Quickly, begone! You may no longer stay,
> For it is dawn.

My love, if there were but some wile or way
To banish hostile morn and prying day —
At least from where we two are fondly lying —
Then filled with thanks would be my gentle sighing,
Alas!
Already I can hear the watchman crying:
Begone!
Quickly, begone! You may no longer stay,
For it is dawn.

My love, I know that he is surely lying
Who tells you there is any sadder sighing
Than of two lovers who bemoan the day
That comes too soon to chase their night away.
Alas!
Already I can hear the watchman crying:
Begone!
Quickly, begone! You may no longer stay,
For it is dawn.

My love, forget me never, for today —
Although I now must rise and go my way —
I leave my heart there, where we two were lying,
To pledge unending love in endless sighing.
Alas!
Already I can hear the watchman crying:
Begone!
Quickly, begone! You may no longer stay,
For it is dawn.

My love, if you were not close by me lying,
Then death would echo in my doleful sighing.
I will return. So does my torment weigh,
That without you I cannot live the day.
Alas!
Already I can hear the watchmen crying:
Begone!
Quickly, begone! You may no longer stay,
For it is dawn.

"Am I, Am I, Am I Fair?"
(Eustache Deschamps, 1346–1410)

Source: *An Anthology of Medieval Lyrics* by Angel Flores (New York: Modern Library, 1962), pp. 72–73, 161–163, 435–436. Reprinted with the permission of the Estate of Angel Flores, c/o The Permission Company, High Bridge, N.J.

Am I, am I, am I fair?   My brow is fair, my face is sweet.
It seems as far as I can tell   And my mouth is red and neat;

Tell me if I'm fair.

I have green eyes and small eyebrows,
My nose is delicate and blond my
hair,
My chin is round, my throat is white;
Am I, am I, am I fair?

My breasts are firm and carried high,
My arms are long, my fingers slim,
And my waist is small and trim;
Tell me if I'm fair.

I have tiny rounded feet,
Good shoes and pretty clothes I wear,
I am gay and full of mirth;
Tell me if I'm fair.

I have cloaks fur-lined in gray,
I have hats and trimmings fine,
I have many a silver pin;
Am I, am I, am I fair?

I've silken sheets and tapestry,
I've sheets of white and beige and
gold,
Many a dainty thing I hold;
Tell me if I'm fair.

I'm fifteen only, I tell you;

Many my pretty treasures are
If I keep the key with care;
Am I, am I, am I fair?

Those who would be my friends
Must indeed be brave
If such a maid they'd have
Tell me if I'm fair.

Before God, I promise too,
That if I live I'll be most true
To him — if I don't falter;
Am I, am I, am I fair?

If he be courteous and kind,
Valiant, well read and gay,
He shall always have his way;
Tell me if I'm fair.

It is an earthly paradise
To have a woman always near
Who is so blossoming and fresh;
Am I, am I, am I fair?

Among yourselves, faint-hearts,
Think on what I say;
Here ends my virelay:
Am I, am I, am I fair?

"Under the Lime Tree"
(Walther von der Vogelweide, c. 1170–1230)

Source: *An Anthology of Medieval Lyrics* by Angel Flores (New York: Modern Library, 1962), pp. 72–73, 161–163, 435–436. Reprinted with the permission of the Estate of Angel Flores, c/o The Permission Company, High Bridge, N.J.

Under the lime tree
On the heath
There our bed was,
There you can see
So fair beneath,
Broken flowers and flattened grass.
Before the forest in the valley,
Tandaradei,
The nightingale sang sweetly.

I had come

To the meadow:
My love had come before.
There I was given such welcome,
Holy Virgin! oh
I am content for evermore.
A thousand times did we not kiss?
Tandaradei,
See how red my mouth is

There he made
So rich and fair

A bed from blooms.
There laughter stayed,
Is still heard there,
When somebody the same way comes.
On the roses, then, he may
Tandaradei,
See where my head lay.

That he lay by me,
If it were known

(Now God forbid!), I'd be ashamed.
What he did with me,
Will be known to none
Except the two of us unnamed,
And a little bird:
Tandaradei,
Who will be the silent third.

"Ballade for Fat Margot"
(François Villon, 1431–after 1463)

Source: *Complete Works of François Villon,* edited by Anthony Bonner, copyright © 1960 by Bantam Books, a division of Random House, Inc., p. 107. Used by permission of Bantam Books, a division of Random House, Inc.

If I love and serve my lovely lady willingly,
should you therefore think me vile and stupid?
She has all the charms a man could want.
For love of her I gird on sword and shield;
when people come I run and grab a pot
to go get wine, as quietly as possible;
I serve them water, cheese, bread and fruit.
If they pay me well, I say, "That's good,
and please come back whenever you're in rut,
to this brothel where we ply our trade."

But then bad feelings start to fly
when she comes home without a cent;
I cannot stand her, and feel a deathly hatred
for her. I grab her dress, her belt and slip,
and swear I'll make them do in place of cash.
Hands on hips, she shouts, "You Antichrist!",
and swears on Jesus' death that I
will not. So then I snatch some club
and with it write a message on her nose,
in this brothel where we ply our trade.

Then we make up in bed, and she more bloated
than a poisonous dung-hill beetle, farts
and laughs and claps me on the head,
says I'm cute and whacks my thigh.
Then, both drunk, we sleep like logs.
When we awake, her belly starts to quiver
and she mounts me, to spare love's fruit;
I groan, squashed beneath her weight —
this lechery of hers will ruin me,
in this brothel where we ply our trade.

Through wind, hail or frost my living's made.
I am a lecher, and she's a lecher with me.
Which one of us is better? We're both alike:
the one as worthy as the other. Bad rat, bad cat.
We both love filth, and filth pursues us;
we flee from honor, honor flees from us,
in this brothel where we ply our trade.

Lais
Marie de France (1140/1150–c. 1190)

Little is known about Marie's background. It may be deduced that she had connections to aristocratic circles because she wrote in the Anglo-Norman form of Old French. She is best known for her twelve short stories, called *lais*, that followed the courtly love tradition. One of the common themes found in courtly love literature was an unmarried knight involved in an adulterous yet unconsummated relationship with an unhappily married aristocratic woman. She often served as his inspiration to do great deeds and to be a good person in order to be truly worthy of her love. This relationship mirrored the economic and political realities of the medieval nobility in which a feudal relationship existed between a knight and his lord to whom he swore an oath of loyalty and fealty. In the following lais, Marie de France uses this literary leitmotif.

Source: *The Lais of Marie de France*, translated by Robert Hanning and Joan Ferrante (Durham, NC: Labyrinth Press, a division of Baker House Book Company, 1978). pp. 155–159. Reprinted with permission.

"Laüstic" ("The Nightingale")

I shall tell you an adventure
about which the Bretons made a *lai*.
Laüstic was the name, I think,
they gave it in their land.
In French it is *rossignol*,
and *nightingale* in proper English.
At Saint-Malo in that country,
there was a famous city.
Two knights lived there,
they both had strong houses.
From the goodness of the two barons
the city acquired a good name.
One had married a woman
wise, courtly, and handsome;
she set a wonderfully high value on
    herself,
within the bounds of customs and
usage.
The other was a bachelor,
well known among his peers
for bravery and great valor;
he delighted in living well.
He jousted often, spent widely
and gave out what he had.
He also loved his neighbor's wife;
he asked her, begged her so persistently,
and there was such good in him,
that she loved him more than any-
    thing,
as much for the good that she heard of
    him
as because he was close by.
They loved each other discreetly and
    well,

concealed themselves and took care
that they weren't seen
or disturbed or suspected.
And they could do this well enough
since their dwellings were close,
their houses were next door,
and so were their rooms and their
    towers;
there was no barrier or boundary
except a high wall of dark stone.
From the rooms where the lady slept,
if she went to the window
she could talk to her love
on the other side, and he to her,
and they could exchange their posses-
    sions,
by tossing and throwing them.
There was scarcely anything to disturb
    them,
they were both quite at ease;
except that they couldn't come
    together
completely for their pleasure,
for the lady was closely guarded
when her husband was in the country.
Yet they always managed,
whether at night or in the day,
to be able to talk together;
no one could prevent
their coming to the window
and seeing each other there.
For a long time they loved each other,
until one summer
when the woods and meadows were
    green
and the orchards blooming.
The little birds, with great sweetness,
were voicing their joy above the flowers.
It is no wonder if he understands them,
he who has love to his desire.
I'll tell you the truth about the knight:
he listened to them intently
and to the lady on the other side,
both with words and looks.
At night, when the moon shone
when her lord was in bed,
she often rose from his side
and wrapped herself in a cloak.
She went to the window

because of her lover, who, she knew
was leading the same life,
awake most of the night.
Each took pleasure in the other's sight
since they could have nothing more;
but she got up and stood there often
that her lord grew angry
and began to question her, to ask
why she got up and where she went.
"My lord," the lady answered him,
"there is no joy in this world
like hearing the nightingale sing.
That's why I stand there.
It sounds so sweet at night
that it gives me great pleasure;
it delights me so and I so desire it
that I cannot close my eyes."
When her lord heard what she said
he laughed in anger and ill will.
He set his mind on one thing:
to trap the nightingale.
There was no valet in his house
that he didn't set to making traps,
    nets, or snares,
which he then had placed in the
    orchard;
there was no hazel tree or chestnut
where they did not place a snare or
    lime
until they trapped and captured him.
When they had caught the nightin-
    gale,
they brought it, still alive, to the lord.
He was very happy when he had it;
he came to the lady's chambers.
"Lady," he said, "where are you?
Come here! Speak to us!
I have trapped the nightingale
that kept you awake so much.
From now on you can lie in peace:
he will never again awaken you."
When the lady heard him,
she was sad and angry.
She asked her lord for the bird
but he killed it out of spite,
he broke its neck in his hands —
too vicious an act —
and threw the body on the lady;
her shift was stained with blood,

a little, on her breast.
Then he left the room.
The lady took the little body;
she wept hard and cursed
those who betrayed the nightingale,
who made the traps and snares,
for they took great joy from her.
"Alas," she said, "now I must suffer.
I won't be able to get up at night
or go and stand in the window
where I used to see my love.
I know one thing for certain:
he'd think I was pretending.
I must decide what to do about this.
I shall send him the nightingale
and relate the adventure."
In a piece of samite,
embroidered in gold and writing,
she wrapped the little bird.
She called one of her servants,
charged him with her message,
and sent him to her love.

He came to the knight,
greeted him in the name of the lady,
related the whole message to him,
and presented the nightingale.

When everything had been told and
   revealed to the knight,
after he had listened well,
he was very sad about the adventure,
but he wasn't mean or hesitant.
He had a small vessel fashioned,
with no iron or steel in it;
it was all pure gold and good stones,
very precious and very dear;
the cover was very carefully attached.
He placed the nightingale inside
and then he had the casket sealed —
he carried it with him always.
This adventure was told,
it could not be concealed for long.
The Bretons made a *lai* about it
which men call *The Nightingale*.

The Art of Courtly Love
Andreas Capellanus

Andrew the Chaplain (Andreas Capellanus) was the chaplain of King Philip Augustus. His work *The Art of Courtly Love (De arte honeste amandi)* is addressed to his nephew, Walter, who sought his advice. It is not clear if this should be considered a serious work. In the first two books, Andreas instructs how to acquire and keep love, but in the third one he condemns it. Much of the work is organized in the form of dialogues between men and women of different social backgrounds and outlines the ways in which a man should set about seducing a woman.

The Art of Courtly Love is meant to depict the literary culture of Eleanor of Aquitaine's court at Poitiers between 1170 and 1174, where courtly love flourished. This is hardly surprising because it was her grandfather, Duke William of Aquitaine, who is credited as the first troubadour. Nevertheless, it was probably written about a decade later. The following excerpts are derived from the second book and show a mock court where ladies of high birth render decisions on cases of love. Among the judges are Queen Eleanor, her daughter Countess Marie of Champagne, and Ermengarde, Countess of Narbonne.

Source: *The Art of Courtly Love: Andreas Capellanus,* translated by John Jay Perry © 1990 Columbia University Press, pp. 167–169, 171, 175–177. Reprinted with the permission of the publisher.

A man who was greatly enamoured of a certain woman devoted his whole heart to the love of her. But when she saw that he was in love with her, she absolutely forbade him to love. When she discovered that he was just as much in love with her as ever, she said to him one day, "I know it is true that you have striven a very long time for my love, but you can never get it unless you are willing to make me a firm promise that you will always obey all my commands and that if you oppose them in any way you will be willing to lose my love completely." The man answered her, "My lady, God forbid that I should ever by so much in error as to oppose your commands in anything; so, since what you ask is very pleasing, I gladly assent to it." After he had promised this she immediately ordered him to make no more effort to gain her love and not to dare to speak a good word of her to others. This was a heavy blow to the lover, yet he bore it patiently. But one day when this lover and some other knights were with some ladies he heard his companions speaking very shamefully about his lady and saying things about her reputation that were neither right nor proper. He endured it for a while with an ill grace, but when he saw that they kept on disparaging the lady he burst out violently against them and began to accuse them of slander and to defend his lady's reputation. When all this came to her ears she said that he ought to lose her love completely because by praising her he had violated her commands.

This point the Countess of Champagne explained as follows in her decision. She said that the lady was too severe in her command, because she was not ashamed to silence him by an unfair sentence after he had wholly submitted himself to her will and after she had given him the hope of her love by binding him to her with a promise which no honorable woman can break without a reason. Nor did the aforesaid lover sin at all when he tried to deliver a well-deserved rebuke to those who were slandering his lady. For although he did make such a promise in order the more easily to obtain her love, it seems unfair of the woman to lay upon him the command that he should trouble himself no more with love for her.

Again. Another man, although he was enjoying the embraces of a most excellent love, asked her for permission to obtain the embraces of a different woman. Having received this he went away and refrained longer than usual from the solaces of the first lady. But after a month had elapsed he came back to the first one and said that he had never received any solaces from the other lady, nor had he wished to receive them, but he had merely wanted to test the constancy of his loved one. This woman refused him her love on the ground that he was unworthy, saying that for him to ask and receive such permission was reason enough for her to deprive him of her love. But the opinion of Queen Eleanor, who was consulted on the matter, seems to be just the opposite of this woman's. She said, "We know that it comes from the nature of love that those who are in love often falsely pretend that they desire new embraces, that they may the better test the faith and constancy of their co-lover. Therefore a woman sins against the nature of love itself if she keeps back her embraces from her lover on this account or forbids him her love, unless she has clear evidence that he has been unfaithful to her."

There were two men who were equal in birth and life and morals and everything else except that one happened to have more property than the other, so that many wondered which was preferable as a lover. From this case came the dictum of the Countess of Champagne, who said, "It would not be right for one to prefer a vulgar rich man to a noble and handsome poor one. Indeed a handsome poor man may well be preferred to a rich nobleman if both are seeking the love of a rich woman, since it is more worthy for a woman who is blessed with an abundance of property to accept a needy lover than one who has great wealth. Nothing should be more grievous to all good men than to see worth overshadowed by poverty or suffering from the lack of anything. It is right, therefore, for men to praise a wealthy woman who disregards money and seeks a needy lover whom she can help with her wealth, for nothing seems so praiseworthy in a lover of either sex as to relieve the necessities of the loved one so far as may be. But if the woman herself is in need, she is more ready to accept the rich lover; for if both lovers are oppressed by poverty there is little doubt that their love will be of short duration. Poverty brings a great feeling of shame to all honorable men and gives them many an anxious thought and is even a greater disturber of quiet sleep; so as a result it commonly puts love to flight...."

A certain lady had a proper enough lover, but was afterward, through no fault of her own, married to an honorable man, and she avoided her love and denied him his usual solaces. But Lady Ermengarde of Narbonne demonstrated the lady's bad character in these words: "The later contracting of a marital union does not properly exclude an early love except in cases where the woman gives up love entirely and is determined by no means to love any more."

A certain man asked the same lady to make clear where there was the greater affection — between lovers or between married people. The lady gave him a logical answer. She said: "We consider that marital affection and the true love of lovers are wholly different and arise from entirely different sources, and so the ambiguous nature of the word prevents the comparison of the things and we have to place them in different classes. Comparisons of more or less are not valid when things are grouped together under an ambiguous heading and the comparison is made in regard to that ambiguous term. It is no true comparison to say that a name is simpler than a body or that the outline of a speech is better arranged than the delivery."

The same man asked the same lady this question. A certain woman had been married, but was now separated from her husband by a divorce, and her former husband sought eagerly for her love. In this case the lady replied: "If any two people have been married and afterwards separate in any way, we consider love between them wholly wicked."...

A certain knight shamefully divulged the intimacies and the secrets of his love. All those who were serving in the camp of Love demanded that this offense should be most severely punished, lest if so serious a transgression went unavenged, the example might give occasion to others to do likewise. A court of ladies was therefore assembled in Gascony, and they decided unanimously that forever after he should be deprived of all hope of love and that in every court of ladies or of knights he should be an object of contempt and abuse to all. And if any woman should dare to violate this rule of the ladies, for example by giving him her love, she should be subject to the same punishment, and should henceforth be an enemy of all honest women.

Another decision very properly belongs with these. A certain knight asked for the love of a certain lady, and she absolutely refused to love him. The knight sent her some rather handsome presents, and these she accepted with eager face and greedy heart; she did not, however, grow any more yielding in the matter of love, but gave him a flat refusal. The knight complained that the woman, by accepting appropriate gifts, had given him a hope of love, which she was trying to take away from him without a cause. To those facts the Queen responded in this fashion. "Let a woman either decline gifts which are offered her with a view to love, or let her pay for them with her love, or let her suffer in patience being classed with the prostitutes."

The Queen was also asked which was preferable: the love of a young man or of one advanced in years. She answered this question with wonderful subtlety by saying, "We distinguish between a good and a better love by the man's knowledge and his character and his praiseworthy manners, not by his age. But as regards that natural instinct of passion, young men are usually more eager to gratify it with older women than with young ones of their own age; those who are older prefer to receive the embraces and kisses of young women rather than of the older ones. But on the other hand a woman whether young or somewhat older likes the embraces and solaces of young men better than those of older ones. The explanation of this fact seems to be a physiological one."

The Countess of Champagne was also asked what gifts it was proper for ladies to accept from their lovers. To the man who asked this the Countess replied, "A woman who loves may freely accept from her lover the following: a handkerchief, a fillet for the hair, a wreath of gold or silver, a breastpin, a mirror, a girdle, a purse, a tassel, a comb, sleeves, gloves, a ring, a compact, a picture, a wash basin, little dishes, trays, a flag as a souvenir, and, to speak in general terms, a woman may accept from her lover any little gift which may be useful for the care of the person or pleasing to look at or which may call the lover to her mind, if it is clear that in accepting the gift she is free from all avarice. But we wish all of Love's knights to be taught that if a woman receives a ring from her lover as a pledge of love she ought to put it on her left hand and on her little finger, and she should always keep the stone hidden on the inside of her hand; this is because the left hand is usually kept freer from dishonesty and shameful contacts, and a man's life and death are said to reside more in his little finger than in the others, and because all lovers are bound to keep their love secret. Likewise, if they correspond with each other by letter they should refrain from signing their own names. Furthermore, if the lovers should for any reason come before a court of ladies, the identity of the lovers should never be revealed to the judges, but the case should be presented anonymously. And they ought not to seal their letters to each other with their own seals unless they happen to have secret seals known only to themselves and their confidants. In this way their love will always be retained unimpaired."

The Romance of the Rose
Guillaume de Lorris (first half of the thirteenth century) and **Jean de Meun** (1240–1305)

This thirteenth-century allegory about love is a work actually written by two authors. The first part was written by Guillaume de Lorris between 1225 and 1230 and the second part by Jean de Meun between 1269 and 1278. The story starts when a young man falls asleep and dreams that he approaches a garden surrounded by a high wall. He falls in love with a rose and wishes to have it. Emotions and feelings associated with love are personified in characters such as Fair Welcome, Fear, and Rebuff. All the characters in the story either help the dreamer attain the rose or thwart him. The ensuing excerpt comes from the section entitled "Advice of a Friend," where the young man is advised to go on the offensive.

Source: *The Romance of the Rose: Guillaume de Lorris and Jean de Meun*, translated and edited by Frances Horgan (Oxford, New York: Oxford University Press, 1994), pp. 116–118. Reprinted by permission of Oxford University Press.

But they should not be in the habit of telling the gatekeepers immediately that they want to make friends with them in order to take the flower from the rose-bush: they should say instead that their love is loyal and true and their thoughts pure and sincere. You may be sure that they can all be conquered, there is no doubt about that; provided he who entreats them does

so properly, he will never be rejected, and no one should be refused. But if
you take my advice, you will not take the trouble to plead with them unless
you achieve your goal, for perhaps if they were not vanquished they might
boast about having been entreated, but they will never boast if they are part-
ners in the deed.

And they are all of such a kind, however haughty their expression, that
if they were not first entreated they would certainly entreat themselves and
give themselves for nothing to anyone who did not treat them harshly. But
those who make hasty speeches and give foolish and extravagant presents
make them so very proud that they increase the price of their roses; while
they expect in this way to advance their suit, they actually do serious harm,
since they could have had everything for nothing if they had never made
any entreaty, provided that everyone did the same and no earlier entreaty
had been made. And if they wanted to sell their services, they could get a
very good price, provided they all agreed that none would ever address the
gatekeepers or give themselves for nothing but that instead, the better to sub-
due them, they would leave their roses to wither. But no man who sold his
body could please me, nor should he ever please me, at least not if he did
so for such a purpose. Do not delay on that account: make your entreaties
and set traps to catch your prey, for you could delay so long that a dozen,
or two or three or four, in fact fifty-two dozens could quickly attack within
fifty-two weeks. The gatekeepers would soon have turned elsewhere if you
had waited too long, and it would be difficult for you to arrive in time
because of your long delay. I do not recommend that any man wait for a
woman to ask for his love, for anyone who waits for a woman to ask him
has too much confidence in his beauty. And anyone who wishes to begin
and to advance his suit quickly should not be afraid that his lady might
strike him, however proud and haughty she may be, or that his ship will not
come to port, provided he behave properly. This, my friend, is how you will
act when you come to the gatekeepers. But if you see that they are angry, do
not make your request: spy out when they are happy, and do not entreat
them when they are sad, unless their sadness is born of mad Jealousy, who
might have beaten them for your sake and caused them to be assaulted by
anger.

And if you manage to take them on one side in so convenient a place
that you have no fear of intruders, and if Fair Welcome, now captured for
your sake, has escaped, then when Fair Welcome has looked as kindly on
you as he can (and he knows very well how to welcome the fair), you must
pluck the rose, even if you see Rebuff himself beginning to abuse you, or
Shame and Fear grumbling at you. They are only pretending to be angry
and putting up a weak defence, since in defending themselves they admit

defeat, as it will seem to you then. Even if you see Fear tremble, Shame blush, and Rebuff shudder, or all three groan and lament, do not give a fig for that but pluck the rose by force and show that you are a man, when the place and time and season are right, for nothing could please them so well as that force, applied by one who understands it. For many people are accustomed to behave so strangely that they want to be forced to give something that they dare not give freely, and pretend that it has been stolen from them when they have allowed and wished it to be taken. And so you may be sure that they would be sad to escape by this defence; however great the joy they feigned, I am afraid that they would be so angry that they would hate you for it, however much they might have grumbled.

But if they speak clearly and you feel that they are really angry and defending themselves vigorously, you must not stretch out your hand but in all cases yield yourself captive and beg for mercy. Then wait until these three gatekeepers who so torture and torment you have gone away and Fair Welcome alone remains, who will vouchsafe you everything. This is how you should behave towards them, as a worthy, valiant, and sensible man.

The Divine Comedy
Dante Alighieri

Dante Alighieri (1265–1321) was a poet born in Florence to a lower aristocratic family. In his first work, *Vita Nuova*, he wrote a series of mystical lyrics dedicated to his beloved Beatrice, whom he loved from afar. His masterpiece is *The Divine Comedy*, which tells of Dante's journey through hell, purgatory, and heaven. He is guided on this journey by a number of different people: The ancient writer Virgil takes him through hell and purgatory, Beatrice takes him through heaven, and St. Bernard leads him into God's presence.

In the book about hell, Dante writes about various historical figures and about his contemporaries. In the following excerpt from Canto 5, Dante relates the story of Francesca da Rimini and Paolo Malatesta. Francesca had been married to Paolo's brother Gianciotta, but she was actually in love with Paolo. When Gianciotta learns of their adultery, he kills them both. Because of their sin, Francesca and Paolo are condemned to hell where those guilty of carnal sins are forever blown around in a whirlwind.

Source: *Dante: The Divine Comedy, Inferno — 2 Vol.*, translated by Charles S. Singleton, © 1970 Princeton University Press, 1998 renewed PUP, pp. 47, 49, 51, 53, 55 (from Vol. 1). Reprinted by permission of Princeton University Press.

Thus I descended from the first circle into the second, which girds less space, and so much greater woe that it goads to wailing. There stands Minos, horrible and snarling: upon the entrance he examines their offenses, and judges and dispatches them according as he entwines. I mean that when the ill-begotten soul comes before him, it confesses all; and that discerner of sins sees which shall be its place in Hell, then girds himself with his tail as many times as the grades he wills that it be sent down. Always before him stands a crowd of them; they go, each in his turn, to the judgment; they tell, and hear, and then are hurled below.

"O you who come to the abode of pain," said Minos to me, when he saw me, pausing in the act of that great office, "beware how you enter and in whom you trust; let not the breadth of the entrance deceive you!" And my leader to him, "Why do you too cry out? Do not hinder his fated going: thus it is willed there where that can be down which is willed; and ask no more."

Now the doleful notes begin to reach me; now I am come where much wailing smites me. I came into a place mute of all light, which bellows like the sea in tempest when it is assailed by warring winds. The hellish hurricane, never resting, sweeps along the spirits with its rapine; whirling and smiting, it torments them. When they arrive before the ruin, there the shrieks, the moans, the lamentations; there they curse the divine power. I learned that to such torment are condemned the carnal sinners, who subject reason to desire.

And as their wings bear the starlings along in the cold season, in wide, dense flocks, so does that blast the sinful spirits; hither, thither, downward, upward, it drives them. No hope of less pain, not to say of rest, ever comforts them. And as the cranes go chanting their lays, making a long line of themselves in the air, so I saw shades come, uttering wails, borne by that strife; wherefore I said, "Master, who are these people that are so lashed by the black air?"

"The first of these of whom you wish to know," he said to me then, "was empress of many tongues. She was so given to lechery that she made lust licit in her law, to take away the blame she had incurred. She is Semiramis, of whom we read that she succeeded Ninus and had been his wife: she held the land the Sultan rules. The next is she who slew herself for love and broke faith to the ashes of Sichaeus; next is wanton Cleopatra. See Helen, for whom so many years of ill revolved; and see the great Achilles, who fought at the last with love. See Paris, Tristan," and more than a thousand shades whom love had parted from our life he showed me, pointing them out and naming them.

When I heard my teacher name the ladies and the knights of old, pity overcame me and I was as one bewildered. "Poet," I began, "willingly would I speak with those two that go together and seem to be so light upon the wind."

And he to me, "You shall see when they are nearer to us; and do you entreat them then by that love which leads them, and they will come."

As soon as the wind bends them to us, I raised my voice, "O wearied souls! come speak with us, if Another forbid it not."

As doves called by desire, with wings raised and steady, come through the air, borne by their will to their sweet nest, so did these issue from the troop where Dido is, coming to us through the malignant air, such force had my compassionate cry.

"O living creature, gracious and benign, that go through the black air visiting us who stained the world with blood, if the King of the universe were friendly to us, we would pray Him for your peace, since you have pity on our perverse ill. Of that which it pleases you to hear and to speak, we will hear and speak with you, while the wind, as now, is silent for us.

"The city where I was born lies on that shore where the Po descends to be at peace with its followers. Love, which is quickly kindled in a gentle heart, seized this one for the fair form that was taken from me — and the way of it afflicts me still. Love, which absolves no loved one from loving, seized me so strongly with delight in him, that, as you see, it does not leave me even now. Love brought us to one death. Caina awaits him who quenched our life."

These words were borne to us from them. And when I heard those afflicted souls I bowed my head and held it bowed until the poet said to me, "What are you thinking of?"

When I answered, I began, "Alas! How many sweet thoughts, what great desire, brought them to the woeful pass!"

Then I turned again to them, and I began, "Francesca, your torments make me weep for grief and pity; but tell me, in the time of the sweet sighs, by what and how did Love grant you to know the dubious desires?"

And she to me, "There is no greater sorrow than to recall, in wretchedness, the happy time; and this your teacher knows. But if you have such great desire to know the first root of our love, I will tell as one who weeps and tells. One day, for pastime, we read of Lancelot, how love constrained him; we were alone, suspecting nothing. Several times that reading urged our eyes to meet and took the color from our faces, but one moment alone it was that overcame us. When we read how the longed-for smile was kissed by so great a lover, this one, who never shall be parted from me, kissed my mouth all trembling. A Gallehault was the book and he who wrote it; that day we read no farther in it."

While the one spirit said this, the other wept, so that for pity I swooned, as if in death, and fell as a dead body falls.

Same-Sex Love Poetry

Poems expressing deep affection and love between men were prevalent throughout the Middle Ages. Usually these poems were written by churchmen, such as abbots, bishops, and monks, and reflected their communal life together with other males and the resulting absence of heterosexual love interests. Other such poems were written by teachers and students, such as the first poem by Paulinus to his teacher Ausonius, revealing the close bonds that form between teacher and student. Many of these poems contain motifs from classical literature, although the lesbian letter is based on the poems found in the Song of Solomon.

Many people today would label these writers as homosexual or gay. However, such assumptions are not necessarily accurate. Medieval people did not think of sexuality in such absolute categories. Many of these individuals may have had strong feelings toward others of the same gender, and they used poetry as a means to communicate these feelings. These writers did not always act upon them sexually nor did they necessarily desire to.

Source: *Medieval Latin Poems of Male Love and Friendship,* translated by Thomas Stehling. © 1984 by Thomas Stehling, pp. 5, 7, 9, 69, 95, 97, 99, 101, 103. Reproduced by permission of Routledge/Taylor & Francis Books, Inc.

"The End of a Letter to Ausonius"
(Paulinus of Nola, c. 353–431)

You and me: for all time which is given
And destined to mortal men,
For as long as I am held in this confining, limping body,
No matter how far I am separated from you in the world,
You will be neither distant from me nor far from my eyes:
I will hold you, intermingled in my very sinews.
I will see you in my heart and with a loving spirit embrace you;
You will be with me everywhere.
And when released from this bodily prison
I fly from earth
To the spot in heaven where our universal Father places me,
There too I will keep you in my spirit;
Nor will the end which frees me from my body
Release me from your love.
For the mind, once it has survived loss of limbs,
Continues to grow out of its heavenly root,
And therefore must keep both its understanding and affections
Along with its life.
And just as it experiences no death, it will experience no loss of memory
But remain forever alive, forever mindful.
Farewell noble master.

"Five Epigrams on an Adulterer and a Voluptuary"
(Ennodius, c. 473–521)

All generations are preserved in Egyptian books:
Laurence never played the slave before Nero
And conquering with his body, he did not fear strong flames.
Your face is masculine, your gestures feminine, but your thighs are both:
You resolve an opposition in nature by negating the difference.
You are a rabbit and trample the neck of a great lion.
Shave off your misleading beard, little tavern wife
Lest manly lips reduce your earnings.
Look at this monster created by promiscuous rule —
Of common gender, or rather, of all genders.
There is a constant deception at play in his double sex:
He's a woman when passive, but when active in shameful deeds, he's a man.

"To a Hermaphrodite Girl"
(Luxorius, early sixth century)

Double-membered monster of the female sex
Whom unnatural desire makes a man,
With your raging cunt why don't you like to be fucked?
Why does this impossible desire make a fool out of you?
The cunt, with which you should submit and act, you don't use.
When you yield the part which proves
You are a woman, then you may be a girl.

"To a Boy of Angers"
(Hilary the Englishman, twelfth century)

Beautiful boy, unparalleled boy,
I pray look kindly
At this letter sent by your suitor,
See, read, and follow what you have read.

I have thrown myself at your knees,
My own knee bent, my hands joined;
As one of your suitors
I use both tears and prayers.

Face to face with you, I am afraid to speak:
Speech fails me and I am seized with silence.
But now at last in a letter I acknowledge my sickness,
And since I acknowledge it, I deserve health.

Miserable enough, I could almost endure it
As long as I wanted to hide my love.
When I could conceal it no longer,
I finally held up my hands in defeat.

Sick, I demand a doctor,
Stretching out my hands like a beggar.
You alone have the only medicine;
Therefore, save me, your cleric.

Long held in this grim prison,
I found no one who wished to help me.
Since I cannot be freed with bribery,
I lead a life worse than death.

O my sadness, my ruin,
How I wish you wanted money!
But it is better that you have decided
Such bargaining is vice.

Nonetheless, boy, it is certainly stupid
To show such want of feeling,
...
Who acts out of modesty to handsome men.

The heavy theme of chastity
Condemned beautiful Hippolytus;
And Joseph almost came to his death
When he opposed the passion of a queen.

Later Graffiti in a Ninth-Century Manuscript
(another unknown, twelfth or thirteenth century)

Now Chartres and Paris make themselves filthy continually
With Sodom's vice, and in Sens Paris becomes Io.
The men of Orleans are the best, if you like
The customs of men who sleep with boys.
Enemy of nature, neglecting procreation
You spill yourself into forbidden Trojan loins.
The greedy woman provides a vessel in three places, and
        guards each well
Thus the sin of Sodom is restored, a sin many can imitate
Since it needs only beautiful boys of tender years.
Nothing is surer than this: Venus would be
Without honey if she were without Ganymede.

Lesbian Love Letter from a German Manuscript
(author unknown, twelfth or thirteenth century)

To C.
To C., sweeter than honey and honeycomb,
B. sends all that love can send to love.
        O unique and special one,
Why do you delay so long in a far-off land?

Why do you want me to die, your one and only
Who loves you, as you yourself know, with her soul and body,
And who, like a hungry little bird,
Sighs for you at every hour and every moment?
For ever since I was cut off from your sweetest presence,
I have not wanted to see or hear anyone else;
Just as a turtledove after it has lost its husband
Remains forever sitting on its barren twig,
So I lament without end
Until I once more enjoy your faithfulness.
I look around and do not find my lover,
Nor anyone to console me with a word.
While I happily
Turn over in my mind the sweetness
Of your conversation and your appearance,
I am oppressed with terrible pain,
For I find nothing like them now.
What should I compare to your love?
It is sweeter than honey and honeycomb.
And compared to it the luster of gold and silver
      becomes worthless.
What else? In you are all sweetness and value.
Thus my spirit always languishes in your absence.
You have none of the poison of treachery;
You are sweeter than milk and honey.
You are singled out from among thousands;
I love you more than all others,
You alone my love and desire,
You the sweet refreshment of my soul.
There is no pleasure for me
Without you.
Everything which was pleasant with you
Is wearisome and dreary without you.
Therefore, I wish to say in all truth
That if I could pay my life for you — I would not hesitate
Because you are the only woman I have chosen after my heart.
Therefore, I always pray to God
That bitter death not come to me
Before I enjoy the sight of you, so long desired and so
      dear to me.
Farewell.
Have all my faith and love;
Accept what I have written and sent you
And my still faithful spirit.

17

Riddles, Songs and Stories

Riddles

The following riddles are taken from the Exeter Book, a manuscript dating back to the middle of the tenth century containing poems (both secular and religious) and riddles. The book was given to Exeter Cathedral by its first bishop, Leofric (died 1072). Although their answers are quite mundane, the riddles themselves are fraught with sexual double meanings.

Source: *The Earliest English Poems*, translated by Michael Alexander (Harmondsworth, Middlesex, England: Penguin, 1966), ©Michael Alexander 1966, 1977, 1991, pp. 130, 138. Reprinted by permission of Penguin Books, Ltd.

While my ghost lives I go on feet,
rend the ground, green leas.

When breath is gone I bind the hands
of swart Welsh; worthier men, too.

I may be a bottle: bold warrior
swigs from my belly.
    Or a bride may set
proudly her foot on me.
    Or, far from her Wales,
a dark-headed girl grabs and squeezes me,
silly with drink, and in the dark night
wets me with water, or warms me up
before the fire. Fetched between breasts
by her hot hand, while she heaves about
I must stroke her swart part.
    Say my name:
who living live off the land's wealth
and, when dead, drudge for men.

Answer: oxhide

I'm the world's wonder, for I make women happy
— a boon to the neighbourhood, a bane to no one,
though I may perhaps prick the one who picks me.
I am set well up, stand in a bed,
have a roughish root. Rarely (though it happens)
a churl's daughter more daring than the rest
— and lovelier! — lays hold of me,
rushes my red top, wrenches at my head,
and lays me in the larder.
She learns soon enough,
the curly-haired creature who clamps me so,
of my meeting with her: moist is her eye!

Answer: onion

Swings by his thigh a thing most magical!
Below the belt, beneath the folds
of his clothes it hangs, a hole in its front end,
stiff-set & stout, but swivels about.
Levelling the head of this hanging instrument,
its wielder hoists his hem above the knee;
it is his will to fill a well-known hole
that it fits fully when at full length.
He has often filled it before. Now he fills it again.

Answer: key

Carmina Burana
Author or authors unknown

The poems below are from a collection of poems and songs contained in a manuscript called the *Codex Buranus* dating to 1230. It contains about 230 poems — satires, drinking songs, love songs, and laments — most of which were written in Latin. It was discovered in 1803 in Benediktbeuern, a Bavarian monastery, and as a result became known as the *Carmina Burana* (*songs of Beuren*).

Source: *Love Lyrics from the Carmina Burana*, translated and edited by P.G. Walsh. Copyright © 1993 University of North Carolina Press, pp. 44, 86–87, 129–130. Used by permission of the publisher.

"Grates ago Veneri" ("I Give Thanks to Venus")

I give thanks to Venus, for through the power of her favoring smile she has bestowed on me the delightful, much desired victory over my maiden.
My service had been long, yet I still could not enjoy these wages; but now I realize that happiness is mine, that Venus' countenance shines bright.
The maiden had allowed me the enjoyment of beholding, conversing, touching, kissing; but absent from my love was the final and best stage. If I do not attain it, the other rewards for the rest are merely fuel for my madness.

I hasten toward the goal, but the girl entreats me with soft tears; the dear maiden hesitates to loosen the bars of her virginity. As she weeps I drink her tears most sweet, and thus intensify my drunkenness and imbibe a deeper draught of love-heat.

Her kisses tear-smeared taste sweeter, and entice my heart more strongly with their innermost delights. So I am enmeshed more completely, and a keener onset of fire inflames me afresh. But Coronis' grief bursts out in welling sobs and does not soften at my entreaties.

I heap prayers on prayers, kisses on kisses; she pours out tears on tears, rebukes on altercations. She fixes me with an eye now grudging, now almost begging, for at one moment she fights and disputes, at another she entreats. As I seek to soothe her with a prayer, she becomes deafer to my supplication.

With overboldness I use force. She rampages with her sharp nails, tears my hair, forcefully repels my violence. She coils herself and entwines her knees to prevent the door of her maidenhead from being unbarred.

But at last my campaign makes progress; I win a triumph for my battle plan. I tighten by embraces our entwined bodies, I pin her arms, I implant hard kisses. In this way Venus' palace is unbarred.

Both gained satisfaction; my lover grew gentler and reproached me less, bestowing honeyed kisses,
and half-smiling with flickering and half-closed eyes, as though she was drugged beneath the weight of troubled sighs.

"Servit aure spiritus" ("The Wind's Breath Is Harsh")

The wind's breath is harsh, and the foliage of the trees is totally disappearing under the violence of the cold. The songs in the groves are silent. Now love between cattle grows sluggish, for it is in heat only in spring. But I am always in love, and I refuse to follow the new changes of the seasons as beasts are wont to do.

Refrain: How sweet are the wages and blessed joys bestowed by my lovely Flora!

I do not complain of my long service, for I am recompensed with notable payment. I rejoice in my happy reward. As Flora greets me with eyebrows that speak volumes, I cannot take in the joy, for my mind cannot contain it, and I glory in the toil.

Refrain.

It is no harsh lot that attends me. As we sport in our sequestered room, Venus is well-disposed and favorable. The couch hugs my naked Flora. Her youthful flesh gleams white, her maiden's bosom is aglow, her breasts rise slightly with modest swelling.

Refrain.

I transcend mere humanity and boast that I am raised to the number of the gods as I fondle her soft bosom, and as my blessed hand is wandering course roams over the region of her breasts, and with lighter touch reaches down to her belly.

Refrain.

From her small, soft bosom her delicate flanks harmoniously extend. Her unblemished flesh does not irritate the gentle touch. Beneath her girdle her slender form makes her navel project just slightly, with her small belly's modest swelling.

Refrain.

Her lower parts, barely sprouting with a maiden's soft hair, fire my desire with their alluring softness. Her soft limbs with their restrained covering of flesh fell smooth as they conceal the line of her sinews, and shine with their whiteness.

Refrain.

If Jupiter happened to lay eyes on her, I fear that he would become as passionate as I, and return to his deceits; for he would either rain down Danae's gold and soften her with the sweet shower, or masquerade as Europa's bull, or turn white once more as Leda's swan.

Refrain.

"Cur suspectum me tenet domina?" ("Why Does My Mistress Hold Me in Suspicion?")

Why does my mistress hold me in suspicion? Why do her eyes frown so upon me? I call heaven and the deities of heaven to witness: I have no knowledge of the sins which she fears!

Refrain. My lady does me wrong!

The sky will whiten with harvests, the lower air will bring forth elms and attendant vines, the sea will provide huntsmen with wild beasts, before I associate with the citizens of Sodom!

Refrain.

Even if a king made me lavish promises and grinding poverty oppressed me, I am not the kind of man to let utility influence me more then propriety.

Refrain.

I am content with natural love and have learned to take the active, not the passive role. I prefer to live pure and poor rather than unchaste and wealthy.

Refrain.

Britain, our native land, was always unblemished by this notoriety. I pray that I may die before my native land should through me embark on such foulness!

Refrain.

Fabliaux

Fabliaux were short, satirical stories written in the French vernacular. They were written anonymously and date from the end of the twelfth century to the early fourteenth century. They were popular among townspeople and have a distinct anti-courtly, anti-aristocratic feel. They contained vulgar language and humor and mocked traditional morality and values. The characters in the fabliaux fell into certain stereotypes — the lecherous churchman, the adulterous wife, and the cuckolded husband.

Source: *Cuckolds, Clerics, and Countrymen: Medieval French Fabliaux*, translated by John DuVal and Raymond Eichmann (Fayetteville: University of Arkansas Press, 1982), pp. 45–46. Reprinted with the permission of Pegasus Press.

"The Priest Who Peeked"

If you will kindly listen well
To my next tale, I'd like to tell
A short and courtly fabliau
As Guerin has it. Long ago
There lived a peasant who had wed
A maiden courteous, well bred,
Wise, beautiful, of goodly birth.
He cherished her for all his worth
And did his best to keep her pleased.
The lady loved the parish priest,
Who was her only heart's desire.
The priest himself was so afire
With love for her that he decided
To tell his love and not to hide it.
So off he started, running hard.
As he came running through their yard,
The peasant and his wife were sitting
Together at the table eating.
   The priest neither called their
   name nor knocked.
He tried the door. The door was locked
And bolted tight. He looked around
And up and down until he found
A hole to spy through and was able
To see the peasant at the table,
Eating and drinking as she served.
The priest indignantly observed
The way the peasant led his life,
Taking no pleasure of his wife.
And when he'd had enough of spying,
He pounded at the doorway, crying,
"Hey there, good people! You inside!
What are you doing?" The man replied,
"Faith, Sir, we're eating. Why not come
In here to join us and have some?"
—"Eating? What a lie! I'm looking
Straight through this hole at you.
 You're fucking."
—"Hush!" said the peasant, "Believe
me,

We're eating, Sir, as you can see."
—"If you are," said the priest, "I'll eat
 my hat.
You're fucking, Sir. I can see that!
Don't try to talk me out of it.
Why not let me go in and sit?
You stand out here and do the spying,
And let me know if I've been lying
About the sight I'm looking at."

The peasant leapt from where he sat,
Unlocked the door and hurried out.
The priest came in, turned about,
Shut and latched and bolted the door.
However hard the peasant bore
The sight of it, the parson sped
To the peasant's wife. He caught her
 head,
Tripped her up and laid her down.
Up to her chest he pulled her gown
And did of all good deeds the one
That women everywhere want done.
He bumped and battered with such
 force
The peasant's wife had no recourse
But let him get what he was seeking.
And there the other man was, peeking
At the little hole, through which he
 spied
His lovely wife's exposed backside
And the priest, riding on top of her.
"May God Almighty help you, Sire,"
The peasant called, "Is this a joke?"
The parson turned his head and spoke:
"No, I'm not joking. What's the matter?
Don't you see: I have your platter.
I'm eating supper at your table."
"Lord, this is like a dream or fable.
If I weren't hearing it from you,
I never would believe it true

That you aren't fucking with my wife."
"I'm not, Sir! Hush! As God's my life,
That's what I thought I saw you do."
The peasant said, "I guess that's true."
    That's how the peasant got
    confused,
Bewitched, befuddled, and confused,

By the priest and by his own weak brain
And didn't even feel the pain.
Because of the door, it still is said,
"Many a fool by God is fed."
Here ends the fabliau of the priest.
The End: Amen.

The Canterbury Tales *by Geoffrey Chaucer*

Chaucer (1343–1400) is regarded as the greatest poet in England before Shakespeare. Born to a middle class family, he was in the royal service of the Countess of Ulster and later served in the army. After he married he was one of the king's yeomen.

Although he wrote many poems, he is most famous for the *Canterbury Tales*, a group of stories told by pilgrims traveling to Canterbury to visit the shrine of Thomas Becket. Chaucer's intent was for each pilgrim to tell two stories on the way to Canterbury and two stories coming back, but he was never able to finish this enormous project. The following excerpt comes from the Prologue of the Wife of Bath, one of the more colorful characters. In it she relates her opinions on sexuality and on husbands, with which she had plenty of experience, having been married five times.

Source: *The Canterbury Tales*, translated by Nevill Coghill (Harmondsworth, Middlesex, England: Penguin Classics, 1977). © 1951 by Nevill Coghill, © the Estate of Nevill Coghill 1958, 1960, 1975, 1977, pp. 261–264, 275, 279–280. Reproduced by permission of Penguin Books, Ltd.

The Wife of Bath's Prologue

'Tell me to what conclusion or
    in aid
Of what were generative organs made?
And for what profit were those creatures wrought?
Trust me, they cannot have been made
    for naught.
Gloze as you will and plead the explanation
That they were only made for the purgation
Of urine, little things of no avail
Except to know a female from a male,
And nothing else. Did somebody say
    no?
Experience knows well it isn't so.

The learned may rebuke me, or be loth
To think it so, but they were made for
    both,
That is to say both use and pleasure in
Engendering, except in case of sin.
Why else the proverb written down
    and set
In books: "A man must yield his wife
    her debt"?
What means of paying her can he
    invent
Unless he use his silly instrument?
It follows they were fashioned at creation
Both to purge urine and for propagation.

'But I'm not saying everyone is
    bound
Who has such harness as you heard
    me expound
To go and use it breeding; that would
    be
To show too much care for chastity.
Christ was a virgin, fashioned as a
    man,
And many of his saints since time began
Were ever perfect in their chastity.
I'll have no quarrel with virginity.
Let them be pure wheat loaves of
    maidenhead
And let us wives be known for barley-
    bread;
Yet Mark can tell that barley-bread
    sufficed
To freshen many at the hand of Christ.
In that estate to which God sum-
    moned me
I'll persevere; I'm not pernickety.
In wifehood I will use my instrument
As freely as my Maker me it sent.
If I turn difficult, God give me sorrow!
My husband, he shall have it eve and
    morrow
Whenever he likes to come and pay
    his debt,
I won't prevent him! I'll have a hus-
    band yet
Who shall be both my debtor and my
    slave
And bear his tribulation to the grave
Upon his flesh, as long as I'm his wife.
For mine shall be the power all his life
Over his proper body, and not he,
Thus the Apostle Paul has told it me,
And bade our husbands they should
    love us well;
There's a command on which I like to
    dwell...'

        'Now, gentlemen, I'll on and
            tell my tale
And as I hope to drink good wine and
    ale
I'll tell the truth. Those husbands that
    I had,

Three of them were good and two
    were bad.
The three that I call "good" were rich
    and old.
They could indeed with difficulty hold
The articles that bound them all to me;
(No doubt you understand my simile).
So help me God, I have to laugh out-
    right
Remembering how I made them work
    at night!
And faith I set no store by it; no plea-
    sure
It was to me. They'd given me their
    treasure,
And so I had no need of diligence
Winning their love, or showing rever-
    ence.
They loved me well enough, so, heav-
    ens above,
Why should I make a dainty of their
    love?
        'A knowing woman's work is
            never done
To get a lover if she hasn't one,
But as I had them eating from my hand
And as they'd yielded me their gold
    and land,
Why then take trouble to provide
    them pleasure
Unless to profit and amuse my leisure?
I set them so to work, I'm bound to
    say;
Many a night they sang, "Alack the
    day!"
Never for them the flitch of bacon
    though
That some have won in Essex at Dun-
    mow!
I managed them so well by my tech-
    nique
Each was delighted to go out and seek
And buy some pretty thing for me to
    wear,
Happy if I as much as spoke them fair.
God knows how spitefully I used to
    scold them...
        'What shall I say? Before the
            month was gone

This gay young student, my delightful
John,
Had married me in solemn festival.
I handed him the money, lands and all
That ever had been given me before;
This I repented later, more and more.
None of my pleasures would he let me
seek.
By God, he smote me once upon the
cheek
Because I tore a page out of his book,
And that's the reason why I'm deaf.
But look,
Stubborn I was, just like a lioness;
As to my tongue, a very wrangleress....
    '...He started up and smote
me on the head,
And down I fell upon the floor for
dead.'
    'And when he saw how
motionless I lay
He was aghast and would have fled
away,
But in the end I started to come to.
"O have you murdered me, you rob-
ber, you,
To get my land?" I said. "Was that the
game?
Before I'm dead I'll kiss you all the
same."
'He came up close and kneeling gently
down
He said, "My love, my dearest Alison,
So help me God, I never again will hit
You, love; and if I did, you asked for it.

Forgive me!" But for all he was so
meek,
I up at once and smote him on the
cheek
And said, "Take that to level up the
score!
Now let me die, I can't speak any
more."
'We had a mort of trouble and heavy
weather
But in the end we made it up together.
He gave the bridle over to my hand,
Gave me the government of house and
land,
Of tongue and fist, indeed of all he'd
got.
I made him burn that book upon the
spot.
And when I'd mastered him, and out
of deadlock
Secured myself the sovereignty in
wedlock,
And when he said, "My own and
truest wife,
Do as you please for all the rest of life,
But guard your honour and my good
estate,"
From that day forward there was no
debate.
So help me God I was as kind to him
As any wife from Denmark to the rim
Of India, and as true. And he to me.
And I pray God that sits in majesty
To bless his soul and fill it with glory.

18

Advice Manuals

Handbook for William
Dhuoda (mid-ninth century)

This manual was written by a Frankish noblewoman in the middle of the ninth century, and it is the only known book authored by a woman during the Carolingian period. It contains advice for her son William and addresses family relations, social order, and religious and military obligations for this young boy who will in time grow to become a Frankish nobleman. Dhuoda lived during turbulent times when Charlemagne's grandsons were warring. Unfortunately, William died a few years after the handbook was completed while trying to avenge his father's death at the hands of Charles the Bald.

In this excerpt, Dhuoda advises William to guard against fornication.

Source: Reprinted from *Handbook for William: A Carolingian Woman's Counsel for Her Son* by Dhuoda, translated and with an introduction by Carol Neel, by permission of the University of Nebraska Press. Copyright ©1991 by the University of Nebraska Press.

If, because of the persuasion of the devil, fornication or some other spur of the flesh should drive your heart to frenzy, set chastity against it, and remember the continence of the blessed patriarch Joseph, and of Daniel,[1] and of those others who faithfully maintained purity in spirit and body in respect to their lords and their neighbors. They were therefore found worthy to be saved and honored, gathered up by the Lord full of praise among the number of his saints. For as the Apostle says, *fornicators and adulterers God will judge.*[2] And the Psalmist says, for behold they who fornicate away from thee shall perish.[3] And the Apostle says likewise, *Every sin that man doth, is without the body; but he that committeth fornication, sinneth against his own body,*[4] and other comments of this sort.

Therefore, my son, flee fornication and keep your mind away from any

1. Cf. Gen. 39:7-20, Dan. 13:45-64.
2. Heb. 13:4.
3. Cf. Ps. 72:27.
4. 1 Cor. 6:18.

prostitute. It is written, *Go not after thy lusts, but turn away from thy own will.*[5] Do not *give to thy soul* to fly away after her evil desires.[6] Surely, if you attend to one or another of these ills and if you consent to them, they will make you fall onto the sword and into the hands of your enemies. They will say with the Prophet, *Bow down, that we may go over you.*[7] May this not happen to you. But if those evils come and sting your mind through an angel of Satan sent against you,[8] fight them, pray, and say with the Psalmist, *Deliver not up to the beasts* of the earth my soul, I beseech you, and forget not the soul of thy poor servant;[9] *give me not the haughtiness of my eyes;*[10] *let not the lusts of the flesh take hold of me, and give me not over to a shameless and foolish mind.*[11]

The haughtiness of my eyes has, I think, not only an outer, corporeal sense but also an inner sense. For if it did not have inner meaning, this saying would be empty. *I have made a covenant with my eyes, that I would not so much as think upon a virgin,*[12] and many similar sayings in many places. You will find consolation in such great accounts so that you may, in petitioning God, escape the thrill of such embraces and the temptation of such turmoil. And although it is in the head that the eyes of the flesh are turned to desire, the struggle against such evils is fought within. For it is written of eyes turning in passionate desire that they perform their wrongful outrages carnally. *For death is coming up through our windows,*[13] and again, *whosoever shall look on a woman to lust after her*[14] does so carnally.

As for those who adhere to continence and who crush beneath their heels the desire of the flesh, you find it written, *The light of the body is thy eye. And if thy eye be single, thy whole body shall be lightsome.*[15] He who said this, *Turn away my eyes that they may not behold vanity,*[16] and many things like it, wished that chastity be inviolable. For as learned men say, "chastity is the angelic life," and it makes whoever participates in it a citizen of heaven. "O," someone says, "how short, short indeed is that moment of fornication by which future life is lost! And how great is the strength and the enduring splendor of chastity, which makes a mortal man like a fellow citizen of the angels."

5. Ecclus. 18:30.
6. Ecclesiastes 18:31.
7. Isa. 51:23.
8. Cf. 2 Cor. 12:7.
9. Ps. 73:19.
10. Ecclus 23:5.
11. Ecclus 23:10.
12. Job 31:1.
13. Jer. 9:21.
14. Matt. 5:28.
15. Matt. 6:22.
16. Ps. 118:37.

For learned authors do not refuse sacred marriage to the union of the flesh, but they try to root out from among us libidinous and wrongful fornication. For Enoch was chaste, and so were Noah, Abraham, Isaac, Jacob, Joseph, and Moses, and all the others who struggled to keep their hearts pure in Christ in the union of marriage. And what more shall I say?

So my son, whether you keep your body in virginity, a resplendent gift, or in the chastity of the union of marriage, you will be free from the origin of this sin. Your mind will be *secure...like a continual feast,*[17] and will rest throughout all you do in all the eight beatitudes. And there will be fulfilled in you in the company of other good men, as it is written, the worthy praise offered for many: take courage, *blessed are the clean of heart, for they shall see God.*[18]

Strategikon
Kekaumenos (early eleventh century)

Kekaumenos was a member of a Byzantine provincial aristocracy. He wrote his *Strategikon*, an advice manual for his sons, around 1078. In this work, Kekaumenos tried to sum up all the wisdom from his life's experiences. He gave advice on morals and manners, the running of a household, money management, and career decisions. The following excerpt instructs his sons to be careful with friends, but it also shows his skepticism on the trustworthiness of women.

Source: *Byzantium: Church, Society, and Civilization Seen Through Contemporary Eyes,* compiled by Deno John Geanakoplos (Chicago: University of Chicago Press, 1986), © 1984 by the University of Chicago Press, pp. 236–237. Reprinted with permission.

If you have a friend living in another place and he passes through the town in which you live, do not install him in your house, but let him go elsewhere. Send him what he needs and he will receive you more favorably. For in your house, hear how many problems you will have: One is that your wife, your daughters, and your daughters-in-law will not be able to come forth from their chambers and therefore will not properly take care of your house. If it is necessary, however, that they appear, your friend will crane his neck to inspect them. In your presence he will pretend merely to acknowledge them; but if he is alone with them, he will note with curiosity how they walk and turn, and their girdle and glance and, in a word, he will study them from head to foot, in order later to imitate them to the great amusement of the members of his own household. Then he will have contempt for your servants, your table, the disposition of your household, and he will

17. Prov. 15:15.
18. Matt. 5:8.

question you about your revenues, whether you own this or that. But why do I say so much? When he finds a chance, he will pursue your wife with amorous attentions and gaze at her with intemperate eyes, and, if he is able to, he will even seduce her. And when he departs, he will brag unworthily about what he did. But even if he does not speak of it, your enemy, in conflict with you, will proclaim it...A certain nobleman notable for his wealth, high station, and very high-birth, who had his residence in the City, had a beautiful wife whose brother was a general. Even more than beauty she was endowed with a fine spirit, intelligence, and virtue, and was knowledgeable in the Scriptures. The emperor, having often heard much praise of her, sent messengers asking to meet with her, promising both to her and her husband honors and many other good things. But her husband did not know of this. So then the emperor sent her husband out to serve as judge in a theme. Since the ruler could not persuade her [to acquiesce], he quieted down. But after three years [of service] the husband returned from his theme and was happy in his own home. Then a certain handsome youth, also of high station but unrelated, presented himself as a relative. And he said to her husband within their palace, "I," he said, "am related to the lady there." And many other things he said to him in order to ingratiate himself with the husband. And so the judge received him in his house. But he [the youth] was deceitful to him and succeeded in getting on friendly terms with him. What is the point of all this? Briefly, he had sexual relations with her who was once happy but now pitiable. When this drama became known, shame and sorrow, and especially pain, possessed her husband and relatives, but the youth prided himself for his act as if he had accomplished one of the labors of Hercules. And that which an emperor and promise of ranks and riches were unable to accomplish, habit and a friend did.

19

Memoirs

Confessions
St. Augustine (354–430)

Augustine wrote at length about his family background, childhood and early adulthood in his *Confessions*. His mother was a devout Christian and his pagan father worked as a local official in the Roman government. In his youth, Augustine was a typical Roman male. He kept concubines while awaiting his arranged marriage. In Augustine's case, his sexual frustration was also complicated by his preoccupation with religion. He experimented with different schools of thought and religious beliefs before converting to Christianity.

Source: *A select Library of Nicene and Post-Nicene Fathers of the Christian Church. Vol. I: The Confessions and Letters of St. Augustine with a Sketch of His Life and Works,* under the editorial supervision of Philip Schaff and Henry Wace (Grand Rapids, MI: WM.B. Eerdmans, reprint 1956), pp. 68–69, 99–100.

Book IV

[From Chapter 2]

In those years I taught the art of rhetoric, and, overcome by cupidity, put to sale a loquacity by which to overcome. Yet I preferred–Lord, Thou knowest — to have honest scholars (as they are esteemed); and these I, without artifice, taught artifices, not to be put in practise against the life of the guiltless, though sometimes for the life of the guilty. And Thou, O God, from afar sawest me stumbling in that slippery path, and amid much smoke[1] sending out some flashes of fidelity, which I exhibited in that my guidance of such as loved vanity and sought after leasing,[2] I being their companion. In those years I had one (whom I knew not in what is called lawful wedlock, but whom my wayward passion, void of understanding, had discovered), yet

1. Isaiah 42:3 and Matthew 12:20
2. Psalms 4: 2.

one only, remaining faithful even to her; in whom I found out truly by my own experience what difference there is between the restraints of the marriage bonds, contracted for the sake of issue, and the compact of a lustful love, where children are born against the parents' will, although, being born, they compel love.

Book VI

[FROM CHAPTER 13]

Active efforts were made to get me a wife. I wooed, I was engaged, my mother taking the greatest pains in the matter, that when I was once married, the health-giving baptism might cleanse me; for which she rejoiced that I was being daily fitted, remarking that her desires and Thy promises were being fulfilled in my faith. At which time, verily, both at my request and her own desire, with strong heartfelt cries did we daily beg of Thee that Thou wouldest by a vision disclose unto her something concerning my future marriage; but Thou wouldest not. She saw indeed certain vain and fantastic things, such as the earnestness of a human spirit, bent thereon, conjured up; and these she told me of, not with her usual confidence when Thou hadst shown her anything, but slighting them. For she could, she declared, through some feeling which she could not express in words, discern the difference betwixt Thy revelations and the dreams of her own spirit. Yet the affair was pressed on, and a maiden sued who wanted two years of the marriageable age; and, as she was pleasing, she was waited for.

Book VI

[FROM CHAPTER 15]

Meanwhile my sins were being multiplied, and my mistress being torn from my side as an impediment to my marriage, my heart, which clave to her, was racked, and wounded, and bleeding. And she went back to Africa, making a vow unto Thee never to know another man, leaving with me my natural son by her. But I, unhappy one, who could not imitate a woman, impatient of delay, since it was not until two years' time I was to obtain her I sought,— being not so much a lover of marriage as a slave to lust,— procured another (not a wife, though), that so by the bondage of a lasting habit the disease of my soul might be nursed up, and kept up in its vigour, or even increased, into the kingdom of marriage. Nor was that wound of mine as yet cured which had been caused by the separation from my former mistress, but after inflammation and most acute anguish it mortified, and the pain became numbed, but more desperate.

Book VIII

[FROM CHAPTER 7]

But now, the more ardently I loved those whose healthful affections I heard tell of, that they had given up themselves wholly to Thee to be cured, the more did I abhor myself when compared with them. For many of my years (perhaps twelve) had passed away since my nineteenth, when, on the reading of Cicero's Hortensius, I was roused to a desire for wisdom; and still I was delaying to reject mere worldly happiness, and to devote myself to search out that whereof not the finding alone, but the bare search, ought to have been preferred before the treasures and kingdoms of this world, though already found, and before the pleasures of the body, though encompassing me at my will. But I, miserable young man, supremely miserable even in the very outset of my youth, had entreated chastity of Thee, and said, "Grant me chastity and continency, but not yet." For I was afraid lest Thou shouldest hear me soon, and soon deliver me from the disease of concupiscence, which I desired to have satisfied rather than extinguished. And I had wandered through perverse ways in a sacrilegious superstition; not indeed assured thereof, but preferring that to the others, which I did not seek religiously, but opposed maliciously.

Memoirs of Guibert of Nogent
Guibert of Nogent (1055–1124)

The abbot of Nogent wrote his autobiography detailing his childhood and the events that led him to become a monk. Guibert came from a family of minor nobility in northern France. His father was a military man, and Guibert would have followed a similar career path had it not been for his difficult birth, which had caused his family to dedicate young Guibert to God. His father died when Guibert was about one year old, and he was brought up by his widowed mother, for whom he showed great adulation and love — as clearly shown in the excerpt below. His world is filled with superstitions and supernatural presences, not atypical of the way medievals perceived the world around them.

Source: *A Monk's Confession: The Memoirs of Guibert of Nogent*, translated by Paul J. Archambault (University Park, PA: Pennsylvania State University Press, 1996), pp. 34–35, 38, 65, 67. Copyright 1996 the Pennsylvania State University. Reproduced by permission of the publisher.

After these digressions I return to you, O my God, to talk about the conversion of that good woman, my mother. When she was barely of marriageable age, my grandfather gave her to my father, who was himself just an adolescent. She was blessed with a lovely face and a naturally and most becomingly sober demeanor, but since her earliest childhood the fear of God's name had been nurtured in her. In fact she had learned so well to detest sin (not out of experience but out of some instinctive fear of God) that her mind was flooded with great fear of sudden death (as she often told me). Thus, when she was older she lamented that her mature mind no longer felt the sting of that same beneficent fear she had felt at a tender and ignorant age.

It so happened that from the very start of their legitimate union, my parents were prevented from consummating the conjugal act by an evil spell cast over them by certain persons. It is said that their marriage had drawn them the envy of a stepmother, who had nieces both beautiful and well-born, and who would have liked to slip one of them into my father's bed. When this attempt failed utterly, she is said to have resorted to evil spells to prevent the consummation of the marriage. Thus my mother preserved her virginity intact for seven full years. This great misfortune was kept secret for a long time, until my father finally revealed it when summoned to speak before his relatives. One can imagine what means these relatives employed to get them to divorce, and how sedulously they counseled my father, who was then young and inexperienced, to become a monk, though at that time they did not mention this matter explicitly. They gave him this advice not to save his soul but because they wanted to take possession of his lands. When they realized that he was not taking their advice they began hounding the young girl persistently. They imagined that being far from her own family she would cave in under the pressure put upon her by strangers to her clan. She would, they thought, be worn out by their attacks and leave of her own volition, without waiting for a divorce. But with serenity she patiently endured the abuse they heaped upon her and pretended to be unaware of the violent arguments that resulted.

To add to this, a few rich men, seeing how she was inexperienced in conjugal matters, began to lay siege to the young girl's heart. But you, Lord, the builder of inner chastity, inspired in her a modesty that neither her nature nor her youth could have maintained. It is because of you that she did not burn, though placed in the midst of fire. It is thanks to you that, in spite of her tender age, she was not morally corrupted by the evil talk that surrounded her, even though oil may be been poured on the fire. Even though temptations from the outside mixed with inner impulses that are common to human nature, the soul of this young girl was always in control. She never allowed any temptation to lead her astray. Surely this was your work and yours alone, Lord...

For seven years and more, the evil charms that prevent the consummation of a natural and legitimate bond did their work. It is easy enough to admit that if the sense of sight can be perturbed by sleight-of-hand tricks — some magicians make people see things where nothing exists, as it were, or make them take one thing for another — sexual energies and activities are incomparably easier to perturb. Indeed, these arts are frequently practiced among the people, and even the uneducated know about them. Finally, an old woman put an end to these evil charms, and my mother submitted to the duties of the marriage bed as faithfully as she had kept her virginity, despite so many pressures to the contrary.

[In another anecdote, Guibert relates how years later his widowed mother dreamt of being accosted by phantoms which resulted in an encounter with her dead husband. — M.B.]

...Once delivered from the phantoms who dwelt in the well, she was standing near the edge when she suddenly saw my father standing next to her looking as he did when he was young. She stared at him and asked in a supplicating tone whether his name was Evrard (for such was his name in life). He answered no.

It should not surprise us that a spirit should refuse to answer to the name it has been in its earthly life. A spirit can only answer another spirit in a manner befitting a spirit. To believe that souls know one another by their names is ridiculous, for if it were so we would be able to have only a limited knowledge of our own kin in the afterlife. It is obviously not necessary for spirits to have names, for their whole vision, as well as the knowledge of that vision is internal. My father's spirit had therefore refused to be called by its name, but my mother continued to be persuaded it was he and asked him where he lived. In reply he pointed to a place not far from where they stood. She then asked him about his condition. In response he bared his arm and his side, and she was horrified to see how both had been torn and flayed by repeated lacerations that she felt sick to her stomach. I might add that the phantom of a small child was present, filling the air with wails that greatly troubled my mother. Shaken by those wails she said to the spirit: "How can you put up with the wailings of this child, my lord?" "I have to put up with them," he answered, "whether I like it or not."

The child's cries and the lacerations on my father's arm and side had the following meaning. In his youth, when the maleficent influence of some people had prevented my father from having legitimate intercourse with my mother, some depraved counselors (his mind still being very immature) suggested to him most perversely that he should experiment to see if he was able to have intercourse with other women. Young as he was, he went along with them, and having had evil relations with some woman of loose morals, had a child by her who soon died without baptism. The laceration in his side signified that he had broken his marriage bond; as to the wails of that confounded voice it meant the damnation of a child conceived in sin. Such, O God of inexhaustible holiness, was your retribution on the soul of this sinner of yours, whose soul was yet "alive through faith."[3] But let us return to the dream and see how it continued.

My mother asked her husband whether prayer, almsgiving, or sacrifice might bring him some relief. (Indeed, he was aware she was doing these things frequently for him). He answered yes and added, "But among you lives a certain Liutgarde." My mother understood that he mentioned this woman's name so that she might ask Liutgarde to remember him. This Liutgarde was truly "poor in spirit"[4] and lived for God in simplicity, not according to the ways of the world.

History of My Calamities
Peter Abelard (1079–1142)

Peter Abelard was a philosopher, logician, and renowned teacher in Paris, famous for his theories about universals. He also wrote *Sic et Non*, which brought together various writings from popes, Church fathers, the Bible and Church councils showing conflicting opinions on theological issues. Abelard, however, also gained fame for his private life. The following excerpt comes from his autobiography, *History of My Calamities*. In it he talks about his affair with Heloise, the teenage niece of canon Fulbert. While he tutored her, she became pregnant, which led to a number of serious complications. Heloise, however, refused to marry Abelard for fear of ruining his career.

Source: *The Letters of Abelard and Heloise*, translated by Betty Radice (Harmondsworth, Middlesex, England: Penguin Classics, 1974), © Betty Radice, 1974, pp. 66–70, 75. Reprinted by permission of Penguin Books, Ltd.

There was in Paris at the time a young girl named Heloise, the niece of Fulbert, one of the canons, and so much loved by him that he had done everything in his power to advance her education in letters. In looks she did not rank lowest, while in the extent of her learning she stood supreme. A gift for letters is so rare in women that it added greatly to her charm and had won her renown throughout the realm. I considered all the usual attractions for a lover and decided she was the one to bring to my bed, confident that I should have an easy success; for at that time I had youth and exceptional good looks as well as my great reputation to recommend me, and feared no rebuff from any woman I might choose to honour with my love. Knowing

3. Romans 1.17.
4. Matthew 5.3.

the girl's knowledge and love of letters I thought she would be all the more ready to consent, and that even when separated we could enjoy each other's presence by exchange of written messages in which we could speak more openly than in person, and so need never lack the pleasure of conversation.

All on fire with desire for this girl I sought an opportunity of getting to know her through private daily meetings and so more easily winning her over; and with this end in view I came to an arrangement with her uncle, with the help of some of his friends, whereby he should take me into his house, which was very near my school, for whatever sum he liked to ask. As a pretext I said that my household cares were hindering my studies and the expense was more than I could afford. Fulbert dearly loved money, and was moreover always ambitious to further his niece's education in letters, two weaknesses which made it easy for me to gain his consent and obtain my desire: he was all eagerness for my money and confident that his niece would profit from my teaching. This led him to make an urgent request which furthered my love and fell in with my wishes more than I had dared to hope; he gave me complete charge over the girl, so that I could devote all the leisure time left me by my school to teaching her by day and night, and if I found her idle I was to punish her severely. I was amazed by his simplicity — if he had entrusted a tender lamb to a ravening wolf it would not have surprised me more. In handing her over to me to punish as well as to teach, what else was he doing but giving me complete freedom to realize my desires, and providing an opportunity, even if I did not make use of it, for me to bend her to my will by threats and blows if persuasion failed? But there were two special reasons for his freedom from base suspicion: his love for his niece and my previous reputation for continence.

Need I say more? We were united, first under one roof, then in heart; and so with our lessons as a pretext we abandoned ourselves entirely to love. Her studies allowed us to withdraw in private, as love desired, and then with our books open before us, more words of love than of our reading passed between us, and more kissing than teaching. My hands strayed oftener to her bosom than to the pages; love drew our eyes to look on each other more than reading kept them on our texts. To avert suspicion I sometimes struck her, but these blows were prompted by love and tender feeling rather than anger and irritation, and were sweeter than any balm could be. In short, our desires left no stage of love-making untried, and if love could devise something new, we welcomed it. We entered on each joy the more eagerly for our previous inexperience, and were the less easily sated....

...And so we were caught in the act as the poet says happened to Mars and Venus. Soon afterwards the girl found that she was pregnant, and immediately wrote me a letter full of rejoicing to ask what I thought she should do. One night then, when her uncle was away from home, I removed her secretly from his house, as we had planned, and sent her straight to my own country. There she stayed with my sister until she gave birth to a boy, whom she called Astralabe.

On his return her uncle went almost out of his mind — one could appreciate only by experience his transports of grief and mortification...

In the end I took pity on his boundless misery and went to him, accusing myself of the deceit love had made me commit as if it were the basest treachery. I begged his forgiveness and promised to make any amends he might think fit. I protested that I had done nothing unusual in the eyes of anyone who had known the power of love, and recalled how since the beginning of the human race women had brought the noblest men to ruin. Moreover, to conciliate him further, I offered him satisfaction in a form he could never have hoped for: I would marry the girl I had wronged. All I stipulated was that the marriage should be kept secret so as not to damage my reputation. He agreed, pledged his word and that of his supporters, and sealed the reconciliation I desired with a kiss. But his intention was to make it easier to betray me.

I set off at once for Brittany and brought back my mistress to make her my wife. But she was strongly opposed to the proposal, and argued hotly against it for two reasons: the risk involved and the disgrace to myself.... Nature had created me for all mankind — it would be a sorry scandal if I should bind myself to a single woman and submit to such base servitude. She absolutely rejected this marriage; it would be nothing but a disgrace and a burden to me....

[Abelard and Heloise are married in secret. Heloise's uncle feels dishonored by this, and he breaks his silence about the marriage. Heloise enters a convent in Argenteuil and her child is given to be raised by Abelard's sister. This only angers Fulbert even more. — M.B.]

At this news her uncle and his friends and relatives imagined that I had tricked them, and had found an easy way of ridding myself of Heloise by making her a nun. Wild with indignation they plotted against me, and one night as I slept peacefully in an inner room in my lodgings, they bribed one of my servants to admit them and there took cruel vengeance on me of such appalling barbarity as to shock the whole world; they cut off the parts of my body whereby I had committed the wrong of which they complained. Then they fled, but the two who could be caught were blinded and mutilated as I had been, one of them being the servant who had been led by greed while in my service to betray his master.

The Book of Margery Kempe
Margery Kempe (c.1373–1438)

Born to a middle-class family in King's Lynn, England, Margery Kempe experienced a spiritual crisis and depression after the birth of her first child. At about the same time, however, she also started to have visions of Christ. She spent much time on pilgrimages to such places as the Holy Land, Assisi, Rome, and Santiago de Compostela, where she was often taken by bouts of intense and relentless crying. As her husband was not as financially success- ful as her family, she was able to negotiate a deal with him — as described in the following excerpt — under which she would keep her chastity in exchange for paying his debts. When she was approximately sixty years old, she dic- tated her memoirs to a priest because she herself could neither read nor write.

Source: *The Book of Margery Kempe*, translated by B.A. Windeatt (Harmondsworth, Mid- dlesex, England: Penguin Classics, 1965). © B.A. Windeatt 1965, pp. 58–60. Reproduced by permission of Penguin Books Ltd.

It happened one Friday, Midsummer Eve, in very hot weather — as this crea- ture was coming from York carrying a bottle of beer in her hand, and her husband a cake tucked inside his clothes against his chest — that her hus- band asked his wife this question: "Margery, if there came a man with a sword who would strike off my head unless I made love with you as I used to do before, tell me on you conscience — for you say you will not lie — whether you would allow my head to be cut off, or else allow me to make love with you again, as I did at one time?"

"Alas, sir," she said, "why are you raising this matter, when we have been chaste for these past eight weeks?"

"Because I want to know the truth of your heart."

And then she said with great sorrow, "Truly, I would rather see you being killed, than that we should turn back to our uncleanness."

And he replied, "You are no good wife."

And then she asked her husband what was the reason that he had not made love to her for the last eight weeks, since she lay with him every night in his bed. And he said that he was made so afraid when he would have touched her, that he dared do no more.

"Now, good sir, mend your ways and ask God's mercy, for I told you nearly three years ago that you[r desire for sex] would suddenly be slain — and this is now the third year, and I hope yet that I shall have my wish. Good sir, I pray you to grant what I shall ask, and I shall pray for you to be saved through the mercy of our Lord Jesus Christ, and you shall have more reward in heaven than if you wore a hair-shirt or wore a coat of mail as a penance. I pray you, allow me to make a vow of chastity at whichever bishop's hand that God wills."

"No," he said, "I won't allow you to do that, because now I can make love to you without mortal sin, and then I wouldn't be able to."

Then she replied, "If it be the will of the Holy Ghost to fulfil what I have said, I pray God that you may consent to this; and if it be not the will of the Holy Ghost, I pray God that you never consent."...

Then this creature thanked our Lord Jesus Christ for his grace and his goodness, and afterwards got up and went to her husband, saying to him, "Sir, if you please, you shall grant me my desire, and you shall have your desire. Grant me that you will not come into my bed, and I grant you that I will pay your debts before I go to Jerusalem. And make my body free to God, so that you never make any claim on me requesting any conjugal debt after this day as long as you live — and I shall eat and drink on Fridays at your bidding."

Then her husband replied to her, "May your body be as freely available to God as it has been to me."

20

Sagas

Laxdaela Saga
Author unknown

Written in 1245, this Icelandic saga covers 150 years of history from the time of Iceland's settlement in the ninth century. The principal narrative of the Laxdaela saga tells of the life of Gudrun Osvifrsdottir (Osvif's daughter) and her four marriages. The following excerpt describes her second husband's marital tribulation with his ex-wife.

Source: *Laxdaela Saga*, translated and introduction by Magnus Magnusson and Hermann Pálsson (Harmondsworth, Middlesex, England: Penguin Classics, 1969). Copyright © Magnus Magnusson and Herman Pálsson, 1969, pp. 126–128. Reproduced by permission of Penguin Books Ltd.

One day Thord Ingunnarson asked Gudrun what the penalty was for a woman who always wore breeches like a man's.

Gudrun replied, "The same penalty applies to women in a case like that as to a man who wears a neck-opening so wide that his nipples are exposed: both are grounds for divorce."

Then Thord said, "Would you advise me to declare myself divorced from Aud here at the Althing, or back in my own district where I can get support from others? For those who are likely to feel offended by this are proud-minded people."

Gudrun answered after a while, "Only idlers wait till evening."

Thord jumped to his feet at once and went to the Law Rock, where he named witnesses and declared himself divorced from Aud, on the ground that she wore gored breeches like masculine women do. Aud's brothers were greatly annoyed, but there the matter rested. Thord rode from the Althing with the Osvifssons.

When Aud heard the news she said:

> *"I'm glad I know
> I've been abandoned."*

After that, Thord rode west to Saurby with eleven men for the division of the estate, and everything went smoothly, for Thord did not quibble about how the money was divided. Thord drove a large number of livestock east to Laugar. Then he asked for the hand of Gudrun; there was no difficulty in reaching agreement with Osvif, and Gudrun raised no objection. The wedding was to take place at Laugar ten weeks before winter. It was a magnificent feast.

The marriage between Gudrun and Thord was happy.

The only reason why Thorkel Whelp and Knut did not bring an action against Thord Ingunnarson was that they could not get any support for it.

Next summer the men of Hol had their shieling in Hvammsdale; Aud was at the shieling too. The men of Laugar had their shieling in Lambadale, which cuts west into the mountains off Saelingsdale. Aud asked the boy who looked after their sheep how often he met the shepherd from Laugar. He said they met all the time, as was to be expected, since there was only a ridge separating the two shielings.

Aud then said, "Go and see the shepherd from Laugar today and find out for me who are at the shieling and who are staying at home on the farm; and remember to speak respectfully about Thord, as you should."

The boy promised to do as she asked. In the evening when the boy came back, Aud asked him what he had to report.

"I've heard news which will please you," said the shepherd. "There's now a wide floor between Thord's bed and Gudrun's, for she is up at the shieling and he is toiling hard at house-building: Osvif and he are the only men at home on the farm."

"You have done well to find this out," she said. "Have two horses ready saddled at bedtime."

The shepherd did as she told him, and a little before sunset Aud mounted her horse, and she was certainly wearing breeches then. The shepherd rode the other horse and could scarcely keep up with her, so furiously did she spur her horse. She rode south across Saelingsdale Heath and did not pull up until she reached the fence of the homefield at Laugar. There she dismounted and told the shepherd to look after the horses while she went to the house. Aud went up to the door, and found it open. She went into the living-room and over to the bed-closet in which Thord lay sleeping. The door of the bed-closet had been pulled to, but the bolt was not fastened. She went into the bed-closet; Thord lay on his back, sound asleep. She woke him up, and he turned on his side when he saw that a man had come in; Aud drew a short-sword and lunged at him with it, wounding him severely; the sword caught his right arm and gashed him across both nipples. So fierce was the thrust that the sword stuck fast in the bed-boards.

With that, Aud went back to her horse and jumped into the saddle, and rode back home. Thord tried to jump to his feet after he received the wounds but could not, for he was weakened by loss of blood. Osvif now woke up and asked what had happened, and Thord said he had been wounded. Osvif asked him if he knew who had done it, and got up and bandaged his injuries. Thord said he thought it had been Aud. Osvif offered to ride after her; he said she probably had not brought many men with her, and that her punishment would not be in doubt. Thord would not hear of it on any account, saying that she had only done what she had to.

Aud got back home about sunrise, and her brothers asked her where she had been. Aud said she had been to Laugar, and told them what she had gone there to do. They were pleased about it, but said she had probably not done enough.

Thord was in bed with his injuries for a long time. His chest wounds healed well, but he never recovered the full use of his arm.

Njal's Saga
Author unknown

This is the longest saga, written about 1280 and loosely based on events from three hundred years earlier. It was written in Iceland by an unknown author about one hundred years after the founding of Iceland by Norsemen. At the very basic level, Njal's Saga details the lives of two families in southern Iceland — Njal Thorgeirsson of Bergthorsknoll and Gunnar of Hlidarend. The following excerpt is about the marriage of Hrut and Unn, the cousin of Gunnar, the failure of which was caused by a spell.

Source: *Njal's Saga*, translated by Magnus Magnusson and Hermann Pálsson (Harmondsworth, Middlesex, England: Penguin Classics, 1960). Copyright © Magnus Magnusson and Hermann Pálsson, pp. 48–49, 52–53. Reproduced by permission of Penguin Books Ltd.

Hrut spent the winter with the king in high favour; but when spring came he grew very silent. Gunnhild noticed this, and when they were alone she asked him, "Are you unhappy, Hrut?"

"Far from home is far from joy, as the saying goes," replied Hrut.

"Do you want to go back to Iceland?" she asked.

"Yes," he replied.

"Have you a woman out there?" she asked.

"No," said Hrut.

"I believe you have, nevertheless," said the queen, and they broke off their conversation.

Hrut went before the king and greeted him.

"What is it you wish, Hrut?" asked the king.

"I beg your leave, my lord, to go to Iceland," said Hrut.

"Will you have greater honour there than here?" asked the king.

"No," replied Hrut, "but each must do as destiny decides."

Gunnhild said, "You cannot pull against a force like this. Give him leave to go wherever he thinks best."

The harvest had been meagre that year, but despite that the king gave him as much flour as he wanted. Ozur and Hrut made ready for the journey to Iceland, and when all their preparations were made, Hrut went to see the king and Gunnhild. Gunnhild took him to one side.

"I want to give you this gold bracelet," she said when they were alone, and clasped it round his arm.

"You have given me many good gifts," said Hrut.

She put her arms round his neck and kissed him, and said, "If I have as much power over you as I think, the spell I now lay on you will prevent your ever enjoying the woman in Iceland on whom you have set your heart. With other women you may have your will, but never with her. And now you must suffer as well as I, since you did not trust me with the truth."...

[Hrut returns home and marries Unn, but the spell placed by Gunnhild causes problems between the newlyweds.]

Then Mord said to his daughter, "Now tell me everything about your relationship, and let nothing deter you."

"Very well," said Unn. "I want to divorce Hrut, and I can tell you the exact grounds I have against him. He is unable to consummate our marriage and give me satisfaction, although in every other way he is as virile as the best of men."

"What do you mean?" asked Mord. "Be more explicit."

Unn replied, "Whenever he touches me, he is so enlarged that he cannot have enjoyment of me, although we both passionately desire to reach consummation. But we have never succeeded. And yet, before we draw apart, he proves that he is by nature as normal as other men."

"You have done well to tell me this," said Mord. "I can give you a plan which will meet the case so long as you carry it out in every detail.

"First, you must ride home now from the Althing. Your husband will have returned, and he will welcome you warmly. You must be affectionate towards him and compliant, and he will think the situation much improved. On no account must you show him any indifference.

"But when spring comes you must feign illness and take to your bed. Hrut will not try to guess the nature of your illness, and will not reproach you; indeed, he will tell everyone to take the greatest care of you. Then he will set off with Sigmund west to the fjords. He will be busy fetching all his goods from the west, and will be away from home far into the summer.

"Later, when it is time for people to ride to the Althing, and when all those who intend to be there have left the Dales, you must get up from your bed and summon men to accompany you on a journey. When you are quite ready to leave, you must walk to your bedside with those who are going to travel with you. There at your husband's bedstead you must name witnesses and declare yourself lawfully divorced from him; do it as correctly as possible in accordance with the procedural rules of the Althing and the common law of the land. You must then name witnesses once again at the main door.

"With that done you must ride away. Take the path over Laxriverdale Heath and across to Holtavord Heath, for no one will search for you as far as Hrutafjord, and then carry straight on until you come to me here. I shall then take care of the case for you, and you will never fall into his hands again."

Unn now rode home from the Althing. Hrut had already returned, and he welcomed her warmly. Unn responded well, and was affectionate towards him. They got on well together that year. But when spring came, Unn fell ill and took to her bed. Hrut rode off west to the fjords, leaving orders that she was to be well looked after.

When the Althing was due, Unn made her preparations for the journey. She followed her father's instructions in every detail, and then rode off to the Althing. The men of the district searched for her, but could not find her. Mord welcomed his daughter and asked her how she had carried out his plan.

"I have not deviated from it at all," she replied.

Mord went to the Law Rock, and there gave notice of Unn's lawful divorce from Hrut.

21

Drama

Dulcitius
Hrotsvit of Gandersheim (935–1001/1003)

Hrotsvit was a German nun, poet, and the earliest known medieval playwright. She came from an aristocratic family in Saxony and, at an early age, entered a convent where she received a good education. She wrote many works, including the history of her monastery and the deeds of Emperor Otto the Great, but she is best known for her six short plays, including *Dulcitius*, the play reproduced here. It was her desire to write plays like those of the Roman playwright Terence. Her plays feature strong Christian themes such as chastity and martyrdom, but treat them in a humorous way. It is believed that many of her plays were acted out in her convent.

Source: *Hrotsvit of Gandersheim: A Florilegium of Her Works*, translated with introduction by Katharina Wilson (Woodbridge, Suffolk; Rochester, NY: D.S. Brewer, 1998), pp. 45–53. Reprinted with permission of Boydell & Brewer.

The martyrdom of the holy virgins Agape, Chionia and Hirena whom, in the silence of the night, Governor Dulcitius secretly visited, desiring to delight in their embrace. But as soon as he entered, he became demented and kissed and hugged the pots and pans, mistaking them for the girls until his face and his clothes were soiled with disgusting black dirt. Afterward Count Sissinus, acting on orders, was given the girls so he might put them to tortures. He, too, was deluded miraculously but finally ordered that Agape and Chionia be burnt and Hirena be slain by an arrow.

> DIOCLETIAN: The renown of your free and noble descent and the brightness of your beauty demand that you be married to one of the foremost men of my court. This will be done according to our command if you deny Christ and comply by bringing offerings to our gods.

> AGAPE: Be free of care, don't trouble yourself to prepare our wedding because we cannot be compelled under any duress to betray Christ's holy name, which we must confess, nor to stain our virginity.

DIOCLETIAN: What madness possesses you? What rage drives you three?

AGAPE: What signs of our madness do you see?

DIOCLETIAN: An obvious and great display.

AGAPE: In what way?

DIOCLETIAN: Chiefly in that renouncing the practices of ancient religion you follow the useless, new-fangled ways of the Christian superstition.

AGAPE: Heedlessly you offend the majesty of the omnipotent God. That is dangerous...

DIOCLETIAN: Dangerous to whom?

AGAPE: To you and to the state you rule.

DIOCLETIAN: She is mad; remove the fool!

CHIONIA: My sister is not mad; she rightly reprehended your folly.

DIOCLETIAN: She rages even more madly; remove her from our sight and arraign the third girl.

HIRENA: You will find the third, too, a rebel and resisting you forever.

DIOCLETIAN: Hirena, although you are younger in birth, be greater in worth!

HIRENA: Show me, I pray, how?

DIOCLETIAN: Bow your neck to the gods, set an example for your sisters, and be the cause for their freedom!

HIRENA: Let those worship idols, Sire, who wish to incur God's ire. But I won't defile my head, anointed with royal unguent by debasing myself at the idols' feet.

DIOCLETIAN: The worship of gods brings no dishonor but great honor.

HIRENA: And what dishonor is more disgraceful, what disgrace is any more shameful than when a slave is venerated as a master?

DIOCLETIAN: I don't ask you to worship slaves but the mighty gods of princes and greats.

HIRENA: Is he not anyone's slave who, for a price, is up for sale?

DIOCLETIAN: For her speech so brazen, to the tortures she must be taken.

HIRENA: This is just what we hope for, this is what we desire, that for the love of Christ through tortures we may expire.

DIOCLETIAN: Let these insolent girls who defy our decrees and words be put in chains and kept in the squalor of prison until Governor Dulcitius can examine them.

DULCITIUS: Bring forth, soldiers, the girls whom you hold sequestered.

SOLDIERS: Here they are whom you requested.

DULCITIUS: Wonderful, indeed, how beautiful, how graceful, how admirable these little girls are!

SOLDIERS: Yes, they are perfectly lovely.

DULCITIUS: I am captivated by their beauty.

SOLDIERS: That is understandable.

DULCITIUS: To draw them to my heart, I am eager.

SOLDIERS: Your success will be meager.

DULCITIUS: Why?

SOLDIERS: Because they are firm in faith.

DULCITIUS : What if I sway them by flattery?

SOLDIERS: They will despise it utterly.

DULCITIUS: What if with tortures I frighten them?

SOLDIERS: Little will it matter to them.

DULCITIUS: Then what should be done, I wonder?

SOLDIERS: Carefully you should ponder.

DULCITIUS: Place them under guard in the inner room of the pantry, where they keep the servants' pots.

SOLDIERS: Why in that particular spot?

DULCITIUS: So that I may visit them often at my leisure.

SOLDIERS: At your pleasure.

DULCITIUS: What do the captives do at this time of night?

SOLDIERS: Hymns they recite.

DULCITIUS: Let us go near.

SOLDIERS: From afar we hear their tinkling little voices clear.

DULCITIUS: Stand guard before the door with your lantern but I will enter and satisfy myself in their longed-for embrace.

SOLDIERS: Enter. We will guard this place.

AGAPE: What is that noise outside the door?

HIRENA: That wretched Dulcitius coming to the fore.

CHIONIA: May God protect us!

AGAPE: Amen.

CHIONIA: What is the meaning of this clash of the pots and pans?

HIRENA: I will check. Come here, please, and look through the crack!

AGAPE: What is going on?

HIRENA: Look, the fool, the madman base, he thinks he is enjoying our embrace.

AGAPE: What is he doing?

HIRENA: Into his lap he pulls the utensils, he embraces the pots and the pans, giving them tender kisses.

CHIONIA: Ridiculous!

HIRENA: His face, his hands, his clothes, are so soiled, so filthy, that with all the soot that clings to him, he looks like an Ethiopian.

AGAPE: It is only right that he should appear in body the way he is in his mind: possessed by the Devil.

HIRENA: Wait! He prepares to leave. Let us watch how he is greeted, and how he is treated by the soldiers who wait for him.

SOLDIERS: Who is coming out? A demon without doubt. Or rather, the Devil himself is he; let us flee!

DULCITIUS: Soldiers, where are you taking yourselves in flight? Stay! Wait! Escort me home with your light!

SOLDIERS: The voice is our master's tone but the look the Devil's own. Let us not stay! Let us run away; the apparition will slay us!

DULCITIUS: I will go to the palace and complain, and reveal to the whole court the insults I had to sustain.

DULCITIUS: Guards, let me into the palace; I must have a private audience.

GUARDS: Who is this vile and detestable monster covered in torn and despicable rags? Let us beat him, from the steps let us sweep him; he must not be allowed to enter.

DULCITIUS: Alas, alas, what has happened? Am I not dressed in splendid garments? Don't I look neat and clean? Yet anyone who looks at my mien loathes me as a foul monster. To my wife I shall return, and from her learn what has happened. But there is my spouse, with disheveled hair she leaves the house, and the whole household follows her in tears.

WIFE: Alas, alas, my Lord Dulcitius, what has happened to you? You are not sane; the Christians have made a laughing stock out of you.

DULCITIUS: Now I know at last. I owe this mockery to their witchcraft.

WIFE: What upsets me so, what makes me more sad, is that you were ignorant of all that happened to you.

DULCITIUS: I command that those insolent girls be led forth, and that they be publicly stripped of all their clothes, so that they experience similar mockery in retaliation for ours.

SOLDIERS: We labor in vain; we sweat without gain. Behold, their garments stick to their virginal bodies like skin, and he who urged us to strip them snores in his seat, and he cannot be awakened from his sleep. Let us go to the Emperor and report what has happened.

DIOCLETIAN: It grieves me very much to hear that Governor Dulcitius has been so greatly deluded, so greatly insulted, so utterly humiliated. But these vile young women shall not boast with impunity of having made a mockery of our gods and those who worship them. I shall direct Count Sissinus to take due vengeance.

SISSINUS: Soldiers, where are those insolent girls who are to be tortured?

SOLDIERS: They are kept in prison.

SISSINUS: Leave Hirena there, bring the others here.

SOLDIERS: Why do you except the one?

SISSINUS: Sparing her youth. Perchance, she may be converted easier, if she is not intimidated by her sisters' presence.

SOLDIERS: That makes sense.

SOLDIERS: Here are the girls whose presence you requested.

SISSINUS: Agape and Chionia, give heed, and to my council accede!

AGAPE: We will not give heed.

SISSINUS: Bring offerings to the gods.

AGAPE: We bring offerings of praise forever to the true Father eternal, and to His Son co-eternal, and also to the Holy Spirit.

SISSINUS: This is not what I bid, but on pain of penalty prohibit.

AGAPE: You cannot prohibit it; neither shall we ever sacrifice to demons.

SISSINUS: Cease this hardness of heart, and make your offerings. But if you persist, then I shall insist that you be killed according to the Emperor's orders.

CHIONIA: It is only proper that you should obey the orders of your Emperor, whose decrees we disdain, as you know. For if you wait and try to spare us, then you could be rightfully killed.

SISSINUS: Soldiers, do not delay, take these blaspheming girls away, and throw them alive into the flames.

SOLDIERS: We shall instantly build the pyre you asked for, and we will cast these girls into the raging fire, and thus we'll put an end to these insults at last.

AGAPE: O Lord, nothing is impossible for Thee; even the fire forgets its nature and obeys Thee; but we are weary of delay; therefore, dissolve the earthly bonds that hold our souls, we pray, so that as our earthly bodies die, our souls may sing your praise in Heaven.

SOLDIERS: Oh, marvel, oh stupendous miracle! Behold their souls are no longer bound to their bodies, yet no traces of injury can be found; neither their hair, nor their clothes are burnt by the fire, and their bodies are not at all harmed by the pyre.

SISSINUS: Bring forth Hirena.

SOLDIERS: Here she is.

SISSINUS: Hirena, tremble at the deaths of your sisters and fear to perish according to their example.

HIRENA: I hope to follow their example and expire, so with them in Heaven eternal joy I may acquire.

SISSINUS: Give in, give in to my persuasion.

HIRENA: I will never yield to evil persuasion.

SISSINUS: If you don't yield, I shall not give you a quick and easy death, but multiply your sufferings.

HIRENA: The more cruelly I'll be tortured, the more gloriously I'll be exalted.

SISSINUS: You fear no tortures, no pain? What you abhor, I shall ordain.

HIRENA: Whatever punishment you design, I will escape with help Divine.

SISSINUS: To a brothel you will be consigned, where your body will be shamefully defiled.

HIRENA: It is better that the body be dirtied with any stain than that the soul be polluted with idolatry.

SOLDIERS: If you are so polluted in the company of harlots, you can no longer be counted among the virginal choir.

HIRENA: Lust deserves punishment, but forced compliance the crown. With neither is one considered guilty, unless the soul consents freely.

SISSINUS: In vain have I spared her, in vain have I pitied her youth.

SOLDIERS: We knew this before; for on no possible score can she be moved to adore our gods, nor can she be broken by terror.

SISSINUS: I shall spare her no longer.

SOLDIERS: Rightly you ponder.

SISSINUS: Seize her without mercy, drag her with cruelty, and take her in dishonor to the brothel.

HIRENA: They will not do it.

SISSINUS: Who can prohibit it?

HIRENA: He whose foresight rules the world.

SISSINUS: I shall see....

HIRENA: Sooner than you wish, it will be.

SISSINUS: Soldiers, be not afraid of what this blaspheming girl has said.

SOLDIERS: We are not afraid, but eagerly follow what you bade.

SISSINUS: Who are those approaching? How similar they are to the men to whom we gave Hirena just then. They are the same. Why are you returning so fast? Why so out of breath, I ask?

SOLDIERS: You are the one for whom we look.

SISSINUS: Where is she whom you just took?

SOLDIERS: On the peak of the mountain.

SISSINUS: Which one?

SOLDIERS: The one close by.

SISSINUS: Oh you idiots, dull and blind. You have completely lost your mind!

SOLDIERS: Why do you accuse us, why do you abuse us, why do you threaten us with menacing voice and face?

SISSINUS: May the gods destroy you!

SOLDIERS: What have we committed? What harm have we done? How have we transgressed against your orders?

SISSINUS: Have I not given the orders that you should take that rebel against the gods to a brothel?

SOLDIERS: Yes, so you did command, and we were eager to fulfill your demand, but two strangers intercepted us saying that you sent them to us to lead Hirena to the mountain's peak.

SISSINUS: That's new to me.

SOLDIERS: We can see.

SISSINUS: What were they like?

SOLDIERS: Splendidly dressed and an awe-inspiring sight.

SISSINUS: Did you follow?

SOLDIERS: We did so.

SISSINUS: What did they do?

SOLDIERS: They placed themselves on Hirena's left and right, and told us to be forthright and not to hide from you what happened.

SISSINUS: I see a sole recourse, that I should mount my horse and seek out those who so freely made sport with us.

SISSINUS: Hmm, I don't know what to do. I am bewildered by the witchcraft of these Christians. I keep going around the mountain and keep finding this track but I neither know how to proceed nor how to find my way back.

SOLDIERS: We are all deluded by some intrigue; we are afflicted with a great fatigue; if you allow this insane person to stay alive, then neither you nor we shall survive.

SISSINUS: Anyone among you, I don't care which, string a bow, and shoot an arrow, and kill that witch!

SOLDIERS: Rightly so.

HIRENA: Wretched Sissinus, blush for shame, and proclaim your miserable defeat because without the help of weapons, you cannot overcome a tender little virgin as your foe.

SISSINUS: Whatever the shame that may be mine, I will bear it more easily now because I know for certain that you will die.

HIRENA: This is the greatest joy I can conceive, but for you this is a cause to grieve, because you shall be damned in Tartarus for your cruelty, while I shall receive the martyr's palm and the crown of virginity; thus I will enter the heavenly bridal chamber of the Eternal King, to whom are all honor and glory in all eternity.

VII

WITCHCRAFT AND HERESY

22

Witchcraft

Summma Theologica
St. Thomas Aquinas (1225-1274)

Impotence had long been considered an impediment to marriage. Theologians often distinguished between permanent impotence and temporary impotence caused by sorcery. In his systematic and logical way, Aquinas sets out to prove in the *Summa Theologica* that witches and demons can affect reproductive functions. Effects can be long-term, short-term, or limited to a relationship with a specific individual.

Source: *The Summa Theologica of St. Thomas Aquinas, Supplement, QQ. 1-99*, translated by Fathers of the English Dominican Province (New York: Benziger Brothers, 1947), pp. 2767-2768.

WHETHER A SPELL CAN BE AN IMPEDIMENT TO MARRIAGE?

Objection 1. It would seem that a spell cannot be an impediment to marriage. For the spells in question are caused by the operation of demons. But the demons have no more power to prevent the marriage act than other bodily actions; and these they cannot prevent, for thus they would upset the whole world if they hindered eating and walking and the like. Therefore they cannot hinder marriage by spells.

Obj. 2. Further, God's work is stronger than the devil's. But a spell is the work of the devil. Therefore it cannot hinder marriage which is the work of God.

Obj. 3. Further, no impediment, unless it be perpetual, voids the marriage contract. But a spell cannot be a perpetual impediment, for since the devil has no power over others than sinners, the spell will be removed if the sin be cast out, or by another spell, or by the exorcisms of the Church which are employed for the repression of the demon's power. Therefore a spell cannot be an impediment to marriage.

Obj. 4. Further, carnal copulation cannot be hindered, unless there be an impediment to the generative power which is its principle. But the generative power of one man is equally related to all women. Therefore a spell cannot be an impediment in respect of one woman without being so also in respect of all.

On the contrary, It is stated in the Decretals[1]: *If by sorcerers or witches...*, and further on, *if they be incurable, they must be separated.* Further, the demons' power is greater than man's: *There is no power upon earth that can be compared with him who was made to fear no one.*[2] Now through the action of man, a person may be rendered incapable of carnal copulation by some power or by castration; and this is an impediment to marriage. Therefore much more can this be done by the power of a demon.

I answer that, Some have asserted that witchcraft is nothing in the world but an imagining of men who ascribed to spells those natural effects the causes of which are hidden. But this is contrary to the authority of holy men who state that the demons have power over men's bodies and imaginations, when God allows them: wherefore by their means wizards can work certain signs. Now this opinion grows from the root of unbelief or incredulity, because they do not believe that demons exist save only in the imagination of the common people, who ascribe to the demon the terrors which a man conjures from his thoughts, and because, owing to a vivid imagination, certain shapes such as he has in his thoughts become apparent to the senses, and then he believes that he sees the demons. But such assertions are rejected by the true faith whereby we believe that angels fell from heaven, and that the demons exist, and that by reason of their subtle nature they are able to do many things which we cannot; and those who induce them to do such things are called wizards.

Wherefore others have maintained that witchcraft can set up an impediment to carnal copulation, but that no such impediment is perpetual: hence it does not void the marriage contract, and they say that the laws asserting this have been revoked. But this is contrary to actual facts and to the new legislation which agrees with the old.

We must therefore draw a distinction: for the inability to copulate caused by witchcraft is either perpetual and then it voids marriage, or it is not perpetual and then it does not void marriage. And in order to put this to practical proof the Church has fixed the space of three years in the same way as we have stated with regard to frigidity. There is, however, this difference between a spell and frigidity, that a person who is impotent through frigidity is equally impotent in relation to one as to another, and consequently when the marriage is dissolved, he is not permitted to marry

---

1. XXXIII, qu. 1, cap. 4.
2. Job 41:24.

another woman; whereas through witchcraft a man may be rendered impotent in relation to one woman and not to another, and consequently when the Church adjudges the marriage to be dissolved, each party is permitted to seek another partner in marriage.

Reply to Obj. 1. The first corruption of sin whereby man became the slave of the devil was transmitted to us by the act of the generative power, and for this reason God allows the devil to exercise his power of witchcraft in this act more than in others. Even so the power of witchcraft is made manifest in serpents more than in other animals according to Gn. 3, since the devil tempted the woman through a serpent.

Reply to Obj. 2. God's work may be hindered by the devil's work with God's permission; not that the devil is stronger than God so as to destroy His works by violence.

Reply to Obj. 3. Some spells are so perpetual that they can have no human remedy, although God might afford a remedy by coercing the demon, or the demon by desisting. For, as wizards themselves admit, it does not always follow that what was done by one kind of witchcraft can be destroyed by another kind, and even though it were possible to use witchcraft as a remedy, it would nevertheless be reckoned to be perpetual, since nowise ought one to invoke the demon's help by witchcraft. Again, if the devil has been given power over a person on account of sin, it does not follow that his power ceases with the sin, because the punishment sometimes continues after the fault has been removed. And again, the exorcisms of the Church do not always avail to repress the demons in all their molestations of the body, if God will it so, but they always avail against those assaults of the demons against which they are chiefly instituted.

Reply to Obj. 4. Witchcraft sometimes causes an impediment in relation to all, sometimes in relation to one only: because the devil is a voluntary cause not acting from natural necessity. Moreover, the impediment resulting from witchcraft may result from an impression made by the demon on a man's imagination, whereby he is deprived of the concupiscence that moves him in regard to a particular woman and not to another.

Defender of Ladies
Martin Le Franc (1440)

Martin Le Franc was a French poet and clerical official of the Duke of Savoy. He wrote *Defender of Ladies* in 1440 and dedicated it to Philip the Good, the Duke of Burgundy. The work is part of a moral debate between the late fourteenth and early sixteenth century centering on the character of women. The "Adversary" attacks women and "Free Will" defends them. At one point in the poem, the topic of witchcraft is raised, and Free Will defends against the misogynistic reasoning of the Adversary.

Source: *Witchcraft in Europe, 1100-1700: A Documentary History*, edited by Alan C. Kors and Edward Peters (Philadelphia: University of Pennsylvania Press, 1972), pp. 167-169. Reprinted by permission of the University of Pennsylvania Press. Copyright © 1972 by the University of Pennsylvania Press, Inc.

The Adversary brightened up a little, responding, You'll surely change your mind when you've heard this case related. It's true. I've heard it. I believe it, that not just two or three old women, but more than three thousand, go together to hidden places to seek out their familiar demons. This is no joke; this isn't fooling. I'm not trying to lie to you in speaking of this sorcery. When you once learn of their whorishness you'll want all of them burned up, because there's no persuasion in this world that could turn them from their tricks and farces. I tell you that I've seen in a written trial record where an old woman confessed how, since the time when she was just sixteen years old that on certain nights she flew on a broomstick from Valpute and went directly to the awful synagogue of devils. Ten thousand old women in a troop were there, as in a great assembly in the shapes of cats or goats, approaching the devil courteously, kissing him openly on his ass as a sign of their obedience, denying God quite openly and all of His great power. There, they all do different things — some were instructed in their arts and perverse sorceries from the devil himself, by which they later committed many evils. Still others pleased themselves in dancing, others still in banqueting and booze. They found there all these things; you wouldn't believe their abundance. Then the devil praised them all, but those who wanted to repent he sternly punished, beating them without stopping. But to all those who consented he gave whatever they wished. He promised them, and was not lying, the sum of everything they wanted. This devil, now in the form of a cat, walked up and down the earth. Like a judge or lawyer, he listened to all requests. Each person paid him the respect that one would pay to God; thus the deceitful being enjoyed the praise and approving looks of all. And know that when they all departed [from the sabbat] each man took any woman sexually. And if any woman had no man, a devil would do the service for her.

Then each returned home, like the wind, upon her broomstick — so much power had Satan given her, that wretched thief of souls. For instance, one old hag told us that when she paid homage to the devil he gave her an ointment made out of awful, varied poisons, with which she made any man impotent, and thus made more than one hundred, and she ruined many fine young innocents that way. And further, that wicked beast of a woman created whirlwinds and raised storms that destroyed both grain and vine, leveled trees and bushes, wasting entire lands. If anyone protested, he was instantly tempested. More than six hundred have deposed to these crimes without having been put to torture that they've raised hailstorms, wind and rain, all against Nature. They've flung these elements wherever they wished, and done many other wicked things by the power of the devils. Then she said more emphatically (about which I shudder to speak) that the devil made himself into a man and had his lustful way with her. Oh God, what horror! Oh God, such coupling is awful — Oh Lord Jesus what a sin! The woman's married to the devil! I didn't want to believe all this, and said it's just a dizzy head, when another confessed witch whom I saw one day said, "I've seen Sohier and Quotin [at sabbat] dancing and leading the festivities, and I know that both Greeks and Latins attend our awful synagogue."

Listen to what I say in answer, said Free Will. There's no old woman so stupid who's done even the least of these things. But in order to have her hanged or burned, the enemy of humankind, who knows well how to set traps to make the mind deceive itself, has made her mind fool itself. There are no broomsticks or rods by which anyone could fly. But when the devil can fool the mind, they *think* they fly to some far place where they take their pleasure and do whatever it is they wish. They've even been heard to speak of Rome, without ever having been there.

[*The Adversary then points out that Simon Magus flew in the air and that the devil can move anyone anywhere at all. The Defender responds that the devils are all chained up in Hell and can't get out by any means. Not so, says the Adversary, because when Lucifer and the rebel angels fell God punished them in different ways, and some of them dwell in the air, making storms, while others tempt ordinary folk. The Adversary then says that wherever we go the wicked enemy follows. If one temptation doesn't succeed, he'll try another, since he has no other purpose in this world:*]

Thus, when the devil sees the wicked *sorcière* who lacks both law and faith, he thinks he can convert her to his service. He promises her this and that and tells her how to overcome her enemies. And so she says, "Fie on you, Jesus Christ, and all your power." The devil has her on a string and does whatever she asks of him, tying her up even tighter. Then he refuses what she asks until she submits to him. Then he bears her off, condemned to the fire. Then the *sorcière* curses the day she was born.

Malleus Maleficarum
Heinrich Kramer and James Sprenger (fifteenth century)

Malleus Maleficarum (*Hammer of Witches*) is the most significant tract ever written on the subject of witchcraft. Its authors were two Dominicans who had been inquisitors in Germany. The tract was first published in 1486. At that time, there was an upsurge of witchcraft trials, prompted at least in part by the undercurrent of fear affecting western Europe, which was struggling with plague and economic difficulties that caused stress and anxiety among the general populace. Pope Innocent VIII's Bull of 1484 authorized Kramer and Sprenger to root out witches after they complained to him that their local ecclesiastical authorities were failing to persecute those engaged in the practice of witchcraft. This bull serves as a preface to the work (not reproduced here).

The tract dealt with the effects of witchcraft, outlined the form in which its investigation should be carried out, and described the judicial proceedings in ecclesiastical and secular courts. There are clear misogynistic overtones with the authors eager to point out that witchcraft is more prevalent among women. The instructions provided by this tract were used for centuries by both Catholics and Protestants.

Source: *Malleus Maleficarum: The Notorious Handbook Once Used to Condemn and Punish Witches by Heinrich Kramer and James Sprenger*, translated by Montague Summers (San Diego, CA: The Book Tree, 2000), pp. 43–47, 112–114, 117-118. Reprinted with permission.

[PART 1, QUESTION VI:] WHY SUPERSTITION IS CHIEFLY FOUND IN WOMEN

...Now the wickedness of women is spoken of in *Ecclesiasticus* xxv: There is no head above the head of a serpent: and there is no wrath above the wrath of a woman. I had rather dwell with a lion and a dragon than to keep house with a wicked woman. And among much which in that place precedes and follows about a wicked woman, he concludes: All wickedness is but little to the wickedness of a woman. Wherefore S. John Chrysostom says on the text, It is not good to marry (S. Matthew xix):[3] What else is woman but a foe to friendship, an unescapable punishment, a necessary evil, a natural temptation, a desirable calamity, a domestic danger, a delectable detriment, an evil of nature, painted with fair colours! Therefore if it be a sin to divorce her when she ought to be kept, it is indeed a necessary torture; for either we commit adultery by divorcing her, or we must endure daily strife. Cicero in his second book of *The Rhetorics* says: The many lusts of men lead them into one sin, but the one lust of women leads them into all sins; for the root of all woman's vices is avarice. And Seneca says in his *Tragedies:* A woman either loves or hates; there is no third grade. And the tears of woman are a deception, for they may spring from true grief, or they may be a snare. When a woman thinks alone, she thinks evil.....

---

3. "*S. Matthew.*" The ninety Homilies on S. Matthew were written about the year 390.

Others again have propounded other reasons why there are more superstitious women found than men. And the first is, that they are more credulous; and since the chief aim of the devil is to corrupt faith, therefore he rather attacks them. See *Ecclesiasticus* xix: He that is quick to believe is lightminded, and shall be diminished. The second reason is, that women are naturally more impressionable, and more ready to receive the influence of a disembodied spirit; and that when they use this quality well they are very good, but when they use it ill they are very evil.

The third reason is that they have slippery tongues, and are unable to conceal from their fellow-women those things which by evil arts they know; and, since they are weak, they find an easy and secret manner of vindicating themselves by witchcraft. See *Ecclesiasticus* as quoted above: I had rather dwell with a lion and a dragon than to keep house with a wicked woman. All wickedness is but little to the wickedness of a woman. And to this may be added that, as they are very impressionable, they act accordingly.

There are also others who bring forward yet other reasons, of which preachers should be very careful how they make use. For it is true that in the Old Testament the Scriptures have much that is evil to say about women, and this because of the first temptress, Eve, and her imitators; yet afterwards in the New Testament we find a change of name, as from Eva to Ave (as S. Jerome says), and the whole sin of Eve taken away by the benediction of MARY. Therefore preachers should always say as much praise of them as possible.

But because in these times this perfidy is more often found in women than in men, as we learn by actual experience, if anyone is curious as to the reason, we may add to what has already been said the following: that since they are feebler both in mind and body, it is not surprising that they should come more under the spell of witchcraft.

For as regards intellect, or the understanding of spiritual things, they seem to be of a different nature from men; a fact which is vouched for by the logic of the authorities, backed by various examples from the Scriptures. Terence says: Women are intellectually like children. And Lactantius (*Institutiones*, III): No woman understood philosophy except Temeste. And *Proverbs* xi, as it were describing a woman, says: As a jewel of gold in a swine's snout, so is a fair woman which is without discretion.

But the natural reason is that she is more carnal than a man, as is clear from her many carnal abominations. And it should be noted that there was a defect in the formation of the first woman, since she was formed from a bent rib, that is, a rib of the breast, which is bent as it were in a contrary direction to a man. And since through this defect she is an imperfect animal, she always deceives. For Cato says: When a woman weeps she weaves snares. And again: When a woman weeps, she labours to deceive a man. And this is shown by Samson's wife, who coaxed him to tell her the riddle he had propounded to the Philistines, and told them the answer, and so deceived him. And it is clear in the case of the first woman that she had little faith; for when the serpent asked why they did not eat of every tree in Paradise, she answered: Of every tree, etc.— lest perchance we die. Thereby she showed that she doubted, and had little in the word of God. And all this is indicated by the etymology of the word; for *Femina* comes from *Fe* and *Minus*, since she is ever weaker to hold and preserve the faith. And this as regards faith is of her very nature; although both by grace and nature faith never failed in the Blessed Virgin, even at the time of Christ's Passion, when it failed in all men.

Therefore a wicked woman is by her nature quicker to waver in her faith, and consequently quicker to abjure the faith, which is the root of witchcraft.

And as to her other mental quality, that is, her natural will; when she hates someone whom she formerly loved, then she seethes with anger and impatience in her whole soul, just as the tides of the sea are always heaving and boiling. Many authorities allude to this cause. *Ecclesiasticus* xxv: There is no wrath above the wrath of a woman. And Seneca (*Tragedies*, VIII): No might of the flames or of the swollen winds, no deadly weapon, is so much to be feared as the lust and hatred of a woman who has been divorced from the marriage bed....

Women also have weak memories; and it is a natural vice in them not to be disciplined, but to follow their own impulses without any sense of what is due; this is her whole study, and all that she keeps in her memory. So Theophrastus says: If you hand over the whole management of the house to her, but reserve some minute detail to your own judgement, she will think that you are displaying a great want of faith in her, and will stir up a strife; and unless you quickly take counsel, she will prepare poison for you, and consult seers and soothsayers; and will become a witch....

And now let us examine the carnal desires of the body itself, whence has arisen unconscionable harm to human life. Justly may we say with Cato of Utica: If the world could be rid of women, we should not be without God in our intercourse. For truly, without the wickedness of women, to say nothing of witchcraft, the world would still remain proof against innumerable dangers. Hear what Valerius said to Rufinus: You do not know that woman is the Chimaera, but it is good that you should know it; for that monster was of three forms; its face was that of a radiant and noble lion, it had the filthy belly of a goat, and it was armed with the virulent tail of a viper. And he means that a woman is beautiful to look upon, contaminating to the touch, and deadly to keep.

Let us consider another property of hers, the voice. For as she is a liar by nature, so in her speech she stings while she delights us. Wherefore her voice is like the song of the Sirens, who with their sweet melody entice the passers-by and kill them. For they kill them by emptying their purses, consuming their strength, and causing them to forsake God. Again Valerius says to Rufinus: When she speaks it is a delight which flavours the sin; the flower of love is a rose, because under its blossom there are hidden many thorns. See *Proverbs* v, 3-4: Her mouth is smoother than oil; that is, her speech is afterwards as bitter as absinthium. [Her throat is smoother than oil. But her end is as bitter as wormwood.]

Let us consider also her gait, posture, and habit, in which is vanity of vanities. There is no man in the world who studies so hard to please the good God as even an ordinary woman studies by her vanities to please men. An example of this is to be found in the life of Pelagia,[4] a worldly woman who was wont to go about Antioch tired and adorned most extravagantly. A holy father, named Nonnus, saw her and began to weep, saying to his companions, that never in all his life had he used such diligence to please God; and much more he added to this effect, which is preserved in his orations....

To conclude. All witchcraft comes from carnal lust, which is in women insatiable. See *Proverbs* xxx: There are three things that are never satisfied, yea, a fourth thing which says not, it is enough; that is, the mouth of the womb. Wherefore for the sake of fulfilling their lusts they consort even with devils. More such reasons could be brought forward, but to the understanding it is sufficiently clear that it is no matter for wonder that there are more women than men found infected with the heresy of witchcraft. And in consequence of this, it is better called the heresy of witches than of wizards, since the name is taken from the more powerful party. And blessed be the Highest Who has so far preserved the male sex from so great a crime: for since He was willing to be born and to suffer for us, therefore He has granted to men this privilege.

[PART 2, QUESTION I, CHAPTER IV:] WHETHER THE RELATIONS OF AN INCUBUS DEVIL WITH A WITCH ARE ALWAYS ACCOMPANIED BY THE INJECTION OF SEMEN

To this question it is answered that the devil has a thousand ways and means of inflicting injury, and from the time of his first Fall has tried to

---

4. *"Pelagia." "Pelagia meretix" or "Pelagia mima," a beautiful actress who led the life of a prostitute at Antioch. She was converted by the holy bishop Nonnus, and disguised as a man went on a pilgrimage to Jerusalem, where for many years she led the life of extremist mortification and penance in a grotto on the Mount of Olives. This "bienheureuse pécheresse" attained to such heights of sanctity that she was canonized, and in the East, where her cult was long very popular, her festival is kept on 8 October, which is also the day of her commemoration in the Roman Martyrology.*

destroy the unity of the Church, and in every way to subvert the human race. Therefore no infallible rule can be stated as to this matter, but there is this probable distinction: that a witch is either old and sterile, or she is not. And if she is, then he naturally associates with the witch without the injection of semen, since it would be of no use, and the devil avoids superfluity in his operations as far as he can. But if she is not sterile, he approaches her in the way of carnal delectation which is procured for the witch. And should she be disposed to pregnancy, then if he can conveniently possess the semen extracted from some man, he does not delay to approach her with it for the sake of infecting her progeny.

But it is asked whether he is able to collect the semen emitted in some nocturnal pollution in sleep, just as he collects that which is spent in the carnal act, the answer is that it is probable that he cannot, though others hold a contrary opinion. For it must be noted that, as has been said, the devils pay attention to the generative virtue of the semen, and such virtue is more abundant and better preserved in semen obtained by the carnal act, being wasted in the semen that is due to nocturnal pollutions in sleep, which arises only from the superfluity of the humours and is not emitted with so great generative virtue. Therefore it is believed that he does not make use of such semen for the generation of progeny, unless perhaps he knows that the necessary virtue is present in that semen.

But this also cannot altogether be denied, that even in the case of a married witch who has been impregnated by her husband, the devil can, by the commixture of another semen, infect that which has been conceived.

WHETHER THE INCUBUS OPERATES MORE AT ONE TIME THAN ANOTHER: AND SIMILARLY OF THE PLACE

To the question whether the devil observes times and places it is to be said that, apart from his observation of certain times and constellations when his purpose is to effect the pollution of the progeny, he also observes certain times when his object is not pollution, but the causing of venereal pleasure on the part of the witch; and these are the most sacred times of the whole year, such as Christmas, Easter, Pentecost, and other Feast Days.

And the devils do this for three reasons. First, that in this way witches may become imbued not only with the vice of perfidy through apostasy from the Faith, but also with that of Sacrilege, and that the greater offence may be done to the Creator, and the heavier damnation rest upon the souls of the witches.

The second reason is that when God is so heavily offended, He allows them greater power of injuring even innocent men by punishing them either in their affairs or their bodies. For when it is said: "The son shall not bear the iniquity of the father," etc., this refers only to eternal punishment, for very often the innocent are punished with temporal afflictions on account of the sins of others. Wherefore in another place God says: "I am a mighty and jealous God, visiting the sins of the fathers unto the third and fourth generation."[5] Such punishment was exemplified in the children of the men of Sodom, who were destroyed for their fathers' sins.

The third reason is that they have greater opportunity to observe many people, especially young girls, who on Feast Days are more intent on idleness and curiosity, and are therefore more easily seduced by old witches. And the following happened in the native country of one of us Inquisitors (for there are two of us collaborating in this work).

A certain young girl, a devout virgin, was solicited one Feast Day by an old woman to go with her upstairs to a room where there were some very beautiful young men. And when she consented, and as they were going upstairs with the old woman leading the way, she warned the girl not to make the sign of the Cross. And though she agreed to this, yet she secretly crossed herself. Consequently it happened that, when they had gone up, the virgin saw no one, because the devils who were there were unable to show themselves in assumed bodies to that virgin. And the old woman cursed her, saying: Depart in the name of all the devils; why did you cross yourself? This I had from the frank relation of that good and honest maiden.

A fourth reason can be added, namely, that they can in this way more easily seduce men, by causing them to think that if God permits such things to be done at the most holy times, it cannot be such a heavy sin as if He did not permit them at such times.

With regard to the question whether they favour one place more than another, it is to be said that it is proved by the words and actions of witches that they are quite unable to commit these abominations in sacred places. And in this can be seen the efficacy of the Guardian Angels, that such places are reverenced. And further, witches assert that they never have any peace except at the time of Divine Service when they are present in the church; and therefore they are the first to enter and the last to leave the church. Nevertheless, they are bound to observe certain other abominable ceremonies at the command of the devils, such as to spit on the ground at the Elevation of the Host, or to utter, either verbally or otherwise, the filthiest thoughts, as: I wish you were in such or such a place....

5. *"Generation." "Exodus" xx, 5: xxxiv, 7.*

[PART 2, QUESTION I, CHAPTER VI:] HOW WITCHES IMPEDE AND PREVENT THE POWER OF PROCREATION.

...But it must be noted that such obstruction is caused both intrinsically and extrinsically. Intrinsically they cause it in two ways. First, when they directly prevent the erection of the member which is accommodated to fructification. And this need not seem impossible, when it is considered that they are able to vitiate the natural use of any member. Secondly, when they prevent the flow of the vital essences to the members in which resides the motive force, closing up the seminal ducts so that it does not reach the generative vessels, or so that it cannot be ejaculated, or is fruitlessly spilled.

Extrinsically they cause it at times by means of images, or by the eating of herbs; sometimes by other external means, such as cocks' testicles. But it must not be thought that it is by the virtue of these things that a man is made impotent, but by the occult power of devils' illusions witches by this means procure such impotence, namely, that they cause a man to be unable to copulate, or a woman to conceive.

And the reason for this is that God allows them more power over this act, by which the first sin was disseminated, than over other human actions. Similarly they have more power over serpents, which are the most subject to the influence of incantations, than over other animals. Wherefore it has often been found by us and other Inquisitors that they have caused this obstruction by means of serpents or some such things.

For a certain wizard who had been arrested confessed that for many years he had by witchcraft brought sterility upon all the men and animals which inhabited a certain house. Moreover, Nider tells of a wizard named Stadlin who was taken in the diocese of Lausanne, and confessed that in a certain house where a man and his wife were living, he had by his witchcraft successively killed in the woman's womb seven children, so that for many years the woman always miscarried. And that, in the same way, he had caused that all the pregnant cattle and animals of the house were during those years unable to give birth to any live issue. And when he was questioned as to how he had done this, and what manner of charge should be preferred against him, he discovered his crime, saying: I put a serpent under the threshold of the outer door of the house; and if this is removed, fecundity will be restored to the inhabitants. And it was as he said; for though the serpent was not found, having been reduced to dust, the whole piece of ground was removed, and in the same year fecundity was restored to the wife and to all the animals.

Another instance occurred hardly four years ago in Reichshofen. There was a most notorious witch, who could at all times and by a mere touch bewitch women and cause an abortion. Now the wife of a certain nobleman in that place had become pregnant and had engaged a midwife to take care of her, and had been warned by the midwife not to go out of the castle, and above all to be careful not to hold any speech or conversation with that witch. After some weeks, unmindful of that warning, she went out of the castle to visit some women who were met together on some festive occasion; and when she had sat down for a little, the witch came, and, as if for the purpose of saluting her, placed both her hands on her stomach; and suddenly she felt the child moving in pain. Frightened by this, she returned home and told the midwife what had happened. Then the midwife exclaimed: "Alas! you have already lost your child." And so it proved when her time came; for she gave birth, not to an entire abortion, but little by little to separate fragments of its head and feet and hands. And this great affliction was permitted by God to punish her husband, whose duty it was to bring witches to justice and avenge their injuries to the Creator.

And there was in the town of Mersburg in the diocese of Constance a certain young man who was bewitched in such a way that he could never perform the carnal act with any woman except one. And many have heard him tell that he had often wished to refuse that woman, and take flight to other lands; but that hitherto he had been compelled to rise up in the night and to come very quickly back, sometimes over land, and sometimes through the air as if he were flying.

23

Heresy

De Haeresibus
St. Augustine (354–430)

Heresy, or the divergence in belief from mainstream Church doctrine, existed since the early days of Christianity. Manichaeanism was one such movement. It was founded by Mani in Persia in the third century. It was a dualist religion that saw the world divided between the forces of light (goodness) and the forces of darkness (evil). It believed that the god of darkness had taken sparks of light and imprisoned them in material bodies of men and women. The purpose of human life was to release these sparks of light by exposing the body to severe asceticism. Before Augustine converted to Christianity, he had been a Manichaean. The following excerpt comes from chapter 46 of Augustine's *De Haeresibus* ("Concerning Heresies"), in which he describes some of the practices of the Manichaeans.

Source: *De Haeresibus: A Translation with an Introduction and Commentary*, by Liguori G. Müller (Washington DC: Catholic University of America Press, 1956), pp. 89–91. Reprinted with permission.

...In this circumstance, or rather because of some demand of their detestable superstition, their Elect are forced to consume a sort of eucharist sprinkled with human seed in order that the divine substance may be freed even from that, just as it is from other foods of which they partake. However, they deny that they do this, claiming that some others do it, using the name of the Manichaeans. But they were exposed in the Church at Carthage, as you know, for you were a deacon there at the time when, under the prosecution of Ursus the tribune, who was then prefect of the palace, some of them were brought to trial. At this time a girl by the name of Margaret gave evidence of their obscene practices and claimed, though she was not yet twelve years old, that she had been violated in the performance of this criminal rite. Then with difficulty he compelled Eusebia, some kind of Manichaean nun, to admit that she had undergone the same treatment in this regard, though at first, she maintained that she was a virgin and insisted on being examined by a midwife. When she was examined and when her true condition was discovered, she likewise gave information on that whole loathsome business at which flour is sprinkled beneath a couple in sexual intercourse to receive and commingle with their seed. This she had not heard when Margaret gave her testimony, for she had not been present. Even in recent times some of them have been exposed and brought before ecclesiastical authority, as the "Episcopal Acts" which you have sent us show. Under careful examination, they admitted that this is no sacrament, but a sacrilege.

One of them, whose name is Viator, claimed that those who commit such acts are properly called Catharists. Nevertheless, though he asserted that there are other groups of the Manichaean sect divided into Mattarii and especially Manichaeans, he could not deny that all of these three forms were propagated by the same founder and that all of them are, generally speaking, Manichaeans. Surely the Manichaean books are unquestionably common to all of them, and in these books are described these dreadful things relating to the transformation of males into females, and of females into males to attract and to loosen through concupiscence the princes of darkness of both sexes so that the divine substance which is imprisoned in them may be set free and escape. This is the source of the obscene practices which some of the Manichaeans refuse to admit pertain to them. For they imagine that they are imitating divine powers to the highest degree and so they attempt to purge a part of their god, which they really believe is held befouled just as much in human seed as it is in all celestial and terrestrial bodies, and in the seeds of all things. And for this reason, it follows that they are just as much obliged to purge it from human seed by eating, as they are in reference to other seed which they consume in their food. This is the reason they are also called Catharists, that is, Purifiers, for they are so attentive to purifying this part that they do not refrain even from such horrifying food as this.

Chronicle of Ralph of Coggeshall
Ralph of Coggeshall

Ralph was abbot of a Cistercian monastery in England between 1207 and 1218. The following story is dated between 1176 and 1180 and comes from his chronicle. It describes a young heretic woman and her "errors" as told to him by Gervais of Tilbury, a well-known storyteller and courtier. It is interesting to note that suspicions regarding the girl's religious convictions were raised for both Gervais and church officials when the girl refused to have sexual relations with him — an irony considering that Christian teaching stressed the importance of chastity.

Source: *Heresies of the High Middle Ages: Selected Sources,* translated and annotated by
Walter L. Wakefield and Austin P. Evans. © 1991 Columbia University Press, pp. 251–254,
305–306. Reprinted with the permission of the publisher.

In the time of Louis, king of France, who fathered King Philip, while
the error of certain heretics, who are called Publicans in the vernacular, was
spreading through several of the provinces of France, a marvelous thing happened in the city of Rheims in connection with an old woman infected with
that plague. For one day when Lord William, archbishop of that city and
King Philip's uncle, was taking a canter with his clergy outside the city, one
of his clerks, Master Gervais of Tilbury by name, noticed a girl walking
alone in a vineyard. Urged by the curiosity of hot-blooded youth, he turned
aside to her, as we later heard from his own lips when he was a canon. He
greeted her and attentively inquired whose daughter she was and what she
was doing there alone, and then, after admiring her beauty for a while, he
at length in courtly fashion made her a proposal of wanton love. She was
much abashed, and with eyes cast down, she answered him with simple ges-
ture and a certain gravity of speech: "Good youth, the Lord does not desire
me ever to be your friend or the friend of any man, for if ever I forsook my
virginity and my body had once been defiled, I should most assuredly fall
under eternal damnation without hope of recall."

As he heard this, Master Gervais at once realized that she was one of
that most impious sect of Publicans, who at that time were everywhere being
sought out and destroyed, especially by Philip, count of Flanders, who was
harassing them pitilessly with righteous cruelty. Some of them, indeed, had
come to England and were seized at Oxford, where by command of King
Henry II they were shamefully branded on their foreheads with a red-hot
key. While the aforesaid clerk was arguing with the girl to demonstrate the
error of such an answer, the archbishop approached with his retinue and,
learning the cause of the argument, ordered the girl seized and brought with
him to the city. When he addressed her in the presence of his clergy and
advanced many scriptural passages and reasonable arguments to confute her
error, she replied that she had not yet been well enough taught to demonstrate the falsity of such statements but she admitted that she had a mistress
in the city who, by her arguments, would very easily refute everyone's objections. So, when the girl had disclosed the woman's name and abode, she was
immediately sought out, found, and haled before the archbishop by his
officials. When she was assailed from all sides by the archbishop himself and
the clergy with many questions and with texts of the Holy Scriptures which
might destroy such error, by perverse interpretation she so altered all the texts
advanced that it became obvious to everyone that the spirit of all error spoke
through her mouth. Indeed, to the texts and narratives of both the Old and

New Testaments which they put to her, she answered as easily, as much by memory, as though she had mastered a knowledge of all the Scriptures and had been well trained in this kind of response, mixing the false with the true and mocking the true interpretation of our faith with a kind of perverted insight. Therefore, because it was impossible to recall the obstinate minds of both these persons from the error of their ways by threat or persuasion, or by any arguments or scriptural texts, they were placed in prison until the following day.

On the morrow they were recalled to the archepiscopal court, before the archbishop and all the clergy, and in the presence of the nobility were again confronted with many reasons for renouncing their error publicly. But since they yielded not at all to salutary admonitions but persisted stubbornly in error once adopted, it was unanimously decreed that they be delivered to the flames. When the fire had been lighted in the city and the officials were about to drag them to the punishment decreed, that mistress of vile error exclaimed, "O foolish and unjust judges, do you think now to burn me in your flames? I fear not your judgment, nor do I tremble at the waiting fire!" With these words, she suddenly pulled a ball of thread from her heaving bosom and threw it out of a large window, but keeping the end of the thread in her hands; then in a loud voice, audible to all, she said "Catch!" At the word, she was lifted from the earth before everyone's eyes and followed the ball out the window in rapid flight, sustained, we believe, by the ministry of the evil spirits who once caught Simon Magus up into the air. What became of that wicked woman, or whither she was transported, the onlookers could in no wise discover. But the girl had not yet become so deeply involved in the madness of that sect; and, since she still was present, yet could be recalled from the stubborn course upon which she had embarked neither by the inducement of reason nor by the promise of riches, she was burned. She caused a great deal of astonishment to many, for she emitted no sigh, not a tear, no groan, but endured all the agony of the conflagration steadfastly and eagerly, like a martyr of Christ. But for how different a cause from the Christian religion, for which they of the past were slaughtered by pagans! People of this wicked sect choose to die rather than be converted from error; but they have nothing in common with the constancy and steadfastness of martyrs for Christ, since it is piety which brings contempt for death to the latter, to the former it is hardness of heart.

These heretics allege that children should not be baptized until they reach the age of understanding; they add that prayers should not be offered for the dead, nor intercession asked of the saints. They condemn marriages; they preach virginity as a cover for their lasciviousness. They abhor milk and anything made thereof and all food which is the product of coition. They do not believe that purgatorial fire awaits one after death but that once the soul is released it goes immediately to rest or to damnation. They accept no scriptures as holy except the Gospels and the canonical letters. They are countryfolk and so cannot be overcome by rational argument, corrected by scriptural texts, or swayed by persuasions. They choose rather to die than to be converted from this most impious sect. Those who have delved into their secrets declare also that these persons do not believe that God administers human affairs or exercises any direction or control over earthly creatures. Instead, an apostate angel, whom they call Luzabel, presides over all the material creation, and all things on earth are done by his will. The body is shaped by the devil, the soul is created by God and infused into the body; whence it comes about that a persistent struggle is always being waged between body and soul. Some also say that in their subterranean haunts they perform execrable sacrifices to their Lucifer at stated times and that there they enact certain sacrilegious infamies.

Historia Albigensis
Pierre des Vaux de Cernay (d. 1248)

Pierre des Vaux de Cernay was a Cistercian monk who travelled with the Albigensian Crusaders in 1212 led by Simon de Montfort to Languedoc in southern France. He wrote a history of the beliefs of the Albigensians in his *Historia Albigensis*, which was completed some time after 1218.

The Cathari, also called the Albigensians after the town of Albi where its adherents were particularly prevalent, practiced a dualist religion. They were a product of both Manichaeanist beliefs and protesters against the corruption of the mainstream Church. Like Manichaeanism, Cathar beliefs held that the universe was divided between the god of good and the god of evil, who were in constant struggle with each other. The god of evil represented material things, while the god of good represented the spiritual, thus souls were trapped in evil material bodies. They believed in reincarnation and hoped that the soul would break out of the physical rebirth. Their elite, known as *perfecti*, lived in rigorous asceticism.

Source: *Heresy and Authority in Medieval Europe: Documents in Translation*, edited by Edward Peters (Philadelphia: University of Pennsylvania Press, 1980), pp. 123–125. Reprinted by permission of the University of Pennsylvania Press. Copyright © 1980 by Edward Peters.

First it is to be known that the heretics held that there are two creators: viz. one of invisible things, whom they called the benevolent god, and another of visible things, whom they named the malevolent god. The New Testament they attributed to the benevolent god, but the Old Testament to the malevolent god, and rejected it altogether, except certain authorities which are inserted in the New Testament from the Old, which, out of reverence to the New Testament, they esteemed worthy of reception. They charged the author of the Old Testament with falsehood, because the Creator said, "In the day that ye eat of the tree of the knowledge of good and evil ye shall die"; nor (as they say) after eating did they die, when, in fact, after the eating the forbidden fruit they were subjected to the misery of death. They also call him a homicide, as well, because he burned up Sodom and Gomorrah and destroyed the world by the waters of the deluge, as because he overwhelmed Pharaoh and the Egyptians in the sea. They affirmed also that all the fathers of the Old Testament were damned, that John the Baptist was one of the greater demons. They said also, in their secret doctrine, [*in secreto suo*] that that Christ who was born in the visible and terrestrial Bethlehem and crucified in Jerusalem was a bad man, and that Mary Magdalene was his concubine; and that she was the woman taken in adultery, of whom we read in the gospel. For the good Christ, as they said, never ate, nor drank, nor took upon him true flesh, nor ever was in this world, except spiritually in the body of Paul. I say in the terrestrial and visible Bethlehem, because the heretics feigned that there was another new and invisible country, and in that country, according to some, the good Christ was born and crucified. Also the heretics said that the good god had two wives, Collant and Colibant, and from them begat sons and daughters. There were other heretics who said that there is one Creator but that he had for sons Christ and the devil. These, also, said that all creatures were good, but that by the daughters of whom we read in the Apocalypse [*marg.* Genesis], all things had been corrupted.

They said that almost all the Church of Rome was a den of thieves, and that it was the harlot of which we read in the Apocalypse. They so far annulled the sacraments of the Church, as publicly to teach that the water of holy baptism was just the same as river water, and that the Host of the most holy body of Christ did not differ from common bread, instilling into the ears of the simple this blasphemy, that the body of Christ, even though it had been as great as the Alps, would have been long ago consumed and annihilated by those who had eaten of it. Confirmation and confession they considered as altogether vain and frivolous. They preached that holy matrimony was meretricious, and that none could be saved in it if they should beget children. Denying also the resurrection of the flesh, they invented some unheard-of notions, saying that our souls are those of angelic spirits who, being cast down from heaven by the apostacy of pride, left their glorified bodies in the air; and that these souls themselves, after successively inhabiting seven terrene bodies of one sort or another, having at length fulfilled their penance, return to those deserted bodies.

It is also to be known that some among the heretics were called "perfect" or "good men"; others "believers" of the heretics. Those who were called perfect wore a black dress, falsely pretended to chastity, abhorred the eating of flesh, eggs and cheese, wished to appear not liars when they were continually telling lies, chiefly respecting God. They also said that they ought not on any account to swear.

Those were called "believers" of the heretics, who lived after the manner of the world, and who though they did not attain so far as to imitate the life of the perfect, nevertheless hoped to be saved in their faith; and though they differed as to their mode of life, they were one with them in belief and unbelief. Those who were called believers of the heretics were given to usury, rapine, homicide, lust, perjury, and every vice; and they, in fact, sinned with more security and less restraint, because they believed that without restitution, without confession and penance, they should be saved, if only, when on the point of death, they could say a Pater Noster, and receive imposition of hands from the teachers.

As to the "perfect" heretics, however, they had a magistracy whom they called deacons and bishops, without the imposition of whose hands, at the time of his death, none of the believers thought he could be saved; but if they laid their hands upon any dying man, however wicked, if he could only say a Pater Noster, they considered him to be so saved that without any satisfaction and without any other aid, he immediately took wing to heaven.

"The Protests of the Heretics That in Matrimony No One Can Be Saved"
James Capelli

Capelli was a Franciscan friar and lector of the Franciscan convent in Milan in the middle of the thirteenth century. Although he believed that the Cathars' beliefs were wrong, he did not vilify them in his writings. Indeed, Capelli tried to portray their beliefs accurately and to disabuse popular misconceptions of them. The following passage argues that heretics were not driven by lust or sexually depraved as many other church writers believed.

Source: *Heresies of the High Middle Ages: Selected Sources*, translated and annotated by Walter L. Wakefield and Austin P. Evans. © 1991 Columbia University Press, pp. 251–254, 305–306. Reprinted with permission of the publisher.

...Now matrimony is the legitimate union of man and woman who seek an inseparable community of life under faith and worship of one God. Against this the ferocious rabies of the heretics foams out false phrases full of idle superstition. They babble that no one can ever be saved in matrimony. Indeed, these most stupid of people, seeking the purity of virginity and chastity, say that all carnal coition is shameful, base, and odious, and thus damnable. Although spiritually they are prostituted and they pollute the word of God, they are, however, most chaste of body. For men and women observing the vow and way of life of this sect are in no way soiled by the corruption of debauchery. Whence, if any one of them, man or woman, happens to be fouled by fornication, if convicted by two or three witnesses, he forthwith either is ejected from their group or, if he repents, is reconsoled by the imposition of their hands, and a heavy penitential burden is placed upon him as amends for sin. Actually, the rumor of the fornication which is said to prevail among them is most false. For it is true that once a month, either by day or by night, in order to avoid gossip by the people, men and women meet together, not, as some lyingly say, for purposes of fornication, but so that they may hear preaching and make confession to their presiding official, as though from his prayers pardon for their sins would ensue. They are wrongfully wounded in popular rumor by many malicious charges of blasphemy from those who say that they commit many shameful and horrid acts of which they are innocent. And, therefore, they vaunt themselves to be disciples of Christ, who said, "If they have persecuted me, they will also persecute you";[1] and "You shall be hated by all men for my name's sake."[2] And, indeed, they believe fulfilled in them the text, "Blessed are ye when they shall revile you and reproach you and speak all that is evil against you untruly for my sake."[3] Furthermore, they gather each month as though to receive the fruit of penitence, since it is written in the Apocalypse, "And on both sides of the river was the tree of life, bearing twelve fruits, yielding its fruits every month."[4] This, by false interpretation, they expound as applying to their conventicles. They are all bound by their superstitious and false religion, as we said, to the vow of continence. Hence, the devil having suggested to them that they condemn marriages, they call all other persons sensuous and lewd, and thus they are cast out from the chaste body the Church and lose the reward of their continence...

1. John 15:20.
2. Mark 13:13.
3. Matt. 5:11, with slight change in wording.
4. Apoc. 22:2.

VIII

JUDAISM

24

Judaic Law

Midrash Rabbah

This is the interpretation and commentary of the Hebrew Scripture that was written from the fifth century BCE onwards and had a heavy influence on both medieval Jews and Christian theologians. The Midrash Rabbah comprises the Torah, which is the first five books of the Old Testament (Genesis, Exodus, Leviticus, Numbers, and Deuteronomy), and the Five Megillot or Scrolls (Song of Songs, Esther, Ruth, Lamentations, and Ecclesiastes). The following excerpt comes from the Leviticus Rabbah, a book that concerns itself primarily with the laws of purity.

Source: *Judaism and Scripture: The Evidence of Leviticus Rabbah*, by Jacob Neusner (Chicago: University of Chicago Press, 1986), pp. 322–323, 424–425, 427–429. Reprinted with permission from Professor Jacob Neusner.

XV:V

1. A. [Returning to the] body [of the matter]: What is written prior to the present topic?

B. "If a woman conceives and bears a male child" (Lev. 12:2)

C. And what is written thereafter?

D. "When a man has on the skin of his body…" (Lev. 13:2)

E. What has one thing got to do with the other?

F. Said R. Tanhum b. R. Hanilai, "[The matter may be compared] to the case of an ass that fell sick and was cauterized [by the veterinarian]. What caused the offspring to come forth with a mark [of cauterization]? It was because its mother had fallen sick and been cauterized.

G. "So who was it that caused the offspring to come forth afflicted with leprosy marks? It was its mother, who did not take precautions [not to have sexual relations during] her menstrual period."

H. Said R. Abin, "[The matter may be compared] to a vegetable patch, in

253

which a spring flowed. So long as the spring flows into it, the patch grows lichen. So too he who has sexual relations with his wife when she is menstruating in the end will cause her to produce offspring afflicted by leprosy."

I. R. Abin cited in regard [to the one afflicted by leprosy the following verse of Scripture]: "'The fathers have eaten sour grapes, and the teeth of the sons are set on edge' [Ez. 18:2].

J. "But they recited concerning their fathers, 'Our fathers sinned, and are no longer [alive], but we have borne the burden of their sins'" (Lam. 5:7).

XXIII:IX

1. A. R. Ishmael taught, "'You shall not do as they do in the land of Egypt, where you dwelt, and you shall not do as they do in the land of Canaan.... I am the Lord your God" [Lev.18: 3–4].

B. "And if not, it is as if I am not the Lord your God."

2. A. R. Hiyya taught, "[The text states,] 'I am the Lord your God' two times [Lev.18: 4,5].

B. "I am the one who exacted punishment from the Generation of the Flood and from the men of Sodom and Gomorrah and from Egypt.

C. "'I am going to exact punishment from anyone who does as they did.'"

3. A. The Generation of the Flood were kings. They were blotted out of the world only because they were drowning in promiscuity.

B. Said R. Simlai, "In every case in which you find prostitution, mass slaughter comes into the world and kills the good and the bad."

C. R. Huna in the name of R. Yosé said, "The Generation of the Flood were blotted out of the world only because they composed hymeneal songs even for pederasty and bestiality."

D. R. Azariah in the name of R. Joshua b. R. Simon and R. Joshua b. Levi in the name of Bar Qappara: "We find that with all things the Holy One, blessed be he, is long-suffering, except for prostitution.

E. "And there are many verses of Scripture [that prove that fact]:

F. "'When men began [to multiply on the face of the ground] ... the sons of God saw that the daughters of men were fair.... The Lord saw that the wickedness of man was great [in the earth].... So the Lord said, I will blot out [man, whom I have created ... for I am sorry that I ever made them']" (Gen. 6:1–7).

4. A. As to the Sodomites:

B. R. Joshua b. Levi in the name of Bar Pedaiah: "That entire night Lot was standing and marshaling arguments in their defense. When they came and said to him, 'Where are the men ... bring them out, that we may know them' [Gen. 19:5] sexually,

C. "forthwith: 'The men said to Lot, Whom else do you have here?' [Gen. 19:12]. Up to this point you had an opening to marshal arguments in their defense. But from this point you have no more opening to marshal arguments in their defense. Rather: 'Your son-in-law, sons, daughters...for we will destroy this place'" (Gen. 19:13).

"I am the Lord" (Lev. 18.4):

5. A. "I am he who exacted punishment from Samson, Amnon, and Zimri, and I am going to exact punishment from whoever does as they did.

B. "I am he who rewarded Joseph, Jael, and Palti. I am going to reward whoever does as they did."

D. What [do we find in the case of] Joseph?

E. Said Rabban Simeon b. Gamaliel, "Joseph was given what belonged to him [by virtue of his righteous deeds]:

F. "Since his mouth did not kiss [a married woman and so commit] a transgression: 'According to your mouth shall all the people be ruled' [Gen. 41: 40].

G. "Since his neck did not bend [to commit] a transgression: 'He put a golden chain around his neck' [Gen. 41:42].

H. "Since his hands did not caress [a married woman] in transgression: 'And Pharaoh removed his seal [from his hand and placed it on the hand of Joseph]' [Gen. 41:42].

I. "Since his body did not touch [a married woman and so commit] a transgression: 'He clothed him in fine linen clothing' [Gen. 41:42].

J. "Since his feet did not carry him to [commit] a transgression, let him come and ride in a chariot: 'He made him ride in the second chariot' [Gen. 41:43].

K. "Since his mind did not plan to [commit] a transgression, let it come and salute [his] wisdom: 'And they called before him, Abrech, [meaning: father as to wisdom, youth as to years].'"

XXIII: XII

1. A. "The eye of the adulterer also waits for the twilight, [saying, 'No eye shall see me,' and he [God] who dwells in secret puts on a face]" (Job 24:15).

B. Said R. Simeon b. Laquish, "you should not say that [only one who] actually commits adultery is called an adulterer. But one who commits adultery merely with his eyes also is called an adulterer,

C. "as it is said, 'The eye of the adulterer waits for the twilight.'"

2. A. Now the adulterer sits and watches, [saying,] "When will twilight come, when will evening come?"

B. "In the twilight, in the evening of the day" (Prov. 7:9).

C. But he does not know that he who sits in the secret place of the world, the Holy One, blessed be he, so shapes the features of the embryo's face as to expose him [as the father of the child].

D. This is in line with what Job says, "'Does it seem good to you to oppress [and to despise the work of your hands and favor the designs of the wicked]?' [Job 10:3].

E. "This one [the woman's husband] supports and feeds [the wife], but [God] shapes the features of the embryo's face in the other man's likeness!

F. "'To despise the work of your hands' [Job 10:3]. Since you have labored all those forty days [to make the embryo] now will you go and spoil it?

G. "'And favor the designs of the wicked' [Job 10:3]. Is this appropriate to your dignity, to stand between the adulterer and the adulteress?"

H. Said to him the Holy One, blessed be he, "Job, you really do owe me an apology. But will people say as you have said, 'Do you have eyes of flesh' [Job 10:4]?

I. "But," said the Holy One, blessed be he, "Lo, I shall so shape the features of the embryo's face in the other's likeness as to expose him [the adulterer, as the father of the child]."

3. A. Said R. Levi, "The matter may be compared to the case of an apprentice of a potter, who stole a lump of potter's clay, and his master found out about the theft.

B. "What did [the master] do?

C. "He went and made it into a utensil and left it before [the disciple].

D. "Why did he do this? To let him know that his master had detected the theft.

E. "So said the Holy One, blessed be he, 'Lo, I shall so shape the features of the embryo's face in his likeness as to expose [the adulterer as the father of the child].'"

4. A. R. Judah b. R. Simon in the name of R. Levi b. Parta: "It is written, 'The Rock that formed you have you weakened (teshi)' [Deut. 32:18].

B. "You have exhausted (hittastem) the strength of the Creator.

C. "The matter may be compared to an artist who was sitting and drawing the features of the king.

D. "Just as he was finishing his drawing, they came and told him, 'The king has been changed.'

E. "Forthwith the artist's hands trembled. He said, 'Whose [picture] shall we make, the one of the former or the one of the new [king]?'

F. "So too for all forty days the Holy One, blessed be he, is engaged in shaping the embryo. At the end of the forty days, the mother goes and plays around with someone else. Forthwith: 'The hands of the Creator tremble. He says, 'Whose [likeness] shall we make, the one of the former or the one of the new [father]?'

G. "This is an example of the statement, 'The Rock that formed you have you weakened.' You have exhausted the strength of the Creator."

H. In the word *teshi* (TSY) the Y is written smaller than the other letters. [There is no similar instance in Scripture.]

5. A. Said R. Isaac, "We find that in the case of all those who commit transgression, the thief benefits, and the victim loses, the robber benefits, and the victim loses.

B. "But here both of them benefit!

C. "Who then is the victim? It is as if it were the Holy One, blessed be he, who [has to] destroy the marks of identification [that he has already given to the embryo]."

Babylonian Talmud

This is the commentary on the oral law that God handed to Moses called the *Mishnah*, recorded about the second century CE. The Babylonian Talmud itself began to be compiled about 550 CE and was probably completed in 800. The Talmud, like the Mishnah, is divided into six institutes or Sedarim. The following tract, called *Ketubot*, deals with marriage contracts and is derived from the Seder Nashim, which pertains to women.

Source: *Tractate Ketubot*, The Talmud of Babylonia, vol. 14 A, translated by Jacob Neusner (Atlanta, GA: Scholars Press, 1992), pp. 37–39, 144–145. Reprinted with permission from Professor Jacob Neusner.

A. *There was a groom who came before Rabban Gamaliei the son of Rabbi. He said to him,* "My lord, I had sexual relations and found no blood."

B. *She said to him,* "My lord, I was a virgin."

C. He said to them, "Bring me the sheet."

D. They brought him the sheet, and they soaked it in water and laundered it and found quite a bit of blood. He said to him, "Go, acquire what you have purchased."

A. *Said Huna Mar b. Raba of Paraziqa to R. Ashi, "So should we do that, too?"*

B. *He said to him, "Our laundry work is like their washing. And if you say, so let's do laundry work, the upshot is that the stone you use to smooth the fabric will remove any blood."*

A. *There was someone who came before Rabban Gamaliel son of Rabbi and said to him,* "My lord, I have had sexual relations and found no blood."

B. She said to him, "My lord, I am still a virgin."

C. He said to them, "Bring me two slave girls, one a virgin, one not."

D. They produced them, and he had them sit on the mouth of a wine cask. In the case of the nonvirgin, the odor of the wine passed through, in the case of the virgin, it didn't. He put the wife on the cask, and the smell didn't pass through. He said to him. "Go, acquire what you have purchased."

A. *Why not examine [in such a manner] to begin with?*

B. *He'd heard a tradition about it, but he'd never seen it done in practice, and he thought, "Maybe it wouldn't work out right, and it would not be proper to treat Israelite women in such a disrespectful way."*

A. *There was someone who came before Rabban Gamaliel the Elder and said to him,* "My lord, I have had sexual relations and found no blood."

B. She said to him, "My lord, I am of the family of Dorqati, and women of our family don't produce menstrual blood or hymeneal blood."

C. Rabban Gamaliel looked into the matter among her female relatives and found that what she said was so. He said to him, "Go, acquire what you have purchased. Fortunate are you that you have had the advantage of marrying into that family."

A. *What is the meaning of the name Dorqait?*

B. *A generation [dor] that is cut off [qatua].*

A. Said R. Hanina, "Rabban Gamaliel accorded that man empty consolation, *for it has been taught as a Tannaite statement by R. Hiyya,* 'Just as leaven is good for dough, so blood is good for a woman.' *And it has been taught on Tannaite authority in the name of R. Meir,* 'Any woman who has a substantial menstrual flow has a large number of children.'"

B. *It has been stated:*

C. R. Jeremiah bar Abba said, "'Acquire what you have purchased' is what he said to him."

D. And R. Yosé bar Abin said, "'You are penalized by what you have bought.'"

E. *Now there is no problem for the one who says that he said to him, "You are penalized by what you have bought," for that is in line with what R. Hanina has said. But from the perspective of him who says that what he said is, "Acquire what you have purchased," what advantage is there to be acquired with such a marriage?*

F. *He will never have any doubts in respect to ascertaining the exact time of menstruation.*

A. *There was someone who came before Rabbi and said to him,* "My lord, I have had sexual relations and found no blood."

B. She said to him, "My lord, I am still a virgin, and it was a time of famine."

C. Rabbi looked into their faces and saw that they were black with hunger. He gave instructions concerning them, and then brought them into the bath and gave them food and drink and put them into a private room. He had sexual relations and found blood.

D. He said to him, "Go, acquire what you have purchased."

E. Rabbi recited in their regard this verse: "Their skin is shriveled upon their bones, it is withered, it has become like a stick" (Lam. 4:8)

Christian Law Pertaining to Jews

Laws passed by secular and ecclesiastical authorities concerning Jews provide a great source of knowledge regarding the condition of life for medieval Jewry. They also illustrate the suspicious attitudes of the Christians of the time toward Jewish customs and beliefs. The following laws are from the early middle ages. The Visigoths were the Germanic peoples who settled in Iberia. The Visigothic Laws come from two seventh century codes — one promulgated in 654 by Reccesvinth and the other promulgated in 681 by Erviga. The second group of laws was passed by various church councils held in Spain. The last source is the penitential of Pseudo-Theodore, written between 830 and 847.

Source: *The Jews in the Legal Sources of the Early Middle Ages,* edited and translated by Amnon Linder, 1997, with the permission of Wayne State University Press. Copyright © 1997 by the Israel Academy of Science and Humanities, pp. 264, 278, 324–325, 483–485, 490, 602.

Laws of the Visigoths

That the Jews Should Not Join Together in Nuptial Contracts According to Their Custom

Not one of the Jews should join in marriage, pollute in adultery, or defile in incest his blood relative. No one should take in sexual intercourse any person within the sixth degree. No one should either adopt or practice nuptial celebrations in any other way except according to the custom of the Christians. For if detected, he shall be punished by the punishments specified for such a condemnation.

THAT THE JEWS SHOULD NOT PRACTICE THE CIRCUMCISION OF THE FLESH

Not one of the Jews should carry out the circumcision of the flesh. No one should suffer this to be done to him and remain unpunished. No slave, no freeborn or freedman, native or foreigner, should either undertake or dare to operate on another the disgrace of this detestable operation on any occasion whatever. For anyone who would be proved to have of his own will done or endured the like shall be punished by the severity of the given law.

ON JUDAIZING CHRISTIANS

Just as Christians ought to bewail the crime of those people who maintain their prevarication against Christ, in the same way it should be fully determined that absolutely no one found guilty of deviating from the better way to the worst should merit forgiveness. And since a savage and stupefying presumption must be eradicated by an even more savage punishment, we decree in the edict of this law that any Christian of either sex, and in particular one born to Christian parents, exposed as having practiced circumcisions or any other Jewish rite (or if, God forbid, one should be exposed in future) should be subjected through the united will and the zeal of the Catholics to the harshest punishments and destroyed in the most degrading death, appropriate to the horrendous and execrable evil that he has most wickedly perpetrated. Their properties should be transferred unquestionably to the fisc if the heirs and relatives of such persons were stained by the deviation of consenting to this deed.

HOW THE CONGREGATION OF JEWS WITH THE BISHOP ON THE DESIGNATED DAYS SHOULD BE CARRIED OUT

Any community of Jews, whatever places or territories they are seen to inhabit, must congregate and join the local bishop or priest on the days of Sabbath or the other holidays that they use to celebrate; and they shall not use on these and similar days the permission they were granted to travel, but they shall not travel anywhere without the consent of their priest during the duration of those days they are suspected of celebrating. On the Sabbath days they shall always congregate with the bishop or the priest, clean after bathing and attached to the benediction given. In those places, indeed, where no priest will be present, any meeting or activity they should engage in shall be done with the judges or with the worthiest Christians; and they shall associate with them in such a way that they shall fearlessly give, when asked, favorable testimony on their conduct.

The women of the Jews, that is, their wives and daughters, shall not find occasion for any deviation or travel on all the above-mentioned holidays, which they misuse according to their deviation. This shall be entirely observed, namely, that a provident decree of the bishops and priests should be made in their regard in the presence of their men, to wit, that just as their men do not take themselves away from the presence of a priest, they, too, should be ordered to stay with certain worthiest Christian women, chosen by the priests and the bishops, during all those days. If anyone should be seen to act against this order, he shall be disgraced by being publicly shorn of his hair and subjected to the punishment of one hundred lashes. This shall be particularly observed, namely, that the hearts of lustful priests, agitated by the execrable contamination of the poison of desire, should not look for any pretext to gratify their desire. We decree, therefore, in a harsher sentence, that every priest shall carry out these directives of our laws in regard to the said women of the Jews in such a way that he shall have no occasion for privacy with these women, by means of which he should intend to defile himself with them. For if it would happen to any of the priests that he should frequently abuse the zeal — which he should use for the sake of Christ's name — as a pretext for his own desire, that priest shall be demoted from this honor and bound to a perpetual exile.

Conciliar Canons

On Faithful Maidens, That They Shall Not be Joined to Infidels [Elvira—c. 306]

If heretics should refuse to cross over to the Catholic Church, Catholic maidens shall not be given to them; and it was resolved to give them neither to Jews nor to heretics, because no association could exist between the faithful and the infidel. It is resolved that if parents should act contrary to the interdiction, they shall be removed for five years.

On the Married Faithful, If They Should Commit Adultery with a Jewess or with a Gentile [Toledo IV—633]

If anyone of the faithful with a wife should commit adultery with a Jewess or with a gentile, he shall be kept away from communion. If he should be exposed by another man, he shall be allowed to join the Lord's communion after he has completed a five-year regular penance.

On the Jews [Toledo IV—633]

On the council's proposal our most glorious lord ordered that it should be entered in the canons, that Jews should not be allowed to have Christian wives or concubines nor to purchase a Christian slave for their own use; yet if any sons were born in such a marriage they must be taken to be baptized; it is necessary that they should not act in any public office that would provide them with the opportunity to inflict punishment on Christians. Indeed, if any Christians have been defiled by them in the Jewish rite or have been even circumcised, they should return to liberty and the Christian religion with no repayment of their price.

ON MARRIAGES BETWEEN CHRISTIANS AND JEWS [TOLEDO VI—638]

Jews who have Christian wives in marriage should be warned by the bishop of their city that if they wish to remain with them, they should become Christians. If they were warned and have refused, they shall be separated, because an infidel cannot remain united to one who has transferred to the Christian faith. The sons issued from such marriages, however, should follow the faith and status of the mother; similarly, also, those born to infidel wives and faithful men should follow the Christian religion, not the Jewish superstition.

Penitential of Pseudo-Theodore

If any Christian woman should take gifts from the perfidious Jews and willingly commit adultery with them, she shall be separated from the Church for a whole year and live with great tribulation and then do penance nine years. If, however, she should give birth to children, she shall do penance twelve years. If she was taken against her will, she shall do penance five years. If, however, a Christian woman should willingly commit adultery with a gentile, she shall do penance seven years. If, however, she was taken against her will, she shall do penance four years unless, perchance, it should happen, as the Apostle says: *The infidel will be saved by a faithful wife.*

25

Judaic Thought

"The Female Nature"
Philo of Alexandria (20 BCE–50 CE)

Philo was a hellenized Jew who tried to reconcile Greek thought with Hebrew traditions and teachings. Jews living in Roman times and later medieval Jews had little interest in Philo's philosophical viewpoint, so they did not preserve his teachings. Interestingly, it was the early Christian churchmen who preserved most of Philo's writings because of the great reputation he enjoyed among theologians. Eusebius of Caesarea mentioned that Philo met St. Peter on a journey to Rome, while St. Jerome actually included Philo on his list of Church fathers.

Source: *The Contemplative Life, The Giants, and Selections: Philo of Alexandria*, translation and introduction by David Winston from the Classics of Western Spirituality, copyright © 1981 David Winston, Paulist Press, Inc., New York/Mahwah, N.J., pp. 280–282. Used with permission of Paulist Press, www.paulistpress.com.

Marketplaces, council chambers, law courts, confraternities, and meetings of vast crowds, life under the open air with its words and actions, befit men both in war and in peace. For women, on the other hand, the domestic life that abides within is appropriate, the maidens taking as their interior boundary the middle door, whereas those who have attained to full womanhood take the outer door. For the nature of communities is twofold, the greater and the smaller; the greater we call cities and the smaller households. As to the management of both forms, men have obtained that of the greater, which bears the name of statesmanship, whereas women have obtained that of the smaller, which goes under the name of household management. A woman, then, should not meddle in matters external to the household, but should seek seclusion....

...Even in wars, expeditions, and dangers threatening the entire community, the law does not deem it right for them to be found, having in view what is proper, which it was minded to maintain unaltered always and everywhere, considering it to be in itself a higher good than victory, freedom, and every form of success. If indeed a woman, learning that her husband is a victim of outrage, is overcome by the love induced by her conjugal attachment and is compelled by the momentary passion to rush forward, she must not in her boldness turn masculine beyond the bounds of nature, but remain within the limits in which women may render aid. For it would be dreadful if any woman in her wish to rescue her husband from outrage should outrage herself displaying her own life as full of disgrace and heavy reproaches attributable to her incurable effrontery...

And though all else could be tolerated, this is hard to take, if a woman become so emboldened as to take hold of the genitals of her adversary. She is not to be spared insofar as she appears to be doing this in aid of her husband. She must be restrained from her excessive boldness by paying a penalty through which, though she wish to repeat the offense, she will be incapable of doing so, and those others of her sex who are more reckless will grow moderate through fear. And the penalty shall consist in the cutting off of the hand that handled what it was forbidden to touch....

...The soul, like the family, has a male element in the male line and a female in the female line. The male soul attaches itself to God alone as the Father and Creator of the universe and Cause of all things. The female is devoted to what comes into being and perishes; it extends its power like a hand to take hold blindly of the fortuitous and welcomes the world of created being with all its innumerable changes and vicissitudes, instead of the unchangeable, blessed, and thrice happy divine nature. Naturally then is it clearly stated in a symbol to cut off the hand that had seized the testicles, not in the sense that the body be mutilated by being deprived of a most essential member, but to excise the godless thoughts that employ as their foundation all that comes into being through birth; for the "testicles" are symbols of sowing and birth. Following the logical sequence of nature, I will add this too. The monad is the image of the first cause, the dyad that of passive and divisible matter. Therefore one who honors and welcomes the dyad before the monad should not be unaware that he is approving of matter rather than of God. It is for this reason that the Law deemed it right to cut off this impulse of the soul as if it were a hand, for there is no greater impiety than to attribute to the passive principle the efficacy of the active one.

The Book of Beliefs and Opinions
Saadia Gaon

A prominent philosopher and scholar, Saadia was "gaon" of Sura, or the head of one of the most important Talmudic academies. Saadia was born in Egypt but later settled in Palestine and lived there the rest of his life. He lived in a place where many Jews were living under Arab control, and he tried to inspire them to go back to their Hebrew roots. He did this by translating the Bible into Arabic, putting together the first Hebrew dictionary, and writing a Hebrew grammar book. During his life he became embroiled in debates with the Karaites, who believed that the laws of the Talmud were not obligatory on Jews because they did not come from God; Jews, they argued, were obligated only to adhere to the Torah. Saadia attempted to reconcile Platonic and Aristotelian thought with Judaism in *The Book of Beliefs and Opinions* which was written in Arabic and was the first study to treat Judaism as a rational body of beliefs. The following example shows how Saadia argued against passion and inordinate love between a man and woman and stressed the importance of moderation.

Source: *Saadia Gaon: The Book of Beliefs and Opinions,* translated by Samuel Rosenblatt (New Haven: Yale University Press, 1948), pp. 373–377. Reprinted with permission. Copyright © 1948, by Yale University Press.

EROTICISM

Even though it is repulsive[1] to mention this subject, it is no more so than to discuss the theories of the nonbelievers. Just, therefore, as we reported these latter for the purpose of refuting them and thereby rendering the minds of men immune against the doubts they might arouse, so, too, shall we make an exposition of this subject in order to refute it and thus protect men's minds against confusion. There are, namely, people who entertain the view that human conduct is best regulated by being geared to some dominant love. This, they believe, has the effect of giving subtlety to the spirit and of refining the temperament to the point where the soul becomes something gossamer-like because of its refinement.

The process [they aver] is one of an extremely delicate character, attributable to the influence of nature. A substance, originating in the look of the eye, is poured into the heart. A desire is thereupon aroused which is further strengthened and intensified by the addition of other elements until it is firmly established.

They go even further in this matter, attributing the workings of this dominant passion to the influence of the stars. Thus they assert that, if two human beings were born in the ascendant of two stars facing each other, in full or in part, and both stand under the influence of one zodiacal sign, they will inevitably love and attract one another.

In fact, they carry their theory still further, attributing the consuming passion to the work of the Creator, magnified and exalted be He. They main-

---

1. Saadia seems to have in mind pederasty, which was prevalent among the ancient Greeks as well as the medieval Arabs.

tain, namely, that God has created the spirits of His creatures in the form
of round spheres, which were thereupon divided by Him into halves, each
half being put into a different person. Therefore does it come about that,
when a soul finds the part complementing it, it becomes irresistibly drawn
to it. From this point they proceed further yet, making a duty of man's sur-
rendering himself to his passion. They assert, namely, that this is only a
means of testing the servants of God, so that by being taught submissiveness to love, they might learn how to humble themselves before their Master and serve Him.

Now the advocates of all that has been mentioned above are really
thoughtless and without intelligence. I, therefore, deem it proper in this
chapter, first of all, effectively to refute the spurious doctrines propounded
by them. After that, I shall demonstrate the very opposite of the theories to
which they cling to be true.

I say, then, that so far as the thing they ascribe to our Lord, magnified
and exalted be He, is concerned, it is inconceivable that He should use as a
means of trial something that has been prohibited by Him. Indeed, it is as
Scripture has said: *God imputeth not unseemliness,*[2] and also: *For Thou art
not a God that hath pleasure in wickedness; evil shall not sojourn with Thee.*[3]
As for the doctrine of the division of the spheres to which they cling so tena-
ciously, since we have already refuted that in our refutation of the theory of
uncreated spiritual beings, making it clear that the soul of every human
being is created simultaneously with the perfection of his form, this theory
has become completely null and void.

As for their allegation in regard to the influence of the stars and the tal-
lying of the two parts of the love-match, as well as of the constellations, if
it were really as they say, it could never happen that Zeid should love Amr
without Amr's reciprocation, seeing that they are both equal. We do not,
however, find the matter to be so.

As for their assertion, again, that this emotion originates from a look,
after which desire is generated in the heart, I say that it was precisely on that
account that our Lord, exalted and magnified be He, commanded us to
devote both our eyes and our hearts to His service, as Scripture says: *My son,
give me thy heart, and let thine eyes observe my ways.*[4] He also forbade us to
employ them in rebellion against him, when He said: *And go not about after
your own heart and your own eyes, after which ye use to go astray.*[5]

This latter warning was issued against the consolidation of this state in

2. Job 24:12.
3. Ps. 5:5.
4. Prov. 23:26.
5. Num. 15:39.

the heart to the point where it would hold the subject in its grip and have such dominance over him that he would cut down on his eating and drinking and all other functions basic to his well-being. The consequence [of such a course] would be that his flesh would waste away and his body fall off and maladies would make their inroads on him in all their severity. And what about the inflammation and the fainting and the heart throbs and the worry and the excitement and the agitation, of which Scripture says: *For they have made ready their heart like an oven, while they lie in wait?*[6]

These effects are sometimes carried to the brain, weakening the faculties of imagination, reflection, and memory, and sometimes even destroying the powers of sensation and motion. It may also happen that, upon catching sight of his beloved, the lover should swoon way and fall into a dead faint, his spirit leaving his body for twenty-four hours, so that he would be thought dead and be carried out and buried. Again it is possible that upon seeing his beloved or hearing him mentioned, the lover might emit a rattle and really die, thus proving the truth of the parable coined by the proverbist: *For she hath cast down many wounded; yea, a mighty host are all her slain.*[7]

How now can a person allow himself and his reason to be taken prisoner [by his passion] to the point where he will not know that he has a Master, nor any strength, nor this world nor the next, outside of that passion, as Scripture has put it: *But they that are godless in heart lay up anger; they cry not for help when He blindeth them?*[8] And what about the slavish submissiveness to the object of one's passion and to his retinue, and the sitting at the gates and waiting upon him everywhere, as Scripture expresses it: *Lift up thine eyes unto the high hills, and see: Where hast thou not been lain with? By the ways hast thou sat for them?*[9] And what about the vigils at night and the rising at dawn and the secrecy practiced so as not to be surprised in the act and the deaths one dies whenever one is discovered in one's shame?

It is just as Scripture has expressed it: *The eye also of the adulterer waiteth for the twilight, saying: "No eye shall see me"; and he putteth a covering on his face.*[10] And what about the murder of the lover or the beloved or of one of their retinue or of both them and those attached to them and of a great many human beings together with them that often results from being madly in love, as Scripture says: *Because they are adulteresses, and blood is in their hands?*[11]

6. Hos. 7:6.
7. Prov. 7:26.
8. Job 36:13.
9. Jer. 3:2.
10. Job 24:15.
11. Ezek. 23:45.

Again, if he should one day be successful in attaining the object of his quest and realize in adequate measure that for which his soul has made such strenuous efforts, he might be filled with remorse and hate what he had loved to an even greater degree than he had loved it, as Scripture remarks: *And Amnon hated her with exceeding great hatred; for the hatred wherewith he hated her was greater than the love wherewith he had loved her.*[12]

It should, therefore, be clear to a person that he has sold his soul and his religion and all his senses, as well as his reason, once this arrow has been released that cannot be taken back by him any more, as has also been expressed by Scripture in its remark: *Till an arrow strike through his liver; as a bird hasteneth to the snare.*[13] This emotional state, therefore, has its appropriate place only in the relationship between husband and wife. They should be affectionate to each other for the sake of the maintenance of the world, as Scripture says: *A lovely hind and a graceful doe, let her breasts satisfy thee at all times; with her love be thou ravished always.*[14] A husband should give vent to his desire for his wife in accordance with the dictates of reason and religion and to the extent required in order to bind them closely together but restrain it vigorously and forcefully beyond that point.

The Guide of the Perplexed
Moses Maimonides aka Moses ben Maimon (1135–1204)

Maimonides, also known as Rambam for the acronym of his name (Rabbi Moses ben Maimon), was one of the leading minds of the twelfth century. His *Guide of the Perplexed* tried to reconcile religious thought with philosophy. In the following excerpt, he explains through the use of reason why the Torah proscribes certain types of behavior such as promiscuity, adultery, and incest. Moreover, he posits the view that not only is circumcision an important part of the Hebrew religion, but it also has health benefits.

Source: *The Guide of the Perplexed*, translated by Shlomo Pines (Chicago: University of Chicago Press, 1963), pp. 602, 606–607, 609–612. Reprinted with permission. ©1963 by the University of Chicago.

...Hence *harlots* are prohibited,[15] because through them lines of ancestry are destroyed. For a child born of them is a stranger to the people; no one knows to what family group he belongs, and no one in his family group knows him; and this is the worst of condition for him and for his father. Another important consideration comes in as a reason for the prohibition of

12. II Sam. 13:15.
13. Prov. 7:23.
14. Prov. 5:19.
15. Cf. Deut. 23:18.

harlots. This is the prevention of an intense lust for sexual intercourse and for constant preoccupation with it. For lust is increased through the change of the individuals that are *harlots,* for man is not stirred in the same way by an individual to whom he has been continuously accustomed as by individuals who are constantly renewed and who differ in shapes and manners. In the prohibition of *harlots* there is a very great utility — namely, the prevention of evils; for if *harlots* were permitted, a number of men might happen to betake themselves at one and the same time to one woman; they would inevitably quarrel and in most cases they would kill one another or kill the woman, this being — as is well known — a thing that constantly happens: *And they assemble themselves in troops at a prostitute's house.*[16] In order to prevent these great evils and to bring about this common utility — namely, knowledge of the lines of ancestry — *harlots* and *male prostitutes* are prohibited and there is no way to engage in permitted sexual intercourse other than through singling out a woman for oneself and marrying her in public. For if it sufficed merely to single her out, most men would bring a harlot to their house for a certain time, having made an agreement with her about this, and say that she is a wife. Therefore a binding ceremony and a certain act have been prescribed signifying that the woman is allotted to the man; this is the *betrothal.* Then when the act is made in public, it is the ceremony of *marriage*: *And Boaz took ten men, and so on.*[17] Sometimes the union of the two may be discordant and matters in their household not in good order. Consequently divorce is permitted. However, if a divorce could become valid merely by means of the utterance of words or through the man's turning the woman out of his house, the woman might watch for some negligence on the part of her husband then go out and claim to be divorced. Or if some individual had fornicated with her, she and the adulterer might claim that she had been divorced beforehand. Therefore the Law has given to us the ordinance that a divorce can only be made valid by means of a writ attesting it: *And he shall write her a bill of divorcement, and so on....*[18]

As for the prohibitions against *illicit unions,* all of them are directed to making sexual intercourse rarer and to instilling disgust for it so that it should be sought only very seldom. The reason for the prohibition against *homosexuality* and against intercourse with *beasts* is very clear. For if the thing that is natural should be abhorred except for necessity, all the more should deviations from the natural way and the quest for pleasure alone be eschewed. All *illicit unions* with females have one thing in common: namely, that in the majority of cases these females are constantly in the company of the male

16. Jer. 5:7
17. Ruth 4:2.
18. Deut. 24:1.

in his house and that they are easy of access for him and can be easily controlled by him — there being no difficulty in making them come into his presence; and no judge could blame the male for their being with him. Consequently if the status of the women with whom *union* is *illicit* were that of any *unmarried woman*, I mean to say that if it were possible to marry them and that the prohibition with regard to them were only due to their not being the man's wives, most people would have constantly succumbed and fornicated with them. However, as it is absolutely forbidden to have intercourse with them, the strongest deterrents making us avoid this — I mean by this a sentence of *death by order of a court of law* and the threat of *being cut off* — so that there is no way to have intercourse with these women, men are safe from seeking to approach them and their thoughts are turned away from them.

It is very clear that relations are easy with all women included in the prohibitions concerning *illicit unions*. For it is very general that if a man has a wife, her mother, her grandmother, her daughter, her granddaughter, and her sister will be in his house most of the time, so that the husband will constantly meet them whenever he enters, goes out, and is engaged upon his business. A wife also is often in contact with her husband's brother, his father, and his son. It is likewise manifest that in most cases a man is often in the company of his sisters, maternal and paternal aunts, and the wife of his paternal uncle, and is brought up together with them. Now these are the women with whom *union* is *illicit* because of their being *relatives*. Consider this, this being one of the reasons why intercourse with *relatives* is prohibited.

The second reason derives, in my opinion, from the wish to respect the sentiment of shame. For it would be a most shameless thing if this act could take place between the root and the branch, I refer to sexual intercourse with the mother or the daughter. On the ground of the root and the branch, sexual intercourse of one of the two with the other has been forbidden. There is no difference between a root having intercourse with a branch or a branch with a root; or the root and the branch joining in having intercourse with a third individual, I mean that one individual reveals his nakedness in intercourse both with a root and a branch. Therefore it is forbidden to take together a woman and her mother and to have intercourse with the wife of one's father and the wife of one's son, for all this is revealing one's nakedness before the nakedness of both a root and a branch. Being brother or sister is like being root and branch. But once the sister was forbidden, also the sister of the wife and the wife of the brother are forbidden. For this would constitute the joining of two individuals who are like root and branch in sexual intercourse with a third individual.

As union between a brother and a sister is strictly forbidden and as they are to have the same relation as a root and a branch or even are considered to be one and the same individual, sexual intercourse with one's maternal aunt is also forbidden, for she has the same status as one's mother, and also intercourse with one's paternal aunt, as she has the same status as one's father. And just as the daughter of one's paternal uncle and the daughter of one's paternal aunt are not forbidden, the daughter of one's brother and the daughter of one's sister are likewise not forbidden because of the analogy. The fact that the wife of a brother's son is permitted to the paternal uncle, whereas the wife of the paternal uncle is forbidden to the son of a brother, may be explained by the first reason. For a brother's son is in most cases to be found in his paternal uncle's house and approaches his paternal uncle's wife just as he approaches his brother's wife; whereas a paternal uncle is not to be found in this way in the house of his brother's son and does not approach the latter's wife. Do you not see that in view of the fact that a father has the same opportunity to approach a wife of his son as the son has to approach a wife of his father, the prohibition is equally strict in both cases, its transgression being punished by *one capital punishment.*

...with regard to *circumcision,* one of the reasons for it is, in my opinion, the wish to bring about a decrease in sexual intercourse and a weakening of the organ in question, so that this activity be diminished and the organ be in as quiet a state as possible. It has been thought that circumcision perfects what is defective congenitally. This gave the possibility to everyone to raise an objection and to say: How can natural things be defective so that they need to be perfected from outside, all the more because we know how useful the foreskin is for that member? In fact this *commandment* has not been prescribed with a view to perfecting what is defective congenitally, but to perfecting what is defective morally. The bodily pain caused to that member is the real purpose of circumcision. None of the activities necessary for the preservation of the individual is harmed thereby, nor is procreation rendered impossible, but violent concupiscence and lust that goes beyond what is needed are diminished. The fact that circumcision weakens the faculty of sexual excitement and sometimes perhaps diminishes the pleasure is indubitable. For if at birth this member has been made to bleed and has had its covering taken away from it, it must indubitably be weakened. The *Sages, may their memory be blessed,* have explicitly stated: *It is hard for a woman with whom an uncircumcised man has had sexual intercourse to separate from him.* In my opinion this is the strongest of the reasons for *circumcision.* Who first began to perform this act, if not *Abraham* who was celebrated for his chastity — as has been mentioned by the *Sages, may their memory be blessed,* with reference to his dictum: *Behold now, I know that thou art a fair woman to look upon.*[19]

19. Gen. 12:11.

According to me *circumcision* has another very important meaning, namely, that all people professing this opinion — that is, those who believe in the *unity of God*— should have a bodily sign uniting them so that one who does not belong to them should not be able to claim that he was one of them, while being a stranger. For he would do this in order to profit by them or to deceive the people who profess this religion. Now a man does not perform this act upon himself or upon a son of his unless it be in consequence of a genuine belief. For it is not like an incision in the leg or a burn in the arm, but is a very, very hard thing.

It is also well known what degree of mutual love and mutual help exists between people who all bear the same sign, which forms for them a sort of covenant and alliance. *Circumcision* is a covenant made by *Abraham our Father* with a view to the belief in the *unity of God*. Thus everyone who is circumcised joins *Abraham's covenant*. This covenant imposes the obligation to believe in the unity of God: *To be a God unto thee and to thy seed after thee.*[20] This also is a strong reason, as strong as the first, which may be adduced to account for *circumcision*; perhaps it is even stronger than the first.

The perfection and *perpetuation* of this Law can only be achieved if circumcision is performed in childhood. For this there are three wise reasons. The first is that if the child were let alone until he grew up, he would sometimes not perform it. The second is that a child does not suffer as much pain as a grown-up man because his membrane is still soft and his imagination weak; for a grown-up man would regard the thing, which he would imagine before it occurred, as terrible and hard. The third is that the parents of a child that is just born take lightly matters concerning it, for up to that time the imaginative form that compels the parents to love it is not yet consolidated. For this imaginative form increases through habitual contact and grows with the growth of the child. Then it begins to decrease and to disappear, I refer to this imaginative form. For the love of the father and of the mother for the child when it has just been born is not like their love for it when it is one year old, and their love for it when it is one year old is not like their love when it is six years old. Consequently if it were left uncircumcised for two or three years, this would necessitate the abandonment of circumcision because of the father's love and affection for it. At the time of its birth, on the other hand, this imaginative form is very weak, especially as far as concerns the father upon whom this *commandment* is imposed.

The fact that *circumcision* is performed on the eighth day is due to the circumstance that all living beings are very weak and exceedingly tender when they are born, as if they were still in the womb. This is so until seven

---

20. Gen. 17:7.

days are past. It is only then that they are counted among those who have contact with the air. Do you not see that this point is also taken into account with regard to beasts?—*Seven days shall it be with its dam, and so on.*[21] It is as if before that period it were an abortion. Similarly with regard to man; he is circumcised after seven days have passed. In this way the matter is fixed: *You do not make out of it something that varies.*

This class of commandments also includes the prohibition against mutilating the sexual organs of all the males of animals,[22] which is based on the principle of *righteous statutes and judgments,*[23] I mean the principle of keeping the mean in all matters; sexual intercourse should neither be excessively indulged, as we have mentioned, nor wholly abolished. Did He not command and say: *Be fruitful and multiply?*[24] Accordingly this organ is weakened by means of circumcision, but not extirpated through excision. What is natural is left according to nature, but measures are taken against excess. *He that is wounded in the stones or hath his privy member cut off*[25] is forbidden to marry a *woman of Israel,* for such cohabitation would be perverted and aimless. Such a marriage would likewise be a *stumbling-block* for the woman and for him who seeks her out. This is very clear.

In order to deter people from *illicit unions,* a *bastard* is forbidden to marry a *daughter of Israel;*[26] so that the adulterous man and adulterous woman should know that by committing their act they attach to their descendants a stigma that can never be effaced. The children born of adultery being, moreover, always despised to every way of life and in every nation, the *seed of Israel* is regarded as too noble to mix with bastards.

Because of the nobility of *Priests* they are forbidden to marry a *prostitute,* a *divorced woman,* and *a woman born of the illicit marriage [of a Priest].* The *High Priest,* who is the noblest among the Priests, is even forbidden to marry a widow and a *woman that is not a virgin.*[27] The reason for all this is clear. Mingling of *bastards* with the *congregation of the Lord*[28] being forbidden, that of *male and female slaves* with it is prohibited all the more.

The reason for the prohibition of intermarriage with the *Gentiles* is explained in the text of the Torah: A*nd thou take of their daughters unto thy sons, and so on.*[29]

21. Exod. 22:29.
22. Cf. Lev. 22:24.
23. Deut. 4:8.
24. Gen. 1:22.
25. Cf. Deut. 23:2.
26. Cf. Deut. 23:3.
27. Cf. Lev. 21:13–14.
28. Deut. 23:3.
29. Exod. 34:16.

26

Jewish Culture

The Jewish War
Josephus (37–100)

Flavius Josephus participated as a commander in Galilee in the Jewish War
(66–70) between the Romans and the Jews resulting in the destruction of
the Temple. He wrote an account of the war. Within his history, however,
there is an interesting passage describing one Jewish sect, the Essenes. The
Essenes lived outside of Jerusalem, away from the Temple and religious lead-
ers, because they thought them to be corrupt. They set up all-male monastic communities overlooking the Dead Sea, where they practiced asceticism
that included celibacy. In many ways, they were precursors to Christian
monks.

Source: *The Jewish War by Josephus*, translated by G.A. Williamson revised by E. Mary
Smallwood (Harmondsworth, Middlesex, England: Penguin Classics 1959, revised edition 1981, © G.A. Williamson, 1959, 1969, p. 133. Reproduced by permission of Penguin Books Ltd.

Among the Jews there are three schools of thought, whose adherents
are called Pharisees, Sadducees, and Essenes, respectively. The Essenes profess a severer discipline: they are Jews by birth and are peculiarly attached
to each other. They eschew pleasure-seeking as a vice and regard temperance and mastery of the passions as virtue. Scorning wedlock, they select
other men's children while still pliable and teachable, and fashion them after
their own pattern – not that they wish to do away with marriage as a means
of continuing the race, but they are afraid of the promiscuity of women and
convinced that none of the sex remains faithful to one man. Contemptuous
of wealth, they are communists to perfection, and none of them will be
found to be better off than the rest: their rule is that novices admitted to
the sect must surrender their property to the order, so that among them all
neither humiliating poverty nor excessive wealth is ever seen, but each man's
possessions go into the pool and as with brothers their entire property belongs
to them all. Oil they regard as polluting, and if a man is unintentionally

smeared with it he scrubs himself off clean; for they think it desirable to keep the skin dry and always to wear white. Men to supervise the community's affairs are elected by the show of hands, chosen for their tasks by universal suffrage.

Jewish Poets

The golden age of Hebrew poetry occurred between the middle of the tenth and the middle of the twelfth centuries in Spain. At that time, communities of Jews lived under Muslim rule, which was tolerant and allowed the educated into positions of power. These educated Jews, known as the "Andalusian courtiers," adopted Arabic literary style and imagery.

Source: *Wine, Women, and Death: Medieval Hebrew Poems on the Good Life*, © 1986 by Raymond P. Scheindlin published by The Jewish Publication Society with the permission of the publisher, The Jewish Publication Society, pp. 91, 97, 107, 111–112.

By Samuel the Nagid (993–1055 or 1056)

Burnt by passion's flame —
How can I refrain?
    Love has ruined me,
    Lain in wait for me,
    Ambushed, then gone free
Followed me amain,
Split my heart in twain.

    On my cheek the tear
    Made my secret clear.
    This please tell my dear:
Tears all men disdain.
How can I explain?

    Speak to him for me,
    Tell him of my plea.
    Do not silent be!
Broken love restrain
From a heart in pain.

    Solace to me bring;
    Ease for me the sting.
    Ah, such suffering!
Sleepless have I lain,
Love my slumber's bane.

    Lovers in distress
    Cry for a caress.
    My heart they oppress.
Come my darling swain,
Cling and kiss again.

    This my love song rings
    [   ]
"May true lover twain
Never part again!"

By Moses Ibn Ezra (c. 1055–after 1135)

Caress a lovely woman's breast by night,
And kiss some beauty's lips by morning light.

    Silence those who criticize you, those
    Officious talkers. Take advice from me:
With beauty's children only can we live.

Kidnapped were they from Paradise to gall
The living; living men are lovers all.

     Immerse your heart in pleasure and in joy,
     And by the bank a bottle drink of wine,
     Enjoy the swallow's chirp and viol's whine.
Laugh, dance, and stamp your feet upon the floor!
Get drunk, and knock at dawn on some girl's door.

     This is the joy of life, so take your due.
     You too deserve a portion of the Ram
     Of Consecration, like your people's chiefs.
To suck the juice of lips do not be shy,
But take what's rightly yours – the breast and thigh!

The joy of my eyes and my heart's delight –
A fawn at my left and a cup in my right!
     Many men fault me, but I don't mind.
     Come, watch me crush them, beautiful hind.
     Old age consume them! Death to their kind!
Come, my gazelle, give me something to eat;
The mead of your lips makes our banquet complete.

     Why do they want to discourage me, why?
     What in the world is the sin if I
     Thrill to your beauty? There's Adonai!
Pay them no heed, and in their despite,
Come and caress me, stubborn wight.

     He listened, and let me come home with him.
     He did what I wanted, obeyed every whim.
     By day and by night we dallied within.
I took off his clothes and he took off mine,
He offered his lips and I drank of their wine.

     Just when my heart was no longer free,
     Just then he started to find fault with me.
     He quarreled and spoke to me angrily,
"Get along with you, and be on your way!
Don't you seduce me and lead me astray!"

     Don't be so angry with me, gazelle.
     Think of me kindly, and love me well.
     Give me a kiss, and do not rebel.
You can bestow on me life, if you will,
Or use the power of your beauty to kill.

By Solomon Ibn Gabirol (c. 1020–c.1057)

Like Amnon sick am I, so call Tamar
And tell her one who loves her is snared by death.
Quick, friends, companions, bring her here to me.
The only thing I ask of you is this:
Adorn her head with jewels, bedeck her well,
And send along with her a cup of wine.
If she would pour for me she might put out
The burning pain wasting my throbbing flesh.

By Judah Halevi (before 1075–1141)

Once when I fondled him upon my thighs
He caught his own reflection in my eyes
And kissed my eyes, deceitful imp; I knew
It was his image he kissed, and not my eyes!

Ethical Wills

Many Jews wrote wills for their children that instructed and advised them how to conduct their lives from a religious, moral, and practical standpoint. These wills show clearly the values of medieval Jewish communities. The following excerpts stress chastity within marriage and the importance of devoting oneself to family, and they examine the roles of sons and daughters.

Source: *Hebrew Ethical Wills*, edited by Israel Abrahams (Philadelphia: Jewish Publication Society of America, 1926), pp. 36, 44–45, 48, 78–79, 209–211.

Will of R. Eleazar the Great (c. 12th century)

My son, when thou wakest from thy sleep at midnight, converse with thy wife in chaste terms, using no indecent expression, even in jest, for this too wilt thou be called to account! If thou wakest at other hours, let not thine heart indulge in impure fancies, for evil thought leads to evil deed. How goodly and how sweet that thou be ever prepared to form one of the righteous company which enters with God, thus drawing o'er thyself the thread of His Love, and finding thy pleasant lot with the righteous in Paradise! Shouldst thou be worthy of this, happy art thou, well will it be with thee!...

My son! Reveal not thy secret to thy wife. Be of faithful spirit to all, betray not another's confidence even when thou art at strife with him....

My son! It is incumbent on thee to beget children, and to rear them for the study of the Torah. For their sake thou wilt be worthy of eternal life. My son! Beware lest thy wife be over generous to her first son-in-law. Appoint not the latter as administrator over thy household. My son! Approach not thy wife near her menstrual period. Avoid all grossness. Hold aloof from what is foul and from what has the appearance of foulness. Pass not behind a woman in the street nor between two women...

My son! Wed not an unworthy woman: woe to the tarnished who tarnishes his seed! Absalom and Adonijah, the offspring of such a union, wrought many evils to Israel. They were unchaste and stirred up rebellion. My son! Have no marital intercourse with thy wife while she is suckling her child. Do not leave an infant in his cradle alone in the house by day or night, nor pass thou the night alone in any abode. For under such circumstances, Lilith seizes man or child in her fatal embrace.

My son! Zealously bring up thy children in the study of the Law. Withdraw them not from it! For he who so acts shortens his life; the Holy One weeps over such a one day by day.

Will of Judah ibn Tibbon (b. 1120)

My son! I command thee to honor thy wife to thine utmost capacity. She is intelligent and modest, a daughter of a distinguished and educated family. She is a good housewife and mother, and no spendthrift. Her tastes are simple, whether in food or dress. Remember her assiduous tendence of thee in thine illness, though she had been brought up in elegance and luxury. Remember how she afterwards reared thy son without man or woman to help her. Were she a hired nurse she would have earned thy esteem and forbearance; how much the more, since she is the wife of thy bosom, the daughter of the great, art thou bound to treat her with consideration and respect. To act otherwise is the way of the contemptible. The Arab philosopher says of women: "None but the honorable honoreth them, none but the despicable despises them." *Ben Mishle* also says:

> Pardon thy child and wife their failings,
> And persevere in thine exhortations;
> As an armorer sharpens the edge of a sword,
> By oft drawing it to and fro on the stone.

If thou wouldst acquire my love, honor her with all thy might; do not exercise too severe an authority over her; our Sages have expressly warned men against this. If thou givest orders or reprovest, let thy words be gentle. Enough is it if thy displeasure is visible in thy look, let it not be vented in actual rage....

Will of Eleazar of Mayence (d. 1357)

My daughters must obey scrupulously the rules applying to women; modesty, sanctity, reverence, should mark their married lives. They should carefully watch for the signs of the beginning of their periods and keep separate from their husbands at such times. Marital intercourse must be modest and holy, with a spirit of restraint and delicacy, in reverence and silence. They shall be very punctilious and careful with their ritual bathing, taking with them women friends of worthy character. They shall cover their eyes until they reach their home, on returning from the bath, in order not to behold anything of an unclean nature. They must respect their husbands, and must be invariably amiable to them. Husbands, on their part, must honor their wives more than themselves, and treat them with tender consideration.

If they can by any means contrive it, my sons and daughters should live in communities, and not isolated from other Jews, so that their sons and daughters may learn the ways of Judaism. Even if compelled to solicit from others the money to pay a teacher, they must not let the young, of both sexes, go without instruction in the Torah. Marry your children, O my sons and daughters, as soon as their age is ripe, to members of respectable families. Let no child of mine hunt after money by making a low match for that object; but if the family is undistinguished only on the mother's side, it does not matter, for all Israel counts descent from the father's side.

Every Friday morning, they shall put themselves in careful trim for honoring the Sabbath, kindling the lamps while the day is still great, and in winter lighting the furnace before dark, to avoid desecrating the Sabbath (by kindling fire thereon). For due welcome to the Sabbath, the women must prepare beautiful candles. As to games of chance, I entreat my children never to engage in such pastimes. During the leisure of the festival weeks they may play for trifling stakes in kind, and the women may amuse themselves similarly on New Moons, but never for money. In their relation to women, my sons must behave continently, avoiding mixed bathing and mixed dancing and all frivolous conversation, while my daughters ought not to speak much with strangers, nor jest nor dance with them. They ought to be always at home, and not be gadding about. They should not stand at the door, watching whatever passes. I ask, I command, that the daughters of my house be never without work to do, for idleness leads first to boredom, then to sin. But let them spin, or cook, or sew.

IX

ISLAM

27

Islamic Religion and law

Qur'an

The Qur'an is the sacred book of Muslims containing the foundations of the Islamic faith. Muslims believe that it is the word of Allah as spoken to Muhammad by the angel Gabriel, who initially approached Muhammad while he was meditating in the caves of Mt. Hira, outside of Mecca. These visions continued over a period of two decades between 610 and 632. Although Muhammad himself was illiterate, he was able to recite the Qur'an to his followers, who wrote it down. The first official copy of the Qur'an was compiled under the Caliph Uthman (644–656). The Qur'an is divided into 114 chapters called *suras* with the longest at the beginning and the short-est at the end. The Qur'an covers many issues such as marriage, divorce, adultery, and illicit sexual relations.

Source: *The Holy Qur'an*, translated by M.H. Shakir (Elmhurst, NY: Tahrike Tarsile Qur'an, 1983). Reprinted with the permission of Tahrike Tarsile Qur'an, Inc. Electronic Text Center, University of Virginia Library. http://etext.lib.virginia.edu/

THE COW

2.197: The pilgrimage is [performed in] the well-known months; so who-ever determines the performance of the pilgrimage therein, there shall be no intercourse nor fornication nor quarrelling amongst one another; and what-ever good you do, Allah knows it; and make provision, for surely the pro-vision is the guarding of oneself, and be careful (of your duty) to Me, O men of understanding.

2.221: And do not marry the idolatresses until they believe, and certainly a believing maid is better than an idolatress woman, even though she should please you; and do not give [believing women] in marriage to idolaters until they believe, and certainly a believing servant is better than an idolater, even though he should please you; these invite to the fire, and Allah invites to the garden and to forgiveness by His will, and makes clear His communi-cations to men, that they may be mindful.

2.222: And they ask you about menstruation. Say: It is a discomfort; therefore keep aloof from the women during the menstrual discharge and do not go near them until they have become clean; then when they have cleansed themselves, go in to them as Allah has commanded you; surely Allah loves those who turn much [to Him], and He loves those who purify themselves.

2.223: Your wives are a tilth for you, so go into your tilth when you like, and do good beforehand for yourselves, and be careful [of your duty] to Allah, and know that you will meet Him, and give good news to the believers.

2.226: Those who swear that they will not go in to their wives should wait four months; so if they go back, then Allah is surely Forgiving, Merciful.

2.228: And the divorced women should keep themselves in waiting for three courses; and it is not lawful for them that they should conceal what Allah has created in their wombs, if they believe in Allah and the last day; and their husbands have a better right to take them back in the meanwhile if they wish for reconciliation; and they have rights similar to those against them in a just manner, and the men are a degree above them, and Allah is Mighty, Wise.

2.229: Divorce may be [pronounced] twice, then keep [them] in good fellowship or let [them] go with kindness; and it is not lawful for you to take any part of what you have given them, unless both fear that they cannot keep within the limits of Allah; then if you fear that they cannot keep within the limits of Allah, there is no blame on them for what she gives up to become free thereby. These are the limits of Allah, so do not exceed them and whoever exceeds the limits of Allah these it is that are the unjust.

2.230: So if he divorces her she shall not be lawful to him afterwards until she marries another husband; then if he divorces her there is no blame on them both if they return to each other [by marriage], if they think that they can keep within the limits of Allah, and these are the limits of Allah which He makes clear for a people who know.

2.231: And when you divorce women and they reach their prescribed time, then either retain them in good fellowship or set them free with liberality, and do not retain them for injury, so that you exceed the limits, and whoever does this, he indeed is unjust to his own soul; and do not take Allah's communications for a mockery, and remember the favor of Allah upon you, and that which He has revealed to you of the Book and the Wisdom, admonishing you thereby; and be careful [of your duty to] Allah, and know that Allah is the Knower of all things.

2.232: And when you have divorced women and they have ended — their term [of waiting], then do not prevent them from marrying their husbands when they agree among themselves in a lawful manner; with this is admonished he among you who believes in Allah and the last day, this is more profitable and purer for you; and Allah knows while you do not know.

2.233: And the mothers should suckle their children for two whole years for him who desires to make complete the time of suckling; and their maintenance and their clothing must be — borne by the father according to usage; no soul shall have imposed upon it a duty but to the extent of its capacity; neither shall a mother be made to suffer harm on account of her child, nor a father on account of his child, and a similar duty [devolves] on the [father's] heir, but if both desire weaning by mutual consent and counsel, there is no blame on them, and if you wish to engage a wet-nurse for your children, there is no blame on you so long as you pay what you promised for according to usage; and be careful of (your duty to) Allah and know that Allah sees what you do.

2.234: And [as for] those of you who die and leave wives behind, they should keep themselves in waiting for four months and ten days; then when they have fully attained their term, there is no blame on you for what they do for themselves in a lawful manner; and Allah is aware of what you do.

2.235: And there is no blame on you respecting that which you speak indirectly in the asking of [such] women in marriage or keep (the proposal) concealed within your minds; Allah knows that you will mention them, but do not give them a promise in secret unless you speak in a lawful manner, and do not confirm the marriage tie until the writing is fulfilled, and know that Allah knows what is in your minds, therefore beware of Him, and know that Allah is Forgiving, Forbearing.

2.236: There is no blame on you if you divorce women when you have not touched them or appointed for them a portion, and make provision for them, the wealthy according to his means and the straightened in circumstances according to his means, a provision according to usage; [this is] a duty on the doers of good [to others].

2.237: And if you divorce them before you have touched them and you have appointed for them a portion, then (pay to them) half of what you have appointed, unless they relinquish or he should relinquish in whose hand is the marriage tie; and it is nearer to righteousness that you should relinquish; and do not neglect the giving of free gifts between you; surely Allah sees what you do.

THE WOMEN
4.3: And if you fear that you cannot act equitably towards orphans, then marry such women as seem good to you, two and three and four; but if you

fear that you will not do justice [between them], then [marry] only one or what your right hands possess; this is more proper, that you may not deviate from the right course.

4.15: And as for those who are guilty of an indecency from among your women, call to witnesses against them four [witnesses] from among you; then if they bear witness confine them to the houses until death takes them away or Allah opens some way for them.

4.16: And as for the two who are guilty of indecency from among you, give them both a punishment; then if they repent and amend, turn aside from them; surely Allah is Oft-returning [to mercy], the Merciful.

4.20: And if you wish to have [one] wife in place of another and you have given one of them a heap of gold, then take not from it anything; would you take it by slandering [her] and [doing her] manifest wrong?

4.21: And how can you take it when one of you has already gone in to the other and they have made with you a firm covenant?

4.22: And marry not women whom your fathers married, except what has already passed; this surely is indecent and hateful, and it is an evil way.

4.23: Forbidden to you are your mothers and your daughters and your sisters and your paternal aunts and your maternal aunts and brothers' daughters and sisters' daughters and your mothers that have suckled you and your foster-sisters and mothers of your wives and your step-daughters who are in your guardianship, (born) of your wives to whom you have gone in, but if you have not gone in to them, there is no blame on you (in marrying them), and the wives of your sons who are of your own loins and that you should have two sisters together, except what has already passed; surely Allah is Forgiving, Merciful.

4.24: And all married women except those whom your right hands possess [this is] Allah's ordinance to you, and lawful for you are [all women] besides those, provided that you seek [them] with your property, taking [them] in marriage not committing fornication. Then as to those whom you profit by, give them their dowries as appointed; and there is no blame on you about what you mutually agree after what is appointed; surely Allah is Knowing, Wise.

4.25: And whoever among you has not within his power ampleness of means to marry free believing women, then [he may marry] of those whom your right hands possess from among your believing maidens; and Allah knows best your faith: you are [sprung] the one from the other; so marry them with the permission of their masters, and give them their dowries justly, they being chaste, not fornicating, nor receiving paramours; and when they are taken in marriage, then if they are guilty of indecency, they shall suffer half the punishment which is [inflicted] upon free women. This is for him among you who fears falling into evil; and that you abstain is better for you, and Allah is Forgiving, Merciful.

4.26: Allah desires to explain to you, and to guide you into the ways of those before you, and to turn to you [mercifully], and Allah is Knowing, Wise.

4.27: And Allah desires that He should turn to you [mercifully], and those who follow [their] lusts desire that you should deviate [with] a great deviation.

4.34: Men are the maintainers of women because Allah has made some of them to excel others and because they spend out of their property; the good women are therefore obedient, guarding the unseen as Allah has guarded; and [as to] those on whose part you fear desertion, admonish them, and leave them alone in the sleeping-places and beat them; then if they obey you, do not seek a way against them; surely Allah is High, Great.

4.46: Of those who are Jews [there are those who] alter words from their places and say: We have heard and we disobey and: Hear, may you not be made to hear! and: Raina, distorting [the word] with their tongues and taunting about religion; and if they had said [instead]: We have heard and we obey, and hearken, and Unzurna it would have been better for them and more upright; but Allah has cursed them on account of their unbelief, so they do not believe but a little.

4.128: And if a woman fears ill usage or desertion on the part of her husband, there is no blame on them, if they effect a reconciliation between them, and reconciliation is better, and avarice has been made to be present in the [people's] minds; and if you do good [to others] and guard [against evil], then surely Allah is aware of what you do.

4.129: And you have it not in your power to do justice between wives, even though you may wish [it], but be not disinclined [from one] with total disinclination, so that you leave her as it were in suspense; and if you effect a reconciliation and guard [against evil], then surely Allah is Forgiving, Merciful.

THE LIGHT

24.2: [As for] the fornicatress and the fornicator, flog each of them, [giving] a hundred stripes, and let not pity for them detain you in the matter of obedience to Allah, if you believe in Allah and the last day, and let a party of believers witness their chastisement.

24.3: The fornicator shall not marry any but a fornicatress or idolatress, and [as for] the fornicatress, none shall marry her but a fornicator or an idolater; and it is forbidden to the believers.

24.4: And those who accuse free women then do not bring four witnesses, flog them, [giving] eighty stripes, and do not admit any evidence from them ever; and these it is that are the transgressors,

24.5: Except those who repent after this and act aright, for surely Allah is Forgiving, Merciful.

24.6: And [as for] those who accuse their wives and have no witnesses except themselves, the evidence of one of these [should be taken] four times, bearing Allah to witness that he is most surely of the truthful ones.

24.7: And the fifth [time] that the curse of Allah be on him if he is one of the liars.

24.8: And it shall avert the chastisement from her if she testify four times, bearing Allah to witness that he is most surely one of the liars;

24.9: And the fifth [time] that the wrath of Allah be on her if he is one of the truthful.

Hadiths

Hadiths are accounts of what Muhammad or one of his contemporaries did or said. They evolved out of oral traditions reporting events and were written down about two centuries after the founding of Islam. Hadiths, however, were not automatically believed, but had to be authenticated by *isnad* or a chain of reliable witnesses who could say, "I was informed by A, who was informed by B, who was informed by C, that the Prophet stated...." Hadiths are sources of authority second only to the Qur'an.

The following are traditions related by Muhammad's female companions. They come from "the Six Books" — six collections of traditions whose authors are considered the most reliable. These are Muhammad b. Ismai'il al-Bukhari (810–870), Abu 'Isa Muhammad al-Tirmidhi (d. 872), Muslim b. al-Hajjaj (817–875), Abu Dawud al-Sijistani (817–889), Abu 'Abd Allah Ibn Maja (824–887), Abu 'Abd al-Rahman al-Nasa'i (830–915)

Source: *Encyclopedia of Muhammad's Women Companions and the Traditions They Related* by Muhammad Hisham Kabbani and Laleh Bakhtiar (Chicago, IL: ABC International Group, Inc./Kazi Publications, 1998), pp. 81–82, 86–87, 93–94, 187, 240–241. Reprinted with the permission of Kazi Publications.

AFTER TOUCHING THE MALE ORGAN
Busra Bint Abu Sufyan
    God's Messenger said, "When anyone of you touches his sexual organ, he should perform ablution."

Disapproval of Touching the Penis With the Right Hand
Ayisha Related:

The Prophet used his right hand to get water for ablution and take food and his left hand for purifying himself after urinating or defecating and for anything repugnant

Experiencing Orgasm Without Moisture
Ayisha Related:

God's Messenger said, "When anyone of you wakes up from his sleep and sees moistness but does not think that he has had a wet dream, he should perform the bath lustration. When he thinks that he has experienced [sexual discharge during sleep] but does not see the moistness, a bath lustration is not incumbent upon him."

How to Perform
Ayisha Related:

When God's Messenger bathed after sexual intercourse, he first washed his hands. He then poured water with his right hand onto his left hand and washed his private parts. He then performed ablution as for prescribed prayer. He then took some water and wet his fingers and moved them through the roots of his hair. And when he found that these had been properly moistened, he poured three handfuls on his head. He then poured water over his body and subsequently washed his feet.

Female Circumcision
Umm Atiyyat Al-ansariya Related:

A woman used to perform circumcision in Madinah. The Prophet said to her, "Do not cut severely, as that is better for a woman and more desirable for a husband." [Abu Dawud remarks that this not a strong Tradition because it has been transmitted in a form missing the link of the Companions].

Menstruation
Umayyah Bint Al-Salt Related:

She quoted a certain woman of the Ghifar tribe [whose name was Layla, the wife of Abu Dhar al-Ghifari according to Awn al-Mabud I, 123] who said that the Messenger of God made her ride behind him on the rear of the camel saddle. The Messenger of God got down in the morning. He made his camel kneel down, and she got down from the back part of his saddle. There was blood on the saddle from her first menstruation. She stuck to the camel and felt ashamed. When the Messenger of God saw what had happened to her and saw the blood, he said, "Perhaps you have begun menstruation." She replied that she had. He then said, "Set yourself right [that is, tie some cloth to prevent bleeding]. Then take a vessel of water and put some salt in it. Then wash the blood from the back part of the saddle and return to your mount." When the Messenger of God conquered Khaybar, he gave her a portion of the booty. Therefore, whenever the woman wished to become purified from her menses, she would put salt in water. When she died, she left a will asking that her dead body be washed with salted water.

COITUS ABOVE A WAIST WRAPPER
Ayisha Related:

When anyone among us [the wives of the Prophet] menstruated, the Messenger asked her to tie a waist-wrapper over her body, and then he lay with her.

EVERYTHING BUT SEXUAL INTERCOURSE PERMISSIBLE
Ayisha Related:

When she menstruated, she left the bed and lay on the reed mat and did not approach the Messenger of God until she was purified. [Al-Tibi says that this Tradition was abrogated. A large number of Traditions permit a husband and wife to lie together and embrace each other even when the wife is menstruating].

FONDLING A MENSTRUATING WIFE
Ayisha Related:

The Prophet and she used to perform the bath lustration from a single pot while they were in a state of impurity following sexual intercourse. When she was menstruating, he ordered her to put on a cloth worn below the waist and he fondled her. While in retreat in the mosque, he put his head near her, and she would wash it while she was menstruating.

IMPURITY OF MENSES AND HOW TO WASH IT
Asma Bint Abu Bakr Related:

A woman came to the Messenger and asked what she should do if the blood of menses stained a garment of hers. The Prophet replied, "You should scrape it, rub it with water, pour water over it, and then offer a prayer."

LENGTHENING OF HAIR ARTIFICIALLY
Asma Related:

A woman told the Prophet that her daughter had gotten measles and her hair had fallen out. The daughter was to be married and her mother wanted to know if her daughter could use false hair. The Messenger said, "God has cursed the woman who lengthens hair artificially and the one who gets her hair lengthened artificially."

How Much Beauty Can a Woman Display?

Ayisha Related:

Asma bint Abu Bakr, wearing thick clothes, arrived where God's Messenger was. God's Messenger turned away from her and said, "O Asma, when a woman reaches the age of menstruation, it does not suit her that she display parts of her body except this and this," and he pointed to her face and hands.

Offering the Prescribed Prayer Without Head Covering

Ayisha Related:

She visited to Safiya Umm Talhat al-Talhat and her daughters. Seeing her daughters she said that the Messenger of God entered her apartment and there was a girl there. He gave his lower garment to Ayisha, and said to tear it into two pieces and give one-half to this girl and give the other half to the daughter of Umm Salama. He said, "I think they have reached puberty."

Ayisha Related:

God's Messenger said, "God does not accept the prayer of a woman who has reached puberty unless she covers her head."

Painting Nails with Henna

Ayisha Related:

A woman stood behind a screen with a letter [addressed] to the Messenger of God in her hand. The Prophet withdrew his hand and said, "I know not whether it is the hand of a man or the hand of a woman." She replied that it was the hand of a woman. He said, "Had you been a woman, you would have painted your nails with henna."

Permissibility of Women Going Out in the Fields to Answer the Call of Nature

Ayisha Related:

Sawda went out into the fields to answer the call of nature after the time that the partition had been prescribed for woman. She was a bulky woman and very tall. She could not easily conceal herself from anyone who knew her. Umar ibn Khattab saw her. He said that he recognized her, and she should be more careful. She turned back. God's Messenger was at that time in Ayisha's house, and there was a bone in his hand. Sawda came in and complained about Umar. Ayisha said that a revelation came to the Prophet. It ended, and the bone was still in his hand. He said, "Permission has been granted to you that you may go out for your needs."

Book on the Etiquette of Marriage
Abu Hamid al-Ghazali (1058–1128)

Abu Hamid Ibn Muhammad Ibn Muhammad al-Tusi al-Shafi'i al-Ghazali
was a theologian, jurist, and mystic who was born in modern-day Iran. The
following excerpt comes from his *Book on the Etiquette of Marriage*, which
examines marriage from the perspective of law and social custom and essentially summarizes preexisting views of marriage from the beginning of Islam
to the eleventh century. According to Islamic law, marriage was a contract
that was made binding by the mutual consent of a man and a woman,
although it could be dissolved if rights and duties were not met. Marriage
had many guidelines in order to ensure accord between husband and wife,
but also to prevent offending Allah.

Source: *Marriage and Sexuality in Islam: A Translation of al-Ghazali's Book on the Etiquette of Marriage*, translated by Madelain Farah (Salt Lake City: University of Utah
Press, 1984), pp. 106–108. Reprinted with the permission of Professor Caesar Farah.

ETIQUETTE OF INTIMATE RELATIONS
    ...It is desirable that it should commence in the name of God and with
the [following] recitation: Say, "He is God, the One and Only" [Kor. 112:1];
then he should glorify (*takbir*) and exalt (*tahlil*) His name saying, "In the
name of God, Most High, Most Great; O God, cause it to be a good progeny if you cause it to issue forth from my loins." The Prophet said, "If one
of you say when he comes upon his wife, 'O God, avert the devil from me
and avert the devil from what You have granted us.' Then should a child
result, the devil shall not hurt him."
    When you near ejaculation, say to yourself without moving your lips:
"Praise be to God Who has created humans out of fluid, and made thereof
relatives and in-laws, for thy Lord is omnipotent." One of the men of hadith
used to raise his voice in praise to the extent that the members of the household could hear his voice. Then he would turn away from the qiblah, and
would not face the qiblah during coitus out of deference for the *qiblah*. He
should also cover himself and his wife with a garment. The Messenger of
God used to cover his head and lower his voice, saying to the woman,
"Remain quiet." A *khabar* says, "If one of you should have intimate relations with his wife, you should not denude yourselves completely like two
onagers," that is, two donkeys.
    Let him proceed with gentle words and kisses. The Prophet said, "Let
none of you come upon his wife like an animal, and let there be an emissary between them." He was asked, "What is this emissary, O Messenger of
God?" He said, "The kiss and [sweet] words." He also said, "There are three
qualities which are considered deficiencies in a man: one, that he should meet

someone whose acquaintance he wishes to make but parts from him before learning his name and lineage; second, that he should be treated kindly and reject the kindnesses done unto him; and third, that he should approach his concubine or wife and have sexual contact with her before exchanging tender words and caresses, consequently, he sleeps with her and fulfills his needs before she fulfills hers."

Intimate relations are undesirable during three nights of the month: the first, the last, and the middle. It is said that the devil is present during copulation on these nights, and it is also said that the devils copulate during these nights. It was related that Ali, Muawiyah, and Abu Hurayrah also frowned upon it [during those nights]. Certain ulema recommended intimate relations on Friday and the night before it [Thursday] in fulfillment of one of the two interpretations of the Prophet's words, "May God bless the one who purifies and performs the ablution, etc."

Once the husband has attained his fulfillment, let him tarry until his wife also attains hers. Her orgasm (*inzal*) may be delayed, thus exciting her desire; to withdraw quickly is harmful to the woman. Difference in the nature of [their] reaching a climax causes discord whenever the husband ejaculates first. Congruence in attaining a climax is more gratifying to her because the man is not preoccupied with his own pleasure, but rather with hers; for it is likely that the woman might be shy.

It is desirable that he should have intimate relations with her once every four nights; that is more just, for the [maximum] number of wives is four which justifies this span. It is true that intimate relations should be more or less frequent in accordance to her need to remain chaste, for to satisfy her is his duty. If seeking intimate relations [by the woman] is not established, it causes the same difficulty in the same demand and the fulfillment thereof.

He should not approach her during menstruation, immediately after it, or before major ablution (*ghusl*), for that is forbidden according to the decree of the Book. It has been said that it would engender leprosy in the offspring. The husband is entitled to enjoy all parts of her body during menstruation but not to have sodomy; intercourse during menstruation is forbidden (*haram*) because it is harmful, and sodomy will cause permanent harm; for that reason it [sodomy] is more strongly prohibited than intimate relations during menstruation. The words of the Almighty state, "so go your tilth as ye will" [Kor. 2:223]; that is, "any time you please." He may achieve emission by her hand and can enjoy what is concealed by the loincloth (*izar*) short of coitus. The woman should cover herself with a loincloth from her groin to [a point just] above the knee during the state of menstruation. This is one of the rules of etiquette. He may partake of meals with the woman during her period of menstruation; he may also sleep beside her, etc. He should not avoid her.

If the husband wishes to have intimate relations with one after having had coitus with another, then he should wash his genitals first. If he has nocturnal emission, then he should not have intercourse before washing his genitals or urinating. Sexual intercourse is frowned upon at the beginning of the night for he should not sleep in an impure state. Should he seek sleep or food, then let him perform first the limited ablution (*wudu*), for that is a recommended practice of the sunna. The son of Umar related, "I said to the Prophet, 'Should any of us sleep in a state of major ritual impurity (*junub*)?' And he replied, 'Yes, if he has performed the limited ablution (*wudu*).'" However, a dispensation was given in this regard: A'ishah said, "The Prophet used to sleep in a state of major ritual impurity having not touched water."

"The Markets of Seville"
Ibn Abdun (twelfth century)

Muhammad ibn Ahmad ibn 'Abdun was a jurist living in Muslim Spain. He wrote a treatise on the laws and customs of Seville under the ruling Almoravid dynasty. The following excerpt comes from laws pertaining to the markets of Seville and emphasizes the protection of "honorable" women.

Source: *Islam: From the Prophet Muhammad to the Capture of Constantinople, Volume 2: Religion and Society*, edited and translated by Bernard Lewis, copyright © 1987 by Bernard Lewis, pp. 161, 163, 165, 243–251. Used by permission of Oxford University Press.

Women should not sit by the river bank in the summer if men appear there. No barber may remain alone with a woman in his booth. He should work in the open market in a place where he can be seen and observed....

The lime stores and [other] empty places must be forbidden, because men go there to be alone with women.

Only good and trustworthy men, known as such among people, may be allowed to have dealings with women in buying and in selling. The tradespeople must watch over this carefully. The women who weave brocades must be banned from the market, for they are nothing but harlots.

On festival days men and women shall not walk on the same path when they go to cross the river....

Muslim women shall be prevented from entering their [the Christians'] abominable churches, for the priests are evil-doers, fornicators, and sodomites. Frankish[1] women must be forbidden to enter the church except on days of religious services or festivals, for it is their habit to eat and drink and fornicate with the priests, among whom there is not one who has not

---

1. That is, Christians from outside Spain and from those parts of Spain not under Muslim rule.

two or more women with whom he sleeps. This has become a custom among them, for they have permitted what is forbidden and forbidden what is permitted. The priests should be ordered to marry, as they do in the eastern lands. If they wanted to, they would.

No women may be allowed in the house of a priest, neither an old woman nor any other, if he refuses marriage. They should be compelled to submit to circumcision, as was done to them by al-Mu'tadid 'Abbad.[2] They claim to follow the rules of Jesus, may God bless and save him. Now Jesus was circumcised, and they celebrate the day of his circumcision as a festival, yet they themselves do not practice this.

The contractor[3] of the bathhouse should not sit there with the women, for this is an occasion for license and fornication. The contractor of hostelries for traders and travelers should not be a woman, for this is indeed fornication. The broker of houses shall not be a young man, but a chaste old man of known good character…. Itinerant fortune-tellers must be forbidden to go from house to house, as they are thieves and fornicators….

Prostitutes must be forbidden to stand bareheaded outside the houses. Decent women must not bedeck themselves to resemble them. They must be stopped from coquetry and party making among themselves, even if they have been permitted to do this [by their husbands]. Dancing girls must be forbidden to bare their heads…

Catamites must be driven out of the city and punished wherever any one of them is found. They should not be allowed to move around among the Muslims nor to participate in festivities, for they are debauchees accursed by God and man alike.

2. Ruler of Seville, 1040–1069. This story is not confirmed by the chroniclers.
3. That is, the tax farmer who operates or controls the establishment.

28

Islamic Culture and History

Selections from Jahiz
Jahiz (776–868)

Abu 'Uthman 'Amr b. Bahr al-Fuqaymi al-Basri al-Jahiz was an Arab writer born in Basra in what is today southern Iraq. He was nicknamed "al-Jahiz" (the bug-eyed) for his protruding eyes, and his ugliness was renowned. Nevertheless, he was considered to be an *adib*, or a man of letters, educated in a broad range of subjects, similar to the modern concept of the Renaissance man. He wrote on zoology, theology, biology, metaphysics, and sociology. Aside from his scholarly knowledge, Jahiz was also a keen observer of human nature, as demonstrated by the following excerpts, which illustrate the relations between men and women.

Source: *The Life and Works of Jahiz: Translations of Selected Texts* by Charles Pellat, translated from the French by D.M. Hawke (Berkeley: University of California Press, 1969), pp. 258–259. Reprinted with the permission of Thomson Publishing Service on behalf of Routledge.

WOMEN'S SUPERIORITY TO MEN

Women are superior to men in certain respects: it is they that are asked in marriage, desired, loved and courted, and they that inspire self-sacrifice and require protection. An indication of the high esteem in which women are held is that if a man be asked to swear by God — there is none greater — and take his solemn oath to go on the pilgrimage to the House of God, or distribute his possessions as alms, or emancipate his slaves, all that comes easily to him and causes him no embarrassment. But let him be asked to swear to put away his wife, and he grows pale, is overcome with rage, protests, expostulates, gets angry and refuses — and this even if the oath be administered by a redoubtable ruler, if he does not love his wife or regard her highly, and if she be ugly, with but a scant dowry and precious little fortune. All this is the result of the place that God has given wives in their husbands' hearts. God created a child out of a woman without the intervention of any man, but He has never created a child out of a man without a woman. Thus it is especially to woman and not to man that He vouchsafed this wonderful sign, this signal token, when He created the Messiah in Mary's bosom, without a man.

FREE WOMEN AND SLAVES

Slave-girls in general have more success with men than free women. Some people seek to explain this by saying that before acquiring a slave a man is able to examine her from every standpoint and get to know her thoroughly, albeit stopping short of the pleasure of an intimate interview with her; he buys her, then, if he thinks she suits him. In the case of a free woman, however, he is limited to consulting other women about her charms; and women know absolutely nothing about feminine beauty, men's requirements, or the qualities to look for. Men, on the other hand, are sounder judges of women; for the latter only notice their outward appearance, and neglect the characteristics that please men. A woman can only say: Her nose is like a sword-blade, she has eyes like a gazelle, her neck is a silver pitcher, her leg is like the pith of a palm tree, her hair is bunches of grapes, etc. But there are other grounds than these for love and hate.

THE CANON OF FEMININE BEAUTY

Most people who know about women, most experts on the subject, agree in preferring the majdula, that is to say the type of woman intermediate between fat and thin. Her figure must be elegant and shapely, her shoulders symmetrical and her back straight; her bones must be well covered, and she must be neither too plump nor too skinny. The word majdula conveys the notion of tautness, of firm flesh without superfluous fat. A graceful walk is the most beautiful thing about a woman, and she cannot walk gracefully if she is portly, fat and overburdened with flesh. Indeed, a majdula is more often slim, and her slenderness is her best-known feature; this is considered preferable both to the fat corpulent woman and to the thin skinny woman.... A majdula is described in prose by the words: the upper part of her body is a stem and lower part a sand-dune.

Meadows of Gold
Al-Masudi (896–965)

Abul Hasan Ali Ibn Husain Ibn Ali al-Masudi was a geographer and historian born in Baghdad. In his works, *Meadows of Gold* and *Quarries of Jewels*, al-Masudi wrote a history of the world and recounted his travels from Europe to India. He was of the belief that an individual who stays at home and looks to others for information about the world cannot claim to have the same authority of knowledge as the person who travels and sees things for himself. He earned the nickname "the Herodotus and Pliny of the Arabs" because of the analytical and critical approach in his historical works.

Source: *The Meadows of Gold: The Abbasids by Masudi*, translated by Paul Lunde and Caroline Stone (London: Kegan Paul, 1989), pp. 345–346. Reprinted with the permission of Kegan Paul.

In 282 AH/895 AD, Khumarawaih ibn Ahmad ibn Tulun had his throat cut at Damascus, in the month of Dhu al-Qa'da, in the palace which he had built at the base of a hill below Dair al-Murran, "The Monastery of the Ash Tree." He was murdered while drinking by night in the company of Tughj. The crime was committed by certain of his palace eunuchs. Arrested some miles away, they were killed and crucified, some being shot full of arrows, while the black slaves of Khumarawaih cut the flesh from the thighs and buttocks of others and ate it.

I have spoken in my Historical Annals of the eunuchs from the Sudan, the Slavic countries, Byzantium and China — for the Chinese, like the Byzantines, will castrate several of their children. I have discussed, in the same work, the contradictions in character of eunuchs which result from the removal of this member and what nature causes to occur in them when that happens, as has often been confirmed and described. Mada'ini tells how Mu'awiya went in one day to his wife Fakhita, a woman gifted with considerable wisdom and tact, accompanied by a eunuch. Fakhita, whose head was bare, hastened to put on her veil when she saw the eunuch. Mu'awaiya pointed out that the man was an eunuch, but she replied:

"Commander of the Faithful, do you imagine that the mutilation which he has suffered frees me from the prohibitions ordained by God?" Mu'awiya repeated the prayer, "We belong to God, and to God we return," and, recognizing the justice of her words, henceforth allowed into his harem only elderly and broken-down eunuchs.

There has been a great deal of discussion on the subject of eunuchs and an effort has been made to establish the difference between those mutilated by cutting and those mutilated by dragging. It has been maintained that they are men with women and women with men. But these are false theories and bad arguments. The truth is that they remain men. Being deprived of one organ is not enough for them to be allotted this double role and lack of a beard does not prevent them from belonging to the male sex. Claiming that they are closer to being women implies that the works of the Creator can be modified, since He created them men and not women, male and not female. The crime which has been perpetrated on their bodies does not alter the constituent elements any more than it destroys the work of the All-Powerful Creator who gave them life.

I have explained in another book why the armpits of a eunuch have no smell and have quoted the reasons for this set forth by the philosophers. It is in fact worth noting that the eunuch, slow in all his movements, has the peculiar advantage of giving off no odor from there.

Selections from Ibn Butlan
Ibn Butlan (d. 1063)

Abu'l-Hasan al-Mukhtar ibn al-Hasan Ibn Butlan was a Christian physician who lived in Baghdad. In the following account, he discusses the characteristics one should seek out or avoid when purchasing slaves. His concern is primarily with female slaves. Under Islamic law, female slavery was closely connected with concubinage. The Qur'an allowed men to have sexual access to an unlimited number of slave women. This right, however, brought with it certain responsibilities and restrictions for the man; for example, a man could not sell or give away a female slave who had borne him a child, and she was often freed upon her master's death. Moreover, when a slave gave birth, the child was always assumed to be the master's, and it had the status of a free person. This underlies Ibn Butlan's warnings to prospective buyers.

Source: *Islam: From the Prophet Muhammad to the Capture of Constantinople, Volume 2: Religion and Society*, edited and translated by Bernard Lewis, © 1987 by Bernard Lewis, pp. 161, 163, 165, 243–251. Used by permission of Oxford University Press.

ON BUYING SLAVES

Useful advice when buying slaves, according to the saying of the wise men and philosophers; ten pieces of advice, of which four equally apply to male and female slaves, viz:

1. Their injunction that the shopper should make a careful examination before buying and should not decide at first glance. They said: one who shops for a thing should not be in dire need of it, for the hungry man approves any food that appeases his hunger, and the naked man finds suitable any rag that warms and covers him. Accordingly they said: a lecher should not shop for slave-girls, for the tumescent has no judgment since he decides at first glance, and there is magic in the first glance and charm in the new and strange. If he feels an urgent need, he will make a choice at first glance which his senses will later belie when the need is no more. Therefore, it is said: Repeated looking wears out novelty, and constant examination reveals artifice and exposes deceit.

2. The warning of the ancient before purchase. They said: beware of buying slaves at fairs and festivals, for it is at such markets that the slave-dealers

perfect their cunning tricks. How often has a scraggy girl been sold as plump, a dirty brown as a golden blond, an aging man as a full-bottomed boy, a bulging paunch as a trim, flat waist, a stinking mouth as perfumed breath. How often do they dye blemishes in the eyes and leprous sores on the body, and make light blue eyes dark blue. How often do they dye yellow cheeks red, make thin cheeks fat, enlarge small orifices, remove hair from cheeks, stain fair hair jet black, curl lanky hair, whiten brown faces, make spindly legs rounded, thicken falling hair, and gild pockmarks, tattoo marks, freckles, and scabies…How often has a sick slave been sold as healthy, and a boy as a girl. All this in addition to the slave-merchants' practice of encouraging the slave-girls in shameless flirtation with passing young men who regard carrion as lawful meat, as well as their bedecking themselves with rouge and henna and soft, dyed garments. We have heard a slave-dealer say, "A quarter of a dirham's worth of henna raises the price of a slave-girl by 100 silver dirhams."…

3. Their injunction not to decide at the first hearing of male and female slaves. They said: Do not decide at first sight of a slave or slave-girl…but be more inclined to doubt than to trust. It is safer to be suspicious.

4. A special warning for the great. They said: Let the great — anyone with an enemy who he fears may seek to murder him or to penetrate his secrets — beware of buying a eunuch or a slave-girl, especially if she can write and has come out of a ruler's household, without thoroughly investigating her; also beware of buying a mulatto slave-girl from a merchant or broker, for this is a trick by which many kings and great ones have perished.

Three pieces of advice relating especially to the purchase of male slaves, viz:

1. Their warning to the purchaser against buying a slave accustomed to beating and argument. They said: do not buy a slave whose master used to beat him very much, and do not omit to inquire about the previous owner and his reason for selling the slave himself and from others, for there is great benefit in such an inquiry, either in binding him to you or in leaving him.

2. [Is the cause] the boldness of the slave in blaming his master and belittling him or the master's resentment at his slave's complaints and disrespect for him? Is the cause of the selling in the master or in the slave?

3. Their advice on what to do before employing him. They said: The slave's character will be determined by your treatment of him from the moment when he first enters your house. If you embolden him, he will be bold; if you train him, he will be obedient; if he associates with bad slaves or other bad people, he will be bad.

Two pieces of advice relating to female slaves, viz:

1. How to make sure that slave-girls are free from pregnancy before purchase. They said: Be careful to ascertain that female slaves are free from pregnancy before taking possession of them, and beware of their spurious discharge and lying claims. Many of them insert other girls' blood in their private parts. The one to ascertain this is a woman who would not wish you to have another man's child foisted on you. Order her to examine her breasts and feel her stomach. You can also know this from the pallor of her complexion and her desire for salty food, for this is a craving due to pregnancy.

2. On taking care after purchase of tricks to become pregnant against the owner's will. They said: Be careful on two points. If you buy a slave-girl who has not yet reached puberty, it often happens that she reaches puberty while in your possession without your knowledge, concealing this from you because she desires motherhood.

Beware of Lesbian [?] slave-girls who fancy they are barren and that they dislike pregnancy, for often they will deceive you in this.

One piece of advice which concerns the seller, not the buyer.

They said: never send a slave-girl from your house to the slave-dealer, except during the menstrual flow. Otherwise she is likely to become pregnant in the slave-quarters and claim that it is yours.

We have indeed seen one in our time who bled during pregnancy, but this is rare.

ON THE DIFFERENT KINDS OF SLAVES, ACCORDING TO THEIR COUNTRIES AND ORIGINS

We shall report what we have found out, what is well-known, what we have gathered from books, what we have learned by inquiry from travelers, concerning the various races of slaves and the differences between them in body and in character, so that we may satisfy the inquirer in this matter with the fruit of experience and trial. Twenty-five sections, as follows:

The first section contains the explanation of terms, the meanings of which the reader needs to know.

If you hear me say "Farisiyya," know that I mean a woman who is born of Fars. Both parents may be Farisi, but the father alone suffices. If the offspring of a Negress mate with whites for three successive generations, thereafter black gives way to white, a flat nose gives way to a long nose, the limbs become dainty, and the character changes accordingly. The same usage is to be understood with reference to all races.

If you hear me speak of a slave-girl as a "fiver," by this I mean that her height is five spans.

If I say *shahwariyya*, this is not the name of a race but is a Persian word derived from [the Arabic] *shahwa* [passion] and means "perfect passion."

If I say Mansuriyya, I am referring to al-Mansura which is beyond the river [Indus], that is, to Multan and not to al- Mansura of the Arabs.

Then come four sections, relating to the four points of the compass.

The first concerns the eastern lands. The color of the people of these lands is white tinged with red. Their bodies are fertile, their voice clear, their sicknesses few, their faces handsome, their characters noble, their sheep plentiful, their trees tall. There is no anger in them and no courage because of their equitable dispositions; they are a people of calm and of meek temper. All this is because of the temperate sun in that region, their temperate food, and their clear water.

The second concerns the western lands. These are almost the exact opposite of what we have described in the eastern lands, since the sun does not rise over them in the mornings.

The third concerns the northern lands. These are the ones whose inhabitants live under the signs of the Bear and the Goat, such as the Slavs. These are broad-chested and brave, of portly build to conserve heat, but with thin legs because the heat escapes from the extremities. They live long because of their excellent digestion, but their women are barren because they are never clean from menstrual blood.

The fourth concerns the southern lands. These are the ones whose people live under the southern Pole [sic], such as the Ethiopians, and their condition is the opposite of that of the people of the northern lands. Their color is black, their waters are brackish and turbid, their stomachs cold, and their digestion bad. Their natures are calm, their lives short, and their bellies soft because of bad digestion.

The following twenty sections dealing with the countries, one by one.

The Indian women are in the southeast. They have good stature, brown color, and a plentiful share of beauty, with pallor, a clear skin, fragrant breath, softness, and grace, but old age comes quickly upon them. They are faithful and affectionate, very reliable, deep, sharp-tongued, and of fine character. They cannot support humiliation but endure pain without complaint until they are killed. They can master great things when compelled or provoked. Their women are good for childbirth, their men, for the protection of persons and property and for delicate handicrafts. They catch cold easily.

The women of Sind are between the east and the south. They closely resemble the Indians whose country adjoins theirs, except that their women are distinguished by their slender waists and long hair.

The women of Medina are brown in color, and of upright stature. They combine sweetness of speech and grace of body with charm, roguishness, and beauty of form and flesh. These women are not jealous of men, are content with little, do not grow angry, and do not scold. There are negresses among them, and they are suitable for training as singing girls.

The women of Ta'if are golden brown and shapely. They are the most cheerful of all God's creatures, the funniest, and the merriest. They are not good mothers of children, for they are slow to pregnancy and die at childbirth. Their men are the most active of mankind in courtship, the most assiduous in company, and the most excellent in song.

The Berber women are from the island of Barbara [sic], which is between the west and the south. Their color is mostly black, though some pale ones can be found among them. If you find one whose mother is of Kutama, whose father is of Sanhaja, and whose origin is Masmuda, then you will find her naturally inclined to obedience and loyalty in all matters, active in service, suited both to motherhood and to pleasure, for they are the most solicitous in caring for their children. Abu 'Uthman the slave-dealer says, "If it happens that a Berber girl with her racial excellence is imported at the age of nine, spends three years in Medina and three years in Mecca, comes to Iraq at the age of fifteen and is educated in Iraq, and is bought at the age of twenty-five, then she adds to the excellence of her race the roguishness of the Medinans, the languor of the Meccans, and the culture of the women of Iraq. Then she is worthy to be hidden in the eyelid and placed in the eye."

The Yemeni women are of the same race as the Egyptians, with the body of the Berbers, the roguishness of the Medinans, and the languor of the Meccans. They are the mothers of handsome children somewhat resembling the Bedouin Arabs.

The Zaranji women are from a country called Zaranj. Ibn Khurradadhbeh says that from this place to the city of Multan is a journey of two months, and Multan is in the middle of India. A peculiarity of this race is that during sexual intercourse they sweat a liquid like musk, but they are not good for motherhood.

The Zanj women have many bad qualities. The blacker they are, the uglier their faces, the more pointed their teeth, the less use they are and the more likely to do some harm. For the most part, they are of bad character, and they frequently run away. It is not in their nature to worry. Dancing and rhythm are innate and ingrained in them. Since their utterance is obscure, they have been compensated with music and dance. It is said that if a Zanji were to fall from heaven to earth, he would beat time as he fell. They have the cleanest teeth of mankind because they have much saliva, and they have much saliva because they have bad digestion. They can endure hard work. If the Zanji has had enough to eat, you can chastise him heavily and he will not complain. There is no pleasure to be got from their women because of their stench and the coarseness of their bodies.

The Ethiopian women. Most of them have gracious, soft, and weak bodies. They are subject to phthisis and hectic fever and are no good for singing or dancing. They are delicate and do not thrive in any country other than that in which they were born. They are good, obliging, tractable, and trustworthy, and are distinguished by strength of character and weakness of body, just as the Nubians are distinguished by strength of body despite their slenderness and also by weakness of character and shortness of life because of their bad digestion.

The women of Mecca are languorous, feminine, with supple wrists and of white color tinged with brown. Their figures are beautiful, their bodies lissom, their mouths clean and cool, their hair curly, their eyes sickly and languid.

The women of Zaghawa are of vicious character and full of grumbles. Their ill nature and evil dispositions lead them to do terrible things. They are worse then the Zanj and than all the black races. Their women are useless for pleasure, and their men are useless for service.

The Bujja women are between the south and the west in the country which lies between Ethiopia and Nubia. They are golden in color, with beautiful faces, smooth bodies, and tender flesh. If, as slave-girls for pleasure, they are imported while they are still young, they are saved from mutilation, for they are circumcised and all the flesh from the upper part of their pudenda is incised with a razor until the bone appears; they have become a byword. Similarly the nipples of men are cut off and a bone removed from the knee.... Bravery and thievery are innate and ingrained in them; they cannot therefore be trusted with money and are unsuitable for use as treasurer or custodian.

The Nubian women, of all the black races, have ease and grace and delicacy. Their bodies are dry, while their flesh is tender; they are strong and at the same time slender and firm. The climate of Egypt suits them, since they drink the water of the Nile, but if they are removed to some place other than Egypt, diseases of the blood and acute sicknesses overcome them and pain racks their bodies. Their characters are pure, their appearance attractive, and there is in them religion and goodness, virtue, chastity, and submissiveness to the master, as if they had a natural bent for slavery.

The women of Qandahar are like the Indian women. They have one merit above all other women, that the widow or divorcee again becomes like a virgin. ....

The Turkish women combine beauty and whiteness and grace. Their faces tend to look sullen, but their eyes, though small, are sweet. They have smooth brownness and their stature is between medium and short. There are very few tall ones among them. The beautiful ones are extremely beautiful and the ugly ones exceptional. They are treasure houses for children, gold mines for generation. It very rarely happens that their children are ugly or badly formed. They are clean and refined. Their pots are their stomachs on which they rely for preparing, cooking, and digesting food [?]. Bad breath is hardly ever found among them, nor any with large buttocks, but they have some nasty characteristics and are of little loyalty.

The Daylami women are both outwardly and inherently beautiful, but they have the worst characters of all and the coarsest natures. They can endure hardship like the women of Tabaristan in every respect.

The women of Allan are reddish-white and well-fleshed. The cold humor predominates in their temperaments. They are better suited for service than for pleasure since they have good characters in that they are trustworthy and honest and are both reliant and compliant. Also, they are far from licentious.

The Greek women are blond, with straight hair and blue eyes. As slaves they are obedient, adaptable, serviceable, well-meaning, loyal, trustworthy, and reliable. They are good as treasurers because they are meticulous and not very generous. Sometimes they are skilled in some fine handicraft.

The Armenians would be beautiful were it not for their peculiarly ugly feet, though they are well-built, energetic, and strong. Chastity is rare or absent among them, and thievery widespread. Avarice is very rare among them, but they are coarse in nature and speech. Cleanliness is not in their language. They are slaves for hard work and service. If you leave a slave for an hour without work, his nature leads him to no good. Only fear and the stick make them behave properly, and their only merit is endurance of toil and heavy labor. If you see one of them idle, it is because of his bad character and not because of any lack of strength; therefore, use the stick. Be watchful in striking him and making him do what you want because this race is untrustworthy even when they are contented, not to speak of when they are angry. Their women are useless for pleasure. In fine, the Armenians are the worst of the whites as the Zanj are the worst of the blacks. And how much do they resemble one another in the strength of their bodies, their great wickedness and their coarse natures!

"The Franks and Marital Jealousy"
Usama ibn Munquidh (1095–1188)

Usama was a poet, courtier, and scholar born in Shayzar in northern Syria and was the son of one of the Munqidhite amirs. He was born into a political family; several members of his family were officials in the Fatimite court. Towards the end of his life, Usama himself was appointed governor of Beirut by Saladin. He is best known for his autobiography, which provides a fascinating portrait of both the writer himself and his Muslim and Frankish contemporaries. The following account makes evident his amazement at the open relations between Frankish men and women.

Source: *Arab Historians of the Crusades*— selected and translated from the Arabic Sources, by Francesco Gabrieli, edited and translated by E.J. Costello. Copyright © 1969 Routledge & Kegan Paul, Ltd., pp. 77–78, 204–207. Reprinted with permission of University of California Press.

The Franks are without any vestige of a sense of honour and jealousy. If one of them goes along the street with his wife and meets a friend, this man will take the woman's hand and lead her aside to talk, while the husband stands by waiting until she has finished her conversation. If she takes too long about it he leaves her with the other man and goes on his way. Here is an example of this from personal experience: while I was in Nablus I stayed with a man called Mu'izz, whose house served as an inn for Muslim travellers. Its windows overlooked the street. On the other side of the road lived a Frank who sold wine for the merchants; he would take a bottle of wine from one of them and publicize it, announcing that such-and-such a merchant had just opened a hogshead of it, and could be found at such-and-such a place by anyone wishing to buy some; "…and I will give him the first right to the wine in this bottle."

Now this man returned home one day and found a man in bed with his wife. "What are you doing here with my wife?" he demanded. "I was tired," replied the man, "and so I came in to rest." "And how do you come to be in my bed?" "I found the bed made up, and lay down to sleep." "And this woman slept with you, I suppose?" "The bed," he replied "is hers. How could I prevent her getting into her own bed?" "I swear if you do it again I shall take you to court!"— and this was his only reaction, the height of his outburst of jealousy!

I hear a similar case from a bath attendant called Salim from Ma'arra, who worked in one of my father's bath-houses. This is his tale: I earned my living in Ma'arra by opening a bath-house. One day a Frankish knight came in. They do not follow our custom of wearing a cloth round their waist while they are at the baths, and this fellow put out his hand, snatched off my loincloth and threw it away. He saw at once that I had just recently shaved my pubic hair. "Salim!" he exclaimed. I came toward him and he pointed to that part of me. "Salim! It's magnificent! You shall certainly do the same for me!" And he lay down flat on his back. His hair there was as long as his beard. I shaved him, and when he had felt the place with his hand and found it agreeably smooth he said: "Salim, you must certainly do the same for my Dama." In their language, Dama means lady, or wife. He sent his valet to fetch his wife, and when they arrived and the valet had brought her in, she lay down on her back, and he said to me: "Do to her what you did to me." So I shaved her pubic hair, while her husband stood by watching me. Then he thanked me and paid me for my services.

You will observe a strange contradiction in their character: they are without jealousy or sense of honour, and yet at the same time they have the courage that as a rule springs only from the sense of honour and a readiness to take offence.

"Frankish Women of the Crusades of Peace and War"
Imad ad-Din (1125–1201)

Imad ad-Din was a secretary to Nur ad-Din, the ruler of Syria, and then to Saladin. He witnessed the Third Crusade (1189–92) and the fall of Jerusalem at the hands of Saladin. His history gives both an excellent description of this conquest and the Muslim view of crusaders and the women who followed them.

Source: *Arab Historians of the Crusades*— selected and translated from the Arabic Sources, by Francesco Gabrieli, edited and translated by E.J. Costello. Copyright © 1969 Routledge & Kegan Paul, Ltd., pp. 77–78, 204–207. Reprinted with permission of University of California Press.

There arrived by ship three hundred lovely Frankish women, full of youth and beauty, assembled from beyond the sea and offering themselves for sin. They were expatriates come to help expatriates, ready to cheer the fallen and sustained in turn to give support and assistance, and they glowed with ardor for carnal intercourse. They were all licentious harlots, proud and scornful, who took and gave, foul-fleshed and sinful, singers and coquettes, appearing proudly in public, ardent and inflamed, tinted and painted, desirable and appetizing, exquisite and graceful, who ripped open and patched up, lacerated and mended, erred and ogled, urged and seduced, consoled and solicited, seductive and languid, desired and desiring, amused and amusing, versatile and cunning, like tipsy adolescents, making love and selling themselves for gold, bold and ardent, loving and passionate, pink-faced and unblushing, black-eyed and bullying, callipygian and graceful, with nasal voices and fleshy thighs, blue-eyed and gray-eyed, broken-down little fools. Each one trailed the train of her robe behind her and bewitched the beholder with her effulgence. She swayed like a sapling, revealed herself like a strong castle, quivered like a small branch, walked proudly with a cross on her breast, sold her graces for gratitude, and longed to lose her robe and her honor. They arrived after consecrating their persons as if to works of piety, and offered and prostituted the most chaste and precious among them. They said that they set out with the intention of consecrating their charms, that they did not intend to refuse themselves to bachelors, and they maintained that they could make themselves acceptable to God by no better sacrifice than this. So they set themselves up each in a pavilion or tent erected for her use, together with other lovely young girls of their age, and opened the gates of pleasure. They dedicated as a holy offering what they kept between their thighs; they were openly licentious and devoted themselves to relaxation; they removed every obstacle to making of themselves free offerings. They plied a brisk trade in dissoluteness, adorned the patched-up fissures, poured themselves into the springs of libertinage, shut themselves up in private under the amorous transports of men, offered their wares for enjoyment, invited the shameless into their embrace, mounted breasts on backs, bestowed their wares on the poor, brought their silver anklets up to touch their golden earrings, and were willingly spread out on the carpet of amorous sport. They made themselves targets for men's darts, they were permitted territory for forbidden acts, they offered themselves to the lances' blows and humiliated themselves to their lovers. They put up the tent and loosed the girdle after agreement had been reached. They were the places where tent-pegs are driven in, they invited swords to enter their sheaths, they razed their terrain for planting, they made javelins rise toward shields, excited the plough to plough, gave the birds a place to peck with their beaks, allowed heads to enter their antechambers and raced under whoever bestrode them at the spur's blow. They took the parched man's sinews to the well, fitted arrows to the bow's handle, cut off sword-belts, engraved coins, welcomed birds into the nest of their thighs, caught in their nets the horns of butting rams, removed the interdict from what is protected, withdrew the veil from what is hidden. They interwove leg with leg, slaked their lovers' thirst, caught lizard after lizard in their holes, disregarded the wickedness of their intimacies, guided pens to inkwells, torrents to the valley bottom, streams to pools, swords to scabbards, gold ingots to crucibles, infidel girdles to women's zones, firewood to the stove, guilty men to low dungeons, money-changers to dinar, necks to bellies, motes to eyes. They contested for tree trunks, wandered far and wide to collect fruit, and maintained that this was an act of piety without equal, especially to those who were far from home and wives. They mixed wine, and with the eye of sin they begged for its hire. The men of our army heard tell of them, and were at a loss to know how such women could perform acts of piety by abandoning all decency and shame. However, a few foolish mamluks[1] and ignorant

---

1. Male slaves who served in the army or government.

wretches slipped away, under the fierce goad of lust, and followed the people of error. And there were those who allowed themselves to buy pleasure with degradation, and those who repented of their sin and found devious ways of retracing their steps, for the hand of any man who shrinks from (absolute) apostasy dares not stretch out, and it is the nature of him who arrives there to steal away from them, suspecting that what is serious, is serious, and the door of pleasure closes in his face. Now among the Franks a woman who gives herself to a celibate man commits no sin, and her justification is even greater in the case of a priest, if chaste men in dire need find relief in enjoying her.

Among the Franks there were indeed women who rode into battle with cuirasses and helmets, dressed in men's clothes; who rode out into the thick of the fray and acted like brave men although they were but tender women, maintaining that all this was an act of piety, thinking to gain heavenly rewards by it, and making it their way of life. Praise be to him who led them into such error and out of the paths of wisdom! On the day of battle more than one woman rode out with them like a knight and showed (masculine) endurance in spite of the weakness (of her sex); clothed only in a coat of mail they were not recognized as women until they had been stripped of their arms. Some of them were discovered and sold as slaves; and everywhere was full of old women. These were sometimes a support and sometimes a source of weakness. They exhorted and incited men to summon their pride, saying that the Cross imposed on them the obligation to resist to the bitter end, and that the combatants would win eternal life only by sacrificing their lives, and that their God's sepulcher was in enemy hands. Observe how men and women led them into error; the latter in their religious zeal tired of feminine delicacy, and to save themselves from the terror of dismay (on the day of Judgment) became the close companions of perplexity, and having succumbed to the lust for vengeance, became hardened, and stupid and foolish because of the harm they had suffered.

Women Poets

The following women poets are from the Abbasid period (780–1258), when the Arabs were at the peak of their economic, political, and cultural development. Many of them were powerful women with familial or other ties to the royal courts. Fadl was a poet in the court of Caliph Mutawakkil; Wallada was the daughter of Caliph Mustakfi; Buthaina was the daughter of the king and queen of Spain, Mu'tamid and I'timad Arrumikiyya. Although the poems are short, they are quite revealing. Wallada was the beloved of Ibn Zaidun, a poet who tried to overthrow the Cordovan dynasty, and Buthaina writes about her ordeal of being sold into slavery after her father is over-thrown.

Source: *Classical Poems by Arab Women*, compiled by Abdullah al-Udhari (London: Saqi Books, 1999), pp. 132, 142, 184, 192, 206. Reprinted with the permission of Saqi Books.

Fadl Ashsha'ira (d. 871)

Riding beasts are no joy to ride unless they're rebridled and mounted.
So pearls are useless unless they're pierced and threaded.

Thawab bint Abdullah al-Hanzaliyya (?)

Your manhood stretch stands no chance of slipping through my body's niche.
So move it away from my body's door and take it back whence it came.

Wallada bint al-Mustakfi (d. 1091)

By Allah, I'm made for higher goals and I walk with grace and style.
I blow kisses to anyone but reserve my cheeks for my man.
Ibn Zaidun, though a man of quality, loves the unbent rods in men's trousers.
If he saw a joystick dangling from a palm tree he'd fly after it like a craving bird.

Buthaina bint al-Mu'tamid ibn Abbad (1070–?)

Listen to my words, echoes of noble breeding.
You cannot deny I was snatched as a spoil of war, I, the daughter of a Banu Abbad king, a great king whose days were soured by time and chased away.
When Allah willed to break us hypocrisy fed us grief and ripped us apart.
I escaped but was ambushed and sold as a slave to a man who saved my innocence so I could marry his kind and honourable son.
And now, father, would you tell me if he should be my spouse, and I hope
   royal Rumaika would bless our happiness.

Moorish Poets

Ibn Sa'id came from Alcala, Spain, and was a widely traveled man. Ulti-mately he entered the service of al-Mustansir, the ruler of Tunis. The fol-lowing poems come from an anthology compiled in 1243 by Ibn Sa'id al-Andalusi from Alcala, Spain, entitled *The Pennants of the Champions and the Standards of the Distinguished*. He collected poems from throughout Mus-lim Spain and North Africa to create this work. The following poems are all of Spanish origin.

Source: *Moorish Poetry: A Translation of The Pennants: An Anthology Compiled in 1243 by the Andalusian Ibn Sa'id*, translated by A.J. Arberry (Cambridge, England: University Press, 1953), pp. 87, 108, 129–130. Reprinted with the permission of Cambridge University Press.

Abu Hafs (12th century — Cordova)

"HIPS"
Her hips, so wide-distended
From her slim waist suspended
Exert their tyranny
On her as much as me

I think upon their treason
And suffer in my reason;
And she has aching thighs
When she attempts to rise.

Abu Bahr (1165–1202 — Murcia)

"THE ABSTINENT LOVER"
Beautiful is she,
Beauty all excelling,
A world of witchery
In her gestures dwelling.

Fairer than the moon
Which, her charms so slender
Beholding, craves the boon
Humbly to attend her.

See, the shining grace
Of its crescent golden
Is but her radiant face
In a glass beholden.

On her cheek the mole
Punctuates and stresses
The calligraphic scroll
Letter by her tresses.

As I lay at night
Nigh to her, night fashioned

Two fires: her beauty bright,
And my sighs impassioned.

Like as o'er his gold
Palpitates the miser,
So yearned I in my hold
Wholly to comprise her.

Yea I bound her well
In my ardent rapture,
Afraid lest my gazelle
Should escape my capture.

Yet I kissed her not,
Chastity denying
My lust, a furnace hot
In my bosom sighing.

Marvel, if you will:
I, of thirst complaining,
While yet the healing rill
On my throat was raining.

Ibn Sa'id (1210–80 — Alcala La Real)

"THE VIRGIN"
A crimson rose was she
When she came to me,
A golden buttercup
When I gave her up.

I robbed her of the flame
Of her virgin shame;
She melted, and was spilled,
And my hopes fulfilled.

Index